How to Play the Property Game

a&b

How to Play the Property Game:
How to Gain Financial Freedom
Through Your Home

Tina Jesson
& Jillian Hinds

First published in Great Britain in 2004 by
Allison & Busby Limited
Bon Marché Centre
241-251 Ferndale Road
London SW9 8BJ
http://www.allisonandbusby.com

A catalogue record for this book is available from
the British Library.

ISBN 0 7490 0634 X

Printed and bound in Wales by
Creative Print & Design, Ebbw Vale

About the Author

Tina Jesson is a successful businesswoman, author and public speaker, considered by many to be a leading property guru in the UK. She is the cofounder of **Home Stagers®** and the **Home Stagers® Network** and has made 'making money from property' her business. After many years working with property developers, investors, and home owners, advising them how to get the most value and profit from their property, Tina now shares her insights with the public and property professionals through seminars and road shows throughout the UK.

As well as being an accomplished public speaker, Tina, the UK's original Home Stager, has made guest appearances on national and regional TV and BBC radio, and has provided expert advice to a number of programmes, including Channel 4's *Selling Houses*.

Tina had first hand experience of negative equity on a property she owned in the 1990s and first started to implement property staging techniques in 1995, before going to market with the concept with her first business in 1999. By 2001, Tina had set-up her existing company with her good friend Jillian Hinds and from there, as they say, Home Stagers was born.

Tina's business, the Home Stagers Network, now has strategic alliances with many estate agents, property developers and property management companies throughout the UK and regularly participates in the National Association of Estate Agents conferences, as well as Home and Property shows across Britain.

Tina and her team of Home Stagers consultants, has helped literally hundreds of people make more profit from their property and now you too can tap into her wealth of knowledge and experience.

You can find out more about Tina Jesson at *www.tinajesson.com*

Prologue

The very idea that ordinary homeowners can think about property in terms of investment is relatively new. But the trend is growing and everyone wants to play the property game.

With the downturn in fortunes from stocks and shares, and even the trusted pension funds now faltering, we are seeing scores of individuals turning to tangible 'bricks and mortar' investments to secure their future.

In the last few years, as the UK property market has steadily risen, the demand for investment property has forced even the high street lenders to provide accessible financing options.

Some people are seeking complete financial freedom through playing the property game, but even on a less adventurous scale, homeowners are seeing property as an investment and making their four walls pay their way.

This book has been written to help those players new to the property game who, with the right kind of information, some timely steering in the right direction, and insider tips on what pitfalls to look out for, can get to a level of financial independence that suits their own situation, no matter how much or how little they have to invest.

In this book we look at different ways that you can make money from 'playing the property game'.

- Maximising the profit in your main residence and moving up the ladder.
- Earning money from the house you live in now.
- What to look out for when purchasing property.
- Finance – de-mystifying the many and varied financial products out there.
- Renovating 'do me up' property.
- Ways to get property earning a revenue, including buy-to-let.
- And, finally, cashing in – how to sell successfully.

CONTENTS

INTRODUCTION

So You Want To Play the Property Game?   13
Getting Into the Property Game   18
Make Your Existing Home Into A Money Spinner   22

INVESTING

Playing the Property Game – Is It a Good Investment? 43
What's Your Game Plan?   46
The Expert Opinion   51
When to Buy, When to Sell   57

BUYING

What to Buy   60
Where to Buy   65
Finding the Right Property   71
Inspection Speaks Louder Than Words   73
Steps to Buying   77
Buying at Auction   83

FINANCING

Show Me the Money   87
Types of Mortgages, Loans and Repayment Options   90

RENOVATING

Kitchens and Bathrooms   117
Floors and Ceilings   129
Building Work and Extensions   136
When to Cash-in   139
Tina's Top Ten Improvement Tips and Seven
Remodelling Secrets   144

RENTING

Getting Someone Else to Pay Your Mortgage   148

Managing the Rental   155
Getting the Right Tenants   157
Overcoming Problems   160

SELLING
Establishing the Price   163
Ways to Sell   164
Property Promotion   173
Top Five Tips to Help You Sell   177

INCREASING THE STAKES
Building a Portfolio   179
Investment Case Studies   188

INSIDER TIPS
The Industry Advice   192
The Wealth Coach   199
The Self-Builder   201
The Negative Equity Success Story   204
The First-time Buyer   207
The Professional Relocator   209
The Professional Investor   212

HOT SPOTS
How to Identify a Property Hot Spot   216
Halifax Hot Spots   224
England's Second Home Hot Spots   249
Bradford & Bingley Report 2003-4   252
Tina's Top Ten Property Hot Spots   256

REFERENCE
Property Portals   282
A to Z of UK Mortgage Lenders   290
Top UK Estate Agency Chains   297
Useful Contacts   299
Reference Summary   300
INDEX   302

INTRODUCTION
So You Want To Play the Property Game?

So your pension fund is non-existent, your shares have taken a dive and you want to play the property game. Whether you want to play as a pawn, a bishop or a king, here is the know-how to get you started.

In the past, making money out of property was seen as the preserve of the already seriously rich, the property professional, or those who are just plain lucky.

The one thing that stops many people from starting is the fear of not getting the funding, or assuming you have to use large amounts of your own money. What I aim to do with this book is to shine a light on the options available for normal home owners to explore, to enable you to make your property 'work for you' to generate wealth. Your potential increase in wealth will range from a little, to quite a lot, depending on your own circumstances, and the level of risks you are prepared to take.

I've based my views and opinions on my own experiences and from other experts who deal in the property market, and while my opinions should never be used to replace the advice of your independent financial advisor, your own research and instincts, it should enable you to think 'outside the box', so that you can discover your own 'creative' ways to make money from the property game.

Let's put it all into perspective for a moment. Investing in property is really not as difficult as managing your own stocks and shares. In fact, if you look at keeping a property for a period of years before selling it on, it can even be less work, and less risky. In the long term, property values have consistently risen. You only have to look at what the market has done in the last 10 years to see that.

The UK property market tends to follow a natural four to seven year cycle, which has been proven and tested over time. The advantage of property investment (and that could mean something as simple as owning your own property to live in) is that it will appreciate over time. Even the houses in negative equity in the mid nineties have doubled in price over the last seven or eight years and negative equity is only a problem IF you are forced to sell. The obvious tip here is not to over-stretch yourself with your mortgage.

TIP: HOW MUCH CAN I BORROW? HOW MUCH CAN I AFFORD TO PAY BACK?

Don't just look at what you can 'borrow' on paper – look at what repayments you can afford – then calculate the repayments as though the interest rate has gone up by a couple of points. That will give you a more comfortable margin and protect you from the future market.

Some brokers are encouraging people to borrow up to SIX times their salary. BEWARE!

As interest rates are at the lowest rate they are ever likely to be, the chance of them increasing in future is high. That means if you are fully 'maxed out' when you take on your new mortgage, you will definitely feel the pinch as interest rates rise. Do not be tempted by some mortgage lenders and brokers who appear to allow people to obtain finance at any more than the industry average of 3.25% of salary – or you may be forced to sell as interest rates go up and even find yourself in the negative equity trap that was so common in the late eighties and nineties.

WAYS TO PLAY THE PROPERTY GAME

There are many ways available for you to invest money, make money, and achieve some level of financial freedom through playing the property game – how much and how quickly you make money will depend on these factors:

The amount of money you have ready to invest
   It is possible to do it with none of your own money.
Your ability to raise finance
   This is not as difficult as it seems.
The level of risk you are willing to take
   You can make money with a low-risk strategy, it just takes a bit longer.

The investment strategy you decide to adopt will be very personal to your own circumstances and what you are trying to achieve. For example your objective may be to maximise your income now with a good rental income; or invest an amount in a renovation project which you will work to develop then sell as quickly as possible to make a fast profit; or it could be to invest money now in order to get the best capital return when you sell in 10 or 15 years time.

   To make money, aim to own your own property as soon as possible and get on the property ladder, then when you sell, the profit you make is tax-free.

   There are some tax advantages to be had if you make money from your principle residence, as you'll not have any capital gains tax to pay if you keep the property for one to two years and keep within the tax limits.

PRINCIPAL RESIDENCE RULE:
For a main residence that you buy as a 'do me up' and then sell within a year or two, there will be no capital gains tax to pay.

Once you own your own property there are a number of things you can do with it to make it work for you that you may never have even thought of:

- Turn it into a Bed & Breakfast
- Hire it out to film-makers
- Take in a lodger
- Work from home
- Open your garden to the public

When you are looking to invest your hard-earned money into property, there are several ways to do that too:

- Buy your next home as a 'do me up' with a view to selling it within a year or so.
- Buy a second property to rent out and you'd be amazed how many ordinary people do it.
- Buy a second property to renovate and sell. A good option if you like DIY and have the skills to do it or if you know good reliable tradesmen.
- Buy a second property as your retirement nest egg with a view to selling it when you retire.

When you play the property game, you should aim to be in it for the long term, not aim to 'get rich quick'. Take it from me, although people have made a lot of money from property in the last couple of years, for many it has been more good luck than judgement. Timing is the key with a get rich quick approach and if this is your aim, I'm sorry to say you have probably missed the boat already unless you get extremely lucky. Property prices will not rise as exponentially as they have in the last few years.

It takes work, time and effort to play the property game successfully in the long term. Many have made some money, only to lose it later on bad decisions. The property market is like any other financial market. It is transient; it keeps changing. What worked 6 months ago, might not work today, what works today, might not work in 6 months. While researching this book, I was amazed at how different 'micro climates' came into play in different areas. One of the biggest mistakes people make is not doing *enough* research – but how much is enough? The key is to keep doing it. Make it part of your daily activity, just like if you owned shares you would make of point of reading the FT and seeing where the share price is today.

RESEARCH, RESEARCH, RESEARCH

This is one thing I can't stress enough. The people who have 'played the property game' and have come unstuck, have not put in the time and effort to make sure they know the market in which they are investing.

You need to investigate a number of factors and be up to date with the market conditions, options and pitfalls.

You need to know:

- when to buy and when to sell
- how to find the right property
- where to buy
- what to buy
- know what you are buying
- know the best financial product for you
- how to sell successfully

GETTING INTO THE PROPERTY GAME

Being a property investor, on whatever scale, should be approached just like running a small business because that's exactly what you will be doing!

TREAT IT LIKE A BUSINESS

I bet you didn't realise you need to run a business to be a property investor? But it will be well worth it. No matter what level you are going to play the property game at, you must approach it as a business. To get full tax benefits you will need a good chartered accountant and a separate bank account to manage your expenditure and rental income. All your receipts need to be kept and simple bookkeeping practices need to be established.

> **TIP:**
> There are tax benefits available to you – a good accountant will guide you through.

If you are looking to make money from the renovation of your main residence, then you will not be subject to capital gains tax.

If you plan to only sell properties that aren't your main residence you can do so within certain limits before you pay capital gains tax. Many smaller developers keep only two properties per year to take advantage of that tax benefit.

> **TIP:**
> Build a good credit rating – having NO credit rating is equally as bad as having a POOR credit rating.

We have all taken out credit from time to time. I recommend taking out the credit option on the purchase of white goods (dishwasher, oven, microwave etc) that have a six-month interest free credit scheme. That way you are building up your credit rating without it costing you any more – providing you pay it off on time.

TIP:
Don't give up the 'day job'.

You'll need a regular job with a regular income if you want to maximise on your leverage at the bank and get the best financial deal. Full financial independence takes time – don't give up the day job just yet.

CASE STUDIES

So, if it's not the very rich who are investing in property, what is the type of person who does take the plunge? And could it be for you?

Over the course of researching for this book, I have met many people who have invested in property in one way or another.

From the single woman who took on a property that 'needed work' and set herself the challenge of doing it up herself in just one year; to the man in corporate employ, who wanted to invest in a small portfolio of rental properties in Manchester; to the lady who had her inheritances to invest and bought a single terraced house to let out to students.

The types of people choosing to 'play the property game' come from very diverse backgrounds.

Sharon is a project manager from Hull who decided to take on a run-down property. Her father was a builder, so she had access to all the right contacts and he kept an eye on the major works that she had done. She converted the loft and turned a two-bedroomed semi into a three-bedroomed house. Her biggest challenge was trying to live in the property whilst all the work was happening and then, when it was time to decorate, having the energy to start after a full day's work. These will be issues you need to consider if you plan to live in a 'do me up' type of property!

William had made investments in rental property for a few years, letting out property to students in the city of Derby. This then gave him enough equity to release sufficient funds to buy a 'do me up' property as a buy-to-sell, in other words a property he didn't have to live in. He would redevelop existing 'old' property in need of modernisation, in very good areas, to ensure he returned the best resale price. This gave him the financial freedom to run his own life management company as his second revenue stream, a business he has a real passion for.

Michael was the typical corporate employee who had got somewhere in his career and decided on property investment over the stock market. He decided to use a property management syndicate to find, and manage, new-build properties off-plan. After he bought his first, and managed to bring in a tenant, he bought a second a few months later. He's happy to let his investment grow as equity builds up in the properties and is quite flexible about when he will sell. If he can hang on to them for long enough, he hopes to retire in 10 years, at 55.

Graham moved to Oxford with his partner. For their first home together, they bought a run-down bungalow in need of some serious modernisation. Realising it had stacks of potential, they set to work remodelling the space to create more rooms and extend into the loft space. Knowing they would be taking on much of the work themselves, Graham's partner took a part-time job at B&Q, which enabled them to get a 20% employee discount on all their building materials. In 18 months they planned to double their investment.

Julie had inherited some money when her father passed away and decided to buy a small terraced house a few streets away. She did a small amount of redecoration and put it up for rent. She brought in a management company to ensure the property was never empty and six years on, the property has doubled in value. She tends to let to young couples for six months at a time and has found this way of investing property very easy. She does have to make sure the property is maintained, but by using the property managers, this is taken care of. Julie plans to sell the property once she retires, to boost her pension income.

So you see, depending on your circumstances and current financial position, it is possible to become a player in the property game, on some scale. What you choose to do will be down to you. But you will need to be sure that you are buying at the right time and in the right place and know when to retire from the game. It's not without its risks of course, but nothing ever is!

In this book I will coach you though the points you need to consider. There is no substitute for doing your own research into your own area, but this book will provide you with a starting point, no matter where you choose to begin.

And the first place we will look is in the home you currently own...

Make Your Existing Home into a Money Spinner

It may not have occurred to you that you can make money from your existing home, but many people do. From running a B&B to registering your house as a film location, there is money to be made if you are aware of the options. The following are my top 5 tips to make some money from the house you currently live in.

RUNNING A BED & BREAKFAST

A good way to earn extra money if you're the sociable type. Your venture can be full-time or just seasonal, and returns are good.

You can charge up to £50 per night for a double room depending on your location, although this will have to be in relation to the services and facilities you are offering.

Do your own market research. If you live in a tourist location (or on the edge of one), near an airport or close to a large city with many attractions, this option might be for you.

You should approach this as a new business venture. To do this, you will need to set-up as a business and get sound professional advice to ensure you pay the correct taxes on your new income. You will need to notify your mortgage lender and the council for a planning permission change of use. There are a myriad of health and safety measures that need to be taken into account. Then, of course, you need to look at your insurance.

All this may seem daunting, but if broken down, they are achievable.

Business advice

This applies equally well to any property game you decide to play. Your local enterprise agency is a good place to start. They will coach you through all the steps needed to start as a business and point you in the right direction for the people you are likely to need to achieve your business objective.

Tax advice

As soon as you start your business and start to spend money, your expenses can be offset against your business. Get a good, friendly accountant. See them as your personal tax advisor. There are many tax benefits to take advantage of, and your accountant will know what is right for you.

Planning Permission

In assessing a planning permission application, most local councils will take into account the effect of the proposal on adjacent residential properties and the character of the residential area. Proposals which significantly alter the character of the property will not be permitted. In addition, certain operations require some form of licence, for example: food for sale/catering (food hygiene and environmental health requirements). The best place for advice before you start is the local planning department.

Listed buildings

Buildings that are listed or located in conservation areas may be subject to additional requirements. Again, the planning department can give you help and advice.

Electricity, Gas and Telephones

Some service providers may charge a different tariff for business customers, so it is important to check the advantages or disadvantages of different tariffs.

Trade waste

Only domestic refuse is collected without charge. If a business activity generates trade waste, arrangements for collection should be discussed with the cleansing section of the District Council's Environmental Services department.

Food Regulations

Any catering activity must comply with strict regulations. You will need to register your operation with the council's envronmental health section.

Health and Safety

The health and safety at work act applies to work being carried out at home. All working areas and equipment must be checked for safety.

Covenants and Other Restrictions

You should ensure that there is no restrictive covenant on your property deeds that prevents you from running a B&B or guesthouse.

Mortgage Lenders

Most mortgage lenders require notification that commercial activities are being undertaken.

Business Rates and Taxation

Any property or part of a property which is used for 'non-domestic purposes' may be subject to the levy of a business rate. The Valuation Agency, which is part of the Inland Revenue, makes the decision on this. It is best to check the likelihood of such a rate at a very early stage. You should check with your accountant or the tax office how setting up a B&B may affect your taxation.

Insurance

You should ensure that property insurance for both buildings and contents provide suitable and adequate cover for business purposes, including liability cover. You should seek the advice of a professional insurance adviser.

Advertising

You can't run a B&B in secret. So you'll need a sign at the very least. Advertisement consent is required for most signs, other than very small unlit signs. The Planning department can advise you on this.

Getting Listed with the AA as a B&B

The best source of B&B referral remains the AA Bed & Breakfast Guide. The guide is available on CD-ROM, and is a bestselling book with 35,000 copies sold in the UK each year. It is available for free online at:
http://www.theaa.com/getaway/hotels/hotels_home.jsp

Hotels and B&Bs listed in the AA Guide receive recognition, inspection and rating. You also get a range of marketing benefits to help promote your B&B to the widest possible audience.

However, you need to budget an annual fee to cover AA Full Recognition costs*:

Room Count	£s inc VAT@17.5%
1 to 4	197.40
5 to 10	246.75
11+	282.00

*correct as at December 2003

B&B Check List
Planning Permission
Licences
Covenants
Landlord/Mortgage Lender
Health & Safety
Business Rates
Insurance
Advertising – Signage
Advertising – AA Listing

TAKING IN LODGERS

There are advantages to taking in lodgers as opposed to running a B&B. You have more consistency, and will be able to build up a relationship with your lodger.

However, you will need to check with either the Citizens Advice Bureau or your accountant how much you can earn from letting out rooms before becoming liable for tax. It is also advisable to have a formal contract drawn up by a solicitor, or get a document from one of the many legal template services available online or from most stationers.

Many thousands of households throughout the country earn extra income in this way. If you live near a college, university or large employers, there is nearly always demand from students and staff looking for living accommodation. Contact your local college or university accommodation office, or company HR department.

You have much more control over the situation with a lodger than you do with full tenants. This is because lodgers occupy your own home and they do not have what is called 'security of tenure'.

In effect, your lodger has a licence to occupy your premises but not a full tenancy; unlike tenants, lodgers cannot call the place their own, therefore it's a much simpler process to remove unsuitable lodgers than it is tenants.

The Inland Revenue allow you to earn up to £4250 per year (just over £350 per month) tax-free through the **rent-a-room scheme**.

However, to avoid full tenancies and to qualify for the rent-a-room scheme, you must meet certain requirements:

1) The room you let must be in your main residence, where you live most of the year – if you move out, the lodger could become a full tenant by default!
2) The lodger must not have **exclusive possession** of a self-contained part of your property – cooking facilities and bathroom etc., are usually shared with you.
3) The room you let must be for the lodger to live in, **not to run a business** from.

4) If you are a tenant yourself you will need **permission from your own landlord** before you take a lodger – get it in writing.
5) You will need to inform your insurers – they may want to change the cover slightly. And it's a good idea to ask the lodger to insure their own possessions – your household insurance may not cover the lodger's possessions.
6) It's a good idea to **inform your mortgage** lender, though it's unlikely they will have any objections.

You will not need planning permission and a lodger should not affect your council tax banding. However, it could affect the amount charged in several ways depending on whether the landlord is in receipt of either of Council Tax Benefit, Council Tax Discount or Council Tax Exemption.

You will not need to worry about health and safety, environmental health and gas checks, as you would with a full tenant, though common sense tells you that you do owe a duty of care for your lodger's health and safety.

This means that any furniture you provide for your lodger MUST meet current safety standards.

You obviously need to be very careful who you take in. As a lodger they will in effect become part of the family.

You need to screen lodgers as you would tenants, by having a formal Lodger Application Form and taking up the same kinds of references and checks etc.

You also need a formal agreement – House and Flat Share (Lodgers) – which sets out house rules and notice periods and such. Usually one-month's notice on either side will suffice.

> Do not be tempted to take in a lodger:
> • Without careful screening
> • Without a written agreement

Letting to a lodger will normally come under the rent-a-room scheme unless you opt-out by informing the Inland Revenue.

In certain circumstances you may be better off opting out of the scheme, though this is less common. Again, check with your accountant or Inland Revenue directly, who will be able to tell you what is right for YOU.

If you share ownership of your home with someone else, you may be able to share the tax-free income or even increase the allowance.

It may also be possible to charge for services such as laundry and meals you provide, and have these incorporated into the tax-free scheme. Check with the Inland Revenue.

You should consider the following issues when taking in a lodger:

- Make modifications to the lodgers' accommodations. You need to have a minimum of a bed and a cupboard with hanging space. You might want to put in a desk and chair.
- Target students and mature lodgers – there has been an increase in male and female single divorcees in their 40s.
- Soaring property prices are forcing more younger people to stay in the rental market for longer.
- Get locks – unless you know the lodger, then you will need to develop a new awareness of your belongings. Get locks for your bedrooms and keep valuable items there. It is also good for your lodger to have locks, as it gives them a sense of privacy.
- Cost – check the local paper to see the trend in charges; this may vary depending on the location, and the lodging arrangements, so tailor your advert to attract the right applicants.
- Get advice on tax – A good internet source is Tax Café: *http://www.taxcafe.co.uk/propertycentre.html*
- Get legal forms and a rent book from Lawpack – £1.50. Also tenants agreements, and lodgers agreements, Lawpack products are available from most stationers – or buy online at *http://www.lawpack.co.uk*
- Do some research – A good internet source for information is: *http://www.landlordzone.co.uk* – It's an online community, a vertical portal for landlords involved in letting property – novice and experienced alike. It provides free access to information, resources and contacts of value to residential and small commercial landlords, tenants, letting agents and other property professionals.

Lodgers: Questions and Answers

Q: Do resident Landlords and Lodgers need to have a written agreement?
A: This is not strictly necessary but always advisable. The agreement sets out the terms on which you are allowing the lodger to occupy your property and what happens if things go wrong; the amount of rent; how it is to be paid (by standing order, cheque or cash); when the amount is to be reviewed and, if necessary, increased.

Q: How much notice is required by either party?
A: How much notice you want your lodger to give you is up to you. I would suggest that if you are renting out a room on a monthly basis that you ask for one month's notice. You will also need to give one month's notice if you want your lodger to leave.

I also recommend that you ask for one month's rent as a deposit up front. That will enable you to find a replacement lodger during the notice period. Don't make the mistake of accepting the deposit amount as the payment for the last month's rent. This is a pitfall many first time landlords fall in to. The deposit is just that, and will cover you for any wear and tear on the room and replacement of any minor breakages. The deposit is only returned if the room and everything in it is left as it was found and everything is accounted for and in good condition. This will be done once the lodger has left and you have had a chance to check that everything is in order. It's always a good idea to provide an inventory of items in the room as part of your agreement. Then you can check against this and get the lodger to sign.

Q: What meals and other services are to be provided? What are the Lodger and Landlord expected to pay for?
A: You can look at renting out on a room only basis around £50 per week. That would exclude bills and not include any meals.

If you are living in the house as your family home, you

may want to include breakfast or other meals. The lodger would then eat with the family and you would be expected to cook and prepare the meals at set times. Not far removed from the Bed & Breakfast idea, this may suit some people as preferable to allowing access to cooking facilities.

You may want your lodger to pay a portion of all the bills and could consider a telephone lock on the landline to prevent misuse when you are away from the property yourself.

Whatever you decide is best for you and your circumstances, all points should all be documented so that it is clear from the start for both you and your lodger. I strongly advise that you make use of a proper House and Flat Share agreement (available from your stationers, or try *www.landlordzone.com*).

Q: Do I need to bother with a Lodger Application Form, references and credit checks?

A: Technically, no. But remember, you are taking a complete stranger into your own home with your family's safety and welfare at stake. You are taking risks if you do not carry out careful checks unless the lodger is either known to you or comes through recommendation. I would always recommend that you do take up references.

Q: What if I want to convert my property to make it more suitable for taking in lodgers?

A: You will possibly need planning permission and you will need to comply with the current building regulations, especially those relating to fire safety.

You may also require additional facilities such as toilets. Contact your local council planning department.

Q: Are there any rules on what rent can be charged?

A: This is purely a matter for the landlord and the lodger to agree between them – a market rent will be at a level similar to other lodgings and tenancies in the area. The agreement may have provision for rent review and increases, for example annually. Some older agreements (entered into before 15 January 1989) may come under the jurisdiction of the rent tribunal where a registered fair rent can be applied for.

RENT A ROOM CHECKLIST
Lodger Application
Landlord/Mortgage Lender
References and Checks
Written Agreement – House and Flat Share (Lodgers)
Standing Order
Locks
Extra Keys
Insurance

WORKING FROM HOME

The use of the home for working is not a new phenomenon. Before the Industrial Revolution, most people worked at home, or close to their home, and "living above the shop" was normal.

With the onset of industrialisation, mass production meant that people travelled to where the work was. This resulted in the building of factories and the creation of new industrial areas. Daily travel or "commuting" became the norm.

The growth of small businesses and flexible home working now plays an important role in business and is likely to become the norm in the future.

Many people now dream of running a business from their home. The business may be the main income earner for the family, or a hobby that has evolved into a part-time additional income.

Another trend is for businesses to try to reduce their overheads by encouraging office and mobile staff to use their homes as a base. Other envisaged benefits are the reduced environmental impact of car usage, and a show of support for "family-friendly" flexibility.

The figures from the Labour Force Survey (LFS) show that currently 25% of the workforce work from home 'sometimes'. This is expected to increase as further rapid growth in information technology and access to high-speed communications enables more and more people to telework.

PLANNING PERMISSION FOR YOUR HOME BUSINESS

You may think that what you do in your own home is your own business, but be aware that you may need planning permission, depending on the nature of your home working business activities.

Some activities, such as operating your mobile office from the dining room table, or even from your study/spare room, are unlikely to change the nature of your residence, and therefore are unlikely to require planning permission.

Other activities, that attract a large number of visitors, and/or deliveries, may be borderline, so check with your Planning department.

You should not presume that because a particular activity did not initially need planning permission, that these requirements will not change as your business grows.

If you have employees, then planning permission is definitely required.

You should always contact the Planning department to find out if you need planning permission for a particular activity in your home. You can get advice in person by visiting the offices of your Council, or by telephoning or writing. I strongly advise that you don't do anything without checking the situation first.

Planning permission is normally required for a business where a material change of use occurs. Whether you need planning permission depends on the scale and character of the business activity and the effect on the character of the property from which it is run.

If you comply with all of the following, you may not need planning permission:

- No part of the dwelling should be separated in such a way that it becomes unsuitable for residential use

- No staff should be employed at the dwelling, whether on a full-time or part-time basis
- Customers or clients should not need to visit the business
- No goods should be stored in or outside your home
- Goods and services should not be sold from the dwelling
- There should be no change in the character of the dwelling when seen from the surrounding area
- Vehicles connected with the business, with the exception of personal transport, should not be stored or parked at the dwelling
- There should not be any significant traffic associated with the business
- No advertisements should be displayed, except for professional nameplates in the case of doctors and dentists.
- The business should not cause harm to the amenities of the area; car repairs and taxi businesses are unlikely to be accepted because of disturbance by traffic and noise.

EXAMPLES OF PLANNING PERMISSION NOT REQUIRED

- Dual business and domestic use of a single room or out-building as an office, not requiring significant deliveries or callers
- Occasional use of domestic kitchen for seasonal produce
- Childminding activity for a few children
- Occasional sale or servicing of vehicles belonging to the household
- Occasional meetings
- Using outbuilding or garage for a low-key hobby
- Use of one or two bedrooms for bed & breakfast
- Overnight parking of a single small trade van or taxi
- Keeping and breeding a few small animals

Always check your individual situation first.
(Additional Information Source: *www.onlineplanningoffices.com*).

LIKELY TO REQUIRE PLANNING PERMISSION:

- Guest house or nursing home
- Commercial kitchen and catering
- Regular day nursery or crèche
- Sale or repair of vehicles belonging to non-residents
- Regular formal meetings and gatherings
- Using outbuilding or garage for manufacturing
- Exclusive business use of one or more rooms or employment of staff
- Parking of a heavy goods vehicle or coach
- Boarding of animals for fees or keeping a significant number of animals

As a general rule, permission will only be granted for part of a dwelling to be used for the purposes of working from home where:

a) the proposed use would be operated by the residential occupier of the dwelling; and

b) the proposed use would be of a small scale and the main use of the property would remain residential.

As with running a B&B, the nature of your home business or home working may also require licences.

Health and Safety

The health and safety at work act applies equally to work being carried out at home. All working areas and equipment must be checked for safety. The Health and Safety Executive produce a useful leaflet called Homeworking.

Covenants

You should ensure that there is no restrictive covenant on your property deeds that prevents the activity you are proposing.

Landlords and Mortgage Lenders

If your accommodation is rented, you should ensure that your landlord is happy with the intended operation. Equally, many mortgage lenders require notification that commercial activities are being undertaken.

Business Rates and Taxation

Any property or part of a property that is used for non-domestic purposes may be subject to the levy of a business rate (national non-domestic rate). The Valuation Agency, which is part of the Inland Revenue, makes the decision on this. It is best to check the likelihood of such a rate at a very early stage. You should check with your accountant or the tax office, how working from home might affect your taxation situation.

Insurance

You should ensure that property insurance for both buildings and contents provide suitable and adequate cover for business purposes, including liability cover. You should seek the advice of a professional insurance adviser to find the right cover to suit your circumstances. If you hold meetings at home, you will need cover. One tip is to use a local hotel to hold any business meetings you have. Most have a lounge area you can use, and those located at motorway junctions are specifically set-up with the business-person in mind. If you have employees coming in to and working from your home, again, you must increase your cover appropriately.

WORKING FROM HOME CHECKLIST

Planning Permission
Licences
Covenants
Landlord/Mortgage Lender
Health and Safety
Business Rates
Insurance

LETTING YOUR HOME AS A TV, FILM OR PHOTOSHOOT LOCATION

In recent years there has been a rush of people registering their homes as locations for film and television companies, and for magazine photoshoots. There are, however, still companies looking for suitable locations. If your home has some unique or outstanding feature and, better still, if it has land nearby where all the vehicles, crew and paraphernalia of filming can be kept, then this might be an option for you. You will need to contact your local film commission. (Try the press and tourism dept of your local council.)

Film Location Companies for you to contact directly:
www.hammer-film-locations.co.uk
www.amazingspace.co.uk

Registering your property can offer both an alternative income and publicity that could, potentially, increase the market value of your property. Some regularly used properties achieve an income of between £15-20,000 a year from location filming – but don't get too excited. Most of these are situated in London and they are the exception rather than the norm.

Everyone has something to offer. Television and film companies have used all kinds of properties from small council flats to large country houses for their locations. However, for interiors, there does need to be enough room to contain both the actors doing their thing, and the crew doing theirs. In practice, it's easier to make a big room look smaller than make a small room look bigger; ultimately the requirement to accommodate a camera crew does make some rooms unsuitable to film in – 8'x10' bedrooms, for example.

It's also worth considering that the economics of commercial filming mean that properties located outside the M25 are less likely to attract work than those closer to London.

STILLS SHOOT

A small stills camera-shoot as part of a magazine editorial could see five or six people and a single van turn up on the day for a six hour shoot – fee £300+. Getting friendly with a local lifestyle magazine is a good way to get an "in". For national magazines who do pay more, you will probably need to be close to London.

FEATURE FILM

A feature film may wish to spend two or three days redecorating and changing your furniture, followed by a further two or three days of shooting their film. It may then take another couple of days to repaint your walls (to the colours you choose) and generally get the place back to the state in which they found it. Preparation (or Build) days can see four to ten people at your property each day, whilst shoot days can mean over 40 people for a 12 hour day – fee £1000+ per day, up to £4000 or so for the largest properties.

THE CONTRACT

Before filming or photo-shoots start you must get a contract you are happy to sign that covers the main areas below:

Fees
What is the fee, when will you be paid, and what happens if the whole project over-runs?

Time
What will be the total duration and number of hours of filming – it can take several hours to get a couple of minutes of action filmed.

Occupation
Are you expected to be present at the property or required to leave it for several days? If so, are alternative accommodation costs covered in the contract?

Condition
Agree the rules for returning property to its original condition, as some film-makers may need to redecorate, and move furniture and other items. This could cost you more than you get if you don't get this one sorted out up front.

Security
How is responsibility for the security for any technical equipment left at the property going to be handled? Make sure you have no liability because this equipment costs thousands of pounds.

Liability
Make sure there is a clause on legal liability, indemnity and insurance. Ensure all breakages are paid for. You don't want to come home to find half your household items lying broken in the bin!

Usage
Make sure you know the exact use of the planned film or pictures. You don't want to end up in a dodgy magazine if you don't expect it ...

TV / FILM LET – CONTRACT CHECKLIST
Fees
Time
Occupation
Condition
Security
Liability
Usage

Opening Your Garden to the Public

I'm not joking. Many 'ordinary' people have extraordinarily beautiful gardens. I know of one local man whose council house garden was so beautiful that people came from miles around to view his dedicated labours. There are a couple of properties in my road who also open their gardens every year to the public – they make a small charge and sell tea, coffee, home-grown vegetables and homemade jam to make a few pounds.

If you do open your garden to the public you will be following in a great tradition, as even Renaissance princes invited strangers into their gardens, and during the 17th century, British monarchs allowed the public into London's Royal Parks, just as an 18th century nobleman's house and garden were accessible for no more than the cost of a servant's tip. In Britain, we are truly a land of gardeners with over 5,000 gardens open to the public in the British Isles alone, which is more than half the total gardens open to the public in rest of Europe.

Gardening remains high on the list of Britain's most popular pastimes and garden visiting is an important way of finding inspiration. If you are located near a tourist attraction, then even better!

If you are particularly green-fingered then why not cultivate your garden? You probably won't make a million, but you'll gain enjoyment from other people's pleasure. If you grow your own vegetables or look to sell plants and cuttings, this can all add to your revenue stream.

A good source for finding other gardens open to the public is the Royal Horticultural Society Garden Finder, available in an annually published directory available online: *www.rhs.org.uk/rhsgardenfinder/gardenfinder.asp*

Another great source of inspiration is:

www.sgd.org.uk/ – The Society of Garden Designers, established in 1981 and the only professional body in the UK dedicated solely to garden design. Active both nationally and internationally, society membership includes Friends, Students, Graduates, Correspondents and Registered Members. Registered Members are approved by the Society as garden designers.

http://www.gardenvisit.com/ – The Garden visit website is a mine of useful information, including reasons for opening one's garden to the public:

- To share your good fortune with the public.
- To raise money for charity.
- To defray the costs of maintaining a large garden.
- To make a profit.
- To let members of the public see a place of importance in the history of garden design.

http://www.ngs.org.uk/ – The National Gardens Scheme has been opening gardens to the public to raise money for charity since 1927. More than £1 million is given to charity each year by the National Gardens Scheme. Over 3,500 gardens in 46 counties in England and Wales are open in aid of the Scheme. If you're interested you will need to be selected by County Organisers and their team members, and selection is based on excellence and interest to the general public.

PUBLIC GARDEN CHECKLIST

The main criteria for selection for the NGS is also worth using as a Checklist for anyone thinking of opening their garden to the public:

Should provide 45 minutes of interest, as visitors often travel some distance to visit gardens.
The garden should be a good example of its type (cottage, alpine, herb, etc.).
There should be something of special interest – the view, a national collection or water feature, for example.
If the garden is acceptable but lacking 45 minutes of interest the County Organiser will sometimes attempt to pair it with a nearby garden or gardens and arrange for them to open on the same day.
The County Organiser must also consider the health and safety aspects of opening a garden (slippery steps, cliffs, etc.) and whether there is sufficient parking if public transportation isn't available.

WHEN SIZE DOESN'T MATTER: MAKE YOUR GARDEN GROW (AND ADD VALUE TO YOUR PROPERTY).

A beautiful garden will also not harm the price of your property when it comes time to sell and you don't need to have a large garden to benefit there. An easy to maintain garden will be more beneficial to the resale value of your property than the size of it. An un-kept or tired garden can reduce your property profit by as much as 10% compared with the same garden that is both tidy well structured. A well-structured garden contains a number of zones, depending on its size, but the key is to entice people to go out in to the garden and enjoy it.

Think of adding decking or a patio with seating and an area to entertain with a BBQ. These are especially important features of your garden when you are looking to market your property at an executive or family homebuyer. But do avoid ponds and deep-water features if you are targeting your property at a young family with small children, as that could even lose you the sale. Keep water features 'children friendly' by keeping them shallow or by covering them with a metal grill.

INVESTING

PLAYING THE PROPERTY GAME – IS IT A GOOD INVESTMENT?
Advice from industry insiders

According to Rightmove (the UK's number one property web-site, which contains 35% of all property for sale in the UK – see *www.rightmove.co.uk*) the year-on-year rate of property asking price inflation is holding steady at just below 10% (as of December 2003).

Demand outstripped supply for the sixth consecutive month, with more buyers than sellers at the end of 2003.

Rightmove also reported a marked increase in market activity, with 35,000 more properties coming off the market than coming on. Good quality properties for both owners and investors remain thin on the ground and this is bound to keep the market strong.

Meanwhile, *The Times*, quoting figures from City Index, predicted property rises for England and Wales of 9.1% for the first half of 2004.

THE FACTS

There is currently a shortage of four million homes in the UK. Builders are finding it impossible to meet demand and this shortage is expected to last at least 25 years.

People are living longer and there are more single person households. The overall UK population is growing by 10% every 10 years.

According to the Royal Institute of Chartered Surveyors

(RICS), if the UK adopts the Euro, house prices are expected to rise by 15-28%.

Smart individuals have recognised that now is the ideal time to invest in property, and are turning to property as a means of boosting their retirement income.

Escalating house prices mean that the lettings market is growing. A mobile workforce and shorter work contracts are fuelling that growth.

Even at an increase of around 9-10% a year, if you are investing in property for the long term, can you really lose out?

Essentially, house prices are expected to double every eight to nine years. That is why property should be seen as a long-term investment.

INVESTOR OR SPECULATOR?

When you are thinking about playing the property game you need to ask yourself one fundamental question: *Are you playing as an investor or as a speculator?*

The Speculator

This type of player will look to buy a property, possibly "off-plan" (i.e. from the plans of a new build property development before it is even built) to obtain a discount and then 'turn' it. They sell the property immediately on the open market, for the full asking price. The money they make is fast and takes into account the discount, plus any immediate increase in the value of the property. This is a high risk, hit and run strategy.

The Investor

This type of player is very different. They are playing the 'long game'. They are in it for the long term and as a property investment should be seen as a long-term investment, a much less risky approach.

These players will look at fixed rate, interest only mort-gages and have relationships with more than one lender. These players never sell. That's right, these players NEVER SELL! They make their money on equity release to buy more properties to build up their portfolios. They will keep on rent-ing these properties out. Okay, they might sell one day – but only when they have to or when they retire maybe.

Don't forget the old quote from Mark Twain:
"Land, buy it now – they won't make any more".

WHAT'S YOUR GAME PLAN?
You will need a strategy to suit your aims. Then build a plan – before you invest a single penny

Your investment strategy will be very personal to your own circumstances and what you end up doing will be governed by what YOU want to achieve.

As we have already seen, it is important to run your investment as a business and you wouldn't start a business without a business plan or a long term strategy, now would you? Well the same applies when you 'Play the Property Game'. You need to have a 'game plan'.

You may want to 'play' with low risk and making a little 'pocket money' on your existing property to meet your needs. Then that's a strategy right for you.

Or you may want to 'play' with a 'real investment' and look to purchase a second property to secure a passive income – that's an income that once you set it up, does the work for you. This form of investment will allow you to use the most leverage from the money you currently have access to. It doesn't have to be all your own money, either. Finding the cash for a deposit may be all you need to enable you to leverage a buy-to-let mortgage. There is more on raising the money later.

Firstly you need to ask yourself 'why do I want to do this?'
- Are you looking for a passive income and a return straight away?
- Are you looking for a long-term investment where capital growth is important, maybe to replace or subsidise a pension plan?

WHAT TYPE OF PROPERTY TO INVEST IN?

If you are looking for a short term passive income (that's regular money in the bank each month) you are best to go with a Home of Multiple Occupancy (HMO), like student accommodation, where a number of rooms are let to various people not within the same family. The rental return you can get will be higher than renting out the whole property to one family and the rental income is very reliable.

If you are looking for a long-term investment where the capital growth is more important to you (that's the value of the property increases significantly over time) – then a new build apartment could be best for you. The rental value may just cover your mortgage and even if it doesn't, paying say £100 to make up your mortgage payments, could be seen as a savings plan or a better investment plan that the stock market. It really does depend on how you look at it.

The best overall long term strategy is to develop what is called 'a mixed portfolio' of a number of different types of property as time goes by, to limit the risk of investment. Then if one property is doing well and the other is not so good, the overall effect on your portfolio will be maintaining the status quo, but you can rest assured, by keeping your property investments for a number of years, the overall increase in value will add value to your assets.

People have said to me, that you can only realise your assets when you sell. That is true for homeowners, but investors tend to re-mortgage to take out the equity as the value rises.

I say, only sell IF you really have to. This is the Golden Rule of property investment and with this strategy you can grow your portfolio. This is the biggest difference between a regular homeowner and an investor and can require a complete shift in mindset.

As a homeowner, you think that paying off the mortgage earlier and becoming 'debt free' can be a bonus, maybe allowing you to retire earlier because you have no monthly mortgage to pay. This thinking saves you money in the form of interest payments.

As a property investor, you think that you will have more overall debt, but you will also own more assets and have more leverage with the equity held in those assets and with someone else paying the mortgage – your tenants, this may allow you to make more money. This thinking *makes* you money in the form of rental payments to you, the landlord.

Knowing your investment strategy will enable you to be focused and able to make the right decisions for YOU.

KNOW YOUR LIMITS

You need to sit down and think about how you view risk. Those people who 'think savings', that's fine, but property investment is probably not for you.

If you have moved to the 'think making money' mindset then you have only just begun. You need to know YOUR limits and what you are comfortable with. This will give you a starting point:

QUESTIONS TO ASK YOURSELF

- Do you give out your mobile number in case of emergencies?
- Will you collect the rent yourself?
- Or does a more 'arm's length' approach appeal to you? Would you prefer to use a managing agent?
- How much time can you put in to 'Playing the Property Game'?
- Would you only be available at evenings and weekends around the day job or would you be full-time?
- Would you consider a property that needs a bit of work?
- Are you any good at DIY and do you have a team of reliable trades to call on if you do take on a property to do up? This can be a sticking point for many people.
- Where would you buy?
- What type of property is right for you?
- How can you raise the deposit?
- What's the right mortgage for you?

This list is by no means exhaustive and you might come up with other questions specific to your own circumstances, but all of these questions will help you to develop your investment strategy and game plan. Without it, it's like playing blindfolded.

Armed with your 'game plan' you will know what to pass up on and what to go after, always remembering that there is always another property just around the corner. Don't be tempted to go after one particular property at any cost, because the numbers do need to stack up. Pay too much and you'll not cover your costs. Get a property at the right price and you will have the winning hand.

My advice:

- Do your research, take your time, don't rush in and buy the first 'cheap' property you can find.
- Invest in one property at a time.

TEN POINT CHECKLIST FOR DESIGNING YOUR OWN 'GAME PLAN.'

What do you want to achieve? Regular monthly income? Long-term capital growth investment?

What will it cost? Rent covers mortgage and I make a profit each month? Rent doesn't have to cover mortgage as I'm investing some of my money each month?

How long term is your plan? 1 - 2 years? Up to 10 years or more?

Condition of property? Little or no maintenance required? Older, 'do me up' property to add initial value?

How much time do you have? Weekends (some evenings)? As much time as it takes?

How do you want to manage the property? Use a property management company? Manage it myself?

What area to buy in? In another part of the country? Within 30 minutes of home?

What type of property? Executive apartment? Traditional house?

How to find the funding? Use all my equity in one property? Spread my equity across multiple properties?

How do you view your investment? A short term project? A long term project?

THE EXPERT OPINION
I asked three seasoned property professionals some key questions to help you get started

When it comes to investing heavily in property, there is a lot more risk and money needed. What better than to ask the seasoned experts for their opinion ...

WHAT WOULD YOU SAY THE TOP 10 PITFALLS WOULD BE FOR THE FIRST TIME INVESTOR?
1) Lack of research – know as much as possible about the market, the area and the property.
2) Paying too much for the property – not enough margin.
3) Not shopping around for the best finance deal – getting a higher interest rate.
4) Taking on more than you can do – especially true when improving a property.
5) Not taking a full survey on older property – and not realising what they've bought.
6) Choosing the wrong mortgage product – not doing enough leg work.
7) Buying in the wrong area – not knowing the local market well enough.
8) Buying in a saturated market – buying at the wrong time.
9) Not consulting a good estate agent for maximum value or returns assessment.
10) Not presenting a property to the profile of the tenants' expectations.

WOULD YOU INVEST IN DIFFERENT TYPES OF PROPERTY WHEN THE MARKET IS BUOYANT – IF SO WHAT TYPE AND WHEN SHOULD YOU DO IT?

You must think of property as a long-term investment; although quick money has been made by buying and selling quickly in a hot market, this is a high risk strategy and you could end up the last one to hold the 'hot potato' at your cost.

If you see property as a longer term investment, it becomes far less of a risk and you really can't lose. You only have to look at the way property has risen in value over the last 10 years to see that.

In a buoyant market you can look to acquire more properties to add to your portfolio as you know there will be demand from the rental sector or you can look to buy property to renovate and buy-to-sell' – more on 'Buy-to-Sell later.

Also consider auction properties and new-build off-plan.

WHAT WOULD YOU SAY WAS THE TYPE OF PROPERTY TO PUT MONEY INTO WHEN THE MARKET IS SLOWING DOWN?

The best investments are in properties which have margin in them from the start. That is where the price you pay is less than the true market value. You can achieve this in two ways:

Buy a "do me up" – or property that is in need of cosmetic improvement (new kitchen and/or bathroom) and can be purchased below market value.

Buy a property that is under market value from 'motivated sellers' – repossession, part-exchange, probate or relocation property. These properties are usually sold below market value to release the value tied up in them by the holding company.

Properties that are at the bottom of the property ladder are always the best investment in a tighter market, as properties at the top will struggle to sell when people in the middle decide to stay put and extend instead of moving up.

One and two bedroom flats and houses have the biggest demand and that will always be from first time buyers in the 21-35 age group, young professionals on approx £15,000-£25,000 p.a. and the relatively new group of 'newly single buyers' – those separated or divorced starting over. This profile also matches lettings demand. A nice two bedroom property appeals to the widest market i.e.: individuals, couple with/without children, two individuals sharing, or a company and don't have issues such as shared access or service charges that flats or apartments might have.

Rent your property if the market is on a downturn rather than trying to sell it. The market conditions will fuel the demand for more rental property. That is, as house prices fall, fewer people will want to sell (unless they have to), leading to a shortage of property becoming available, meaning that rental will seem the only option. People have to live somewhere.

Lock into the best fixed rate mortgage you can find and keep three months' overheads in your bank account. Batten down the hatches and ride it out. Remember, property prices double every eight to nine years. It's just a matter of time.

WHERE WOULD YOU GO FOR FINANCING A BUY-TO-LET AND WHAT'S THE BEST DEAL TO LOOK OUT FOR?

Always use an Independent Mortgage Advisor to get an 'agreement in principle' facility with an immediate online quotation. The rates vary currently between 4.79%–6.25%. The various lending institutions re-package their deals quite often. The secret is to decide whether to lock into a fixed deal or stay on a variable rate. Once decided, unless there is an interest rate cut looming, take the best deal on the day after considering any penalties.

Depending on your personal circumstances, there are several options, with a variety of products to choose from.
1) The high street bank is a good starting point. You will need to meet the following criteria:

- Demonstrate that you can manage a bank account – going to your existing bank makes this much easier.
- Have a good credit rating.
- Having a steady job – the bank will need to see that you can afford a second mortgage.
- Have a clear and well-considered business plan – investing in property is a business venture and all the small business start-up issues will need to be addressed.

2) The mortgage broker will have more products to choose from. Some lenders are now offering **buy-to-let** mortgages – these are based solely on your expected rental income as long as the property is not your main residence.

If you have equity in your main residence, you could apply for a second mortgage through a broker.

WHAT TYPE OF PROPERTY GIVES THE GREATEST RENTAL RETURN?

You should look at the rental market in terms of what the average rental on a particular property type is in your area.

You need to consider the cost of purchasing such a property. To do that, compare the rent you will receive with the mortgage payments you make. You need to have somewhere between 6-10% margin for the property to be worthwhile. (The 'margin' is the difference between your repayment on the mortgage and the rental value you hope to receive.)

The rent you anticipate charging should cover the costs of:

- buying (solicitors, registration, tax)
- management and maintenance (renovation, decoration, furnishing, décor refresh between tenancies)
- any vacant months
- and, most importantly, the cost of mortgage repayments.

As time goes by, the equity in the property (the difference between what you owe and what the property is worth) will increase. As property values increase, achievable rent will also increase and your margins will go up.

You will also have more collateral to borrow against for your next property.

Student properties in Manchester, for example, are a good investment right now, as Manchester has the largest student population in Europe. Similarly, **any** student city in the UK is a good place to invest.

What can you tell me about the advantages of joining a property syndicate?

Property syndicates buy up new build apartments at a discounted price, up to 20% below market price of the finished development, because they buy off-plan (before a new property is even built) and the builder gets his money earlier than having to wait for the development to be fully finished.

The syndicate can then offer these properties for resale to investors who have joined the syndicate. There is usually a join up fee of anywhere from £500 to £2,000.

Benefits of joining a property syndicate:

- Bulk buying at discounts.
- Strength in numbers attracts larger discounts.
- The larger the syndicate the more influence upon the developer.
- As the syndicate grows, many associated links are formed with related companies. For instance:
- Banks who offer a strong buy-to-let option and who take the discount negotiated as the 15% deposit required
- Insurance companies
- Maintenance companies on call-out contracts
- Letting and Management agents
- Property staging companies to ensure the syndicate maintains the best return.
- Finally, some syndicates with strong connections with the mortgage lenders can negotiate even better rates of finance for your buy-to-let mortgage than you could get as an individual.

There is always a downside to every good idea. If a syndicate is selling a number of properties in one development you need to find out what types of people are buying the others. If it's all investors who will be renting out all the properties at the same time as you, you may struggle to let your own investment. The research in the market is vital. Being first in can be of benefit but if the projected tenants don't materialise than your property could be faced with being left empty unless you consider a reduced rental return. It's not to say this type of property is a poor investment – because new builds will return a better rate of capital growth over the years (that is, the property will go up in price significantly over time) – but you will be forced to make less monthly income. Buying this type of property is very dependent on your Investment Strategy.

HOW CAN I TELL IF THERE IS A MARKET FOR A GIVEN TYPE OF PROPERTY AT A GIVEN RENTAL FIGURE?

This is the question I asked James McGing, a Fellow of the NAEA who owns his own Lettings Management Company and now has grown his own portfolio of over 50 properties in the last 7 years. He gave these valuable tips for the first time investor.

- Get three independent views on the rental property – BEFORE you buy, from local lettings and Estate Agents.
- Make sure your proposed letting agent is a member of one of the three industry standards (ARLA – Association of Rental Lettings agencies, RICS – Royal Institute of Chartered Surveyors or NAEA – National Association of Estate Agents). You will be covered by their professional Indemnity Insurance/Fidelity Bonding Insurance, should the agent go bankrupt.
- Test the Rent Exercise: By advertising the property in the local newspaper (which will cost about £40) for the rental price you need to achieve and measuring the response. If you get the calls, great – just tell the caller the property has been taken. If you don't get the calls – THINK AGAIN! It's the most direct way to test the local market and will be the best £40 you spend, before you start forking out thousands.

WHEN TO BUY, WHEN TO SELL
The principle is to buy low and sell high – so how do you do that exactly?

> Q: When is the right time to buy?
> A: Property should always be seen as a long term investment and...
> ...the best time to BUY is NOW!

In an ideal world you should be looking to buy a property in the winter when the property market is very sluggish. Many 'bargains' can be made in December because the number of people looking to buy reduces, and competition for property disappears, and in January when sellers who were on the market prior to Christmas will be in the right frame of mind to accept all reasonable offers, meaning you could get a bargain.

Then, if you can, if you *have to sell*, sell in the spring once the market starts to wake up again. There will be more property coming on the market to choose from, but the very best will sell extremely quickly as more buyers move into the market.

> Q: When is the right time to sell?
> A: Property should always be seen as a long term investment and...
> ...the best time to SELL is NEVER!

Why do you have to sell? We are always brought up to think that you have to sell a property in order to move up the ladder and buy the next property. This will allow you to get a bigger and better house or move to a more prestigious neighbourhood. But it's not the only way.

As an investor, you could chose to keep the house you currently own and do one of two things:

Live in your current home and buy a second property to

rent out. You would get a buy-to-let mortgage on your new property.

Rent out your current property and live in the new house. You would get a buy-to-let mortgage on your current property and a new mortgage on your new property. This can be a good way to get equity released from your existing property too.

There may be reasons you want to sell your existing house, especially if you need to move area, and want to raise capital but you DON'T have to sell as a matter of course. It's just that's how our parents did it and how you've been programmed to do it. To succeed at the property game, your thinking has to change! When you've done that, THEN you can start thinking about how to find the right property for you.

DEMAND FACTORS

In order to help you to assess the market at any one point in time you will need to look closely at a number of demand factors. Demand factors are all the external issues that can affect the property market at any one point in time and as timing is everything, you need to be aware of what is going on around you. These include:

- The economy – recession/war/inflation.
- Employment – where are the major employers/new jobs creation/job losses/type of jobs.
- Interest rates – level of affordability.
- Stock market performance.
- Speculation in the market – too many sales could depress prices.
- Political factors – taxes, changes in law.
- Population factors – demographics, migration across the country.
- Taste – lifestyle choices, age differences.

REGIONAL VS NATIONAL DEMAND FACTORS

There are a number of local trends to look out for in your own area:

- Property development in an area – is there a good supply of property to buy?
- Schools – good schools always have a positive affect on property prices in the catchment area, bad schools depress prices.
- Amenities in the neighbourhood, leisure centres, shopping centres, cultural and entertainment venues.
- Travel facilities, proximity of good rail, road links, tram and underground links.
- Number of listings this year compared to same time last year. There are sources on the internet that can give an indication of this but asking a couple of local Estate Agents can give you a more accurate local view.
- Spread of sale trends – in other words, how long does it take to sell a property in the area? (The national average is between 8–12 weeks.) Again, ask local Estate Agents.
- Asking price vs sale price. Is property in the neighbourhood getting the full asking price, or achieving above or below it? One tip for identifying a 'below asking price' cycle is to see how many 'new price' or 'reduced' labels are on property in the local property section of the newspaper.
- Offers per sold listing – how many offers a property receives before an offer is accepted. This indicates how much real interest there is in a property (and hence the market in general). Again, Estate Agents can give you the low down on this.
- Market trends – check the press pages of the National Association of Estate Agents for latest updates on the market trends. You can also use the internet to find out the overview of what's happening around the country. See *www.naea.co.uk*

BUYING

WHAT TO BUY
Knowing the right type of property to buy for your needs and the market will always pay dividends

What to buy is all about researching your area and finding out as much as you can about the property 'microclimate'. Every area has its own microclimate and that is driven by the local demand factors we have already covered. You need to understand that what is a good buy in one area will not necessarily work in others. It's good to understand why.

> **TIP:**
> Buying at the *bottom* of the market will protect you if prices start to fall.

Many couples are choosing to wait to buy their first property until their late twenties/early thirties. This fits in with a more flexible lifestyle of moving from job to job, even city to city. That's good news for people who are looking to invest in buy-to-let properties, as single people are choosing to rent rather than to buy. When they do decide to buy, they often do so as a couple and choose to buy the three or four bed detached, missing out the typical 'first time buyer' type property.

Another target group to think about is with the increasing number of marriage break ups, older single people are looking for smaller properties to buy or rent.

If you want to live in the property yourself, then you can start to move up in size. Period property is a good buy if this is the case. With their larger plot size than most modern houses, their principal rooms and garden are often bigger and will allow room for extension and remodelling to bring the property up to a modern day specification. If you ensure you retain or add back as many period features as appropriate for the property, you'll make the property even more desirable when you come to sell it.

If you are purchasing a property to let, then you will need to consider the property type. Are you looking for a flat or a house? The points below may help.

POINTS TO CONSIDER WHEN CHOOSING A PROPERTY

- A two-bedroom property will be easier to let/sell than a one-bedroom property.
- Consider the rent/mortgage cover for each property type.
- Where is the demand – where do tenants prefer to live?
- If there is a garden – who will look after it?
- What is the maintenance bill likely to be?

LOOK AT EACH ITEM IN MORE DETAIL

The more bedrooms you have to offer, the wider the appeal. More rooms generally means more rent.

The rent to mortgage ratio. This is perhaps the most important consideration. By how much does the rent cover your mortgage payment? If the rental income will only just cover the mortgage payment then you will not be able to build up a fund to cover you for periods when the property is empty. If the market rental income is insufficient then you may find it difficult to get a mortgage.

Where do tenants prefer to live? This is best answered by a letting agent who will have extensive experience of letting in the area you are considering. Always ask this as part of your initial research rather than when you have your eye on a property. You are much more likely to get an unbiased opinion then. Never take the advice of the selling agent at face value – they are trying to convince you to buy – get 2-3 other opinions before making your mind up.

A large garden may be a huge plus to a gardener, but if left unkempt, could develop into an ongoing problem. You could employ a gardener but this will be another outgoing to contend with.

You need to budget for mortgage payments and other regular outgoings. It's not so easy to predict repair and maintenance costs. As a landlord you will be responsible for repairs and maintenance issues and tenants are likely to demand a swift response when things go wrong. A modern central heating system is likely to be less of a problem than an old system. If your property is thatched then you should budget for re-thatching perhaps every 10-15 years at a cost that could exceed £10,000. If you buy a property with a flat roof then the flat roof will need replacing over a similar length of time.

Wooden windows will need regular maintenance if they are to last. Such maintenance will need to be considered.

From the landlord's point of view, the most desirable of factors is that there is a continuous tenancy at the property. If there are no tenants, then you, the landlord, will have to pay the mortgage.

Location and appearance of the property are important factors in determining whether your property will be considered desirable by potential tenants.

The safest area to buy in is the town or city where you live. You know the good and bad areas. You have an inside knowledge of employment, traffic and new developments. In addition to your local knowledge, you will be able to keep an eye on your investment. This is the main disadvantage IF you look to buy in a lower priced part of the country outside of your local area and local knowledge. If you do that, I would say a management company is essential.

Make sure you seek the advice of a local letting agent. The letting agent will know what type of people are looking for accommodation and what type of accommodation they are looking for.

If the letting agent is keen for your business then they will be only too pleased to advise you on location. Try to speak to more than one letting agent. If the advice given is similar then it is likely to be sound advice so for goodness' sake take it.

Don't go off half-cocked thinking you know best – or you will lose money and potentially loads of it.

Think about location from your tenant's point of view. Local factors may well be important. For example, there is likely to be good demand for property close to hospitals, universities or factories.

If you live in London or another big city then proximity to the tube or bus routes could be of prime importance.

Some factors are likely to be important wherever the property is situated:

Parking:
Most people drive a car so make sure there is space to park.

Security:
People like to feel safe. What kind of area is the property in? Check out *www.upmystreet.co.uk*, which gives you useful information about the area of your proposed property.

Lifestyle:
Proximity to pubs, restaurants and sports facilities will all help.

Road links:
Are major roads accessible?

Public transport:
A railway station close by could attract commuters from neighbouring towns and cities. Brighton is becoming a fashionable home to commuters working in London.

If your letting agent identifies families or single parents as prospective tenants then proximity of schools WILL be a primary concern.

When looking at different types of property, you do need to be aware that some properties are easier to mortgage than others. A multi-storey flat in a tower-block will be very difficult to mortgage. A flat over a shop (particularly a food shop) will present some problems. Mortgage lenders view these properties as the first to suffer in the event of a property downturn.

POOR PROPERTY TYPES

A mortgage is agreed on the basis that the property is a good security. Lenders in general do not like lending on the following properties:

- Property that requires major structural work or remedial works. If the property requires any significant work doing to it, then make sure your mortgage advisor is aware of it.
- Freehold flats, studio flats, ex-local authority flats, high rise flats, flats above commercial premises (particularly food).
- Non-standard construction, i.e. prefabricated buildings, timber framed buildings or concrete walls are all considered non-standard. Brick built structures are still considered standard structures in the UK

Where to Buy

Location, Location, Location! A key element of your research – knowing which areas to go for

Finding the best location to buy is another key element of the Property Game. Buy wisely and you'll be laughing all the way to the bank – get it wrong and you'll inevitably come unstuck.

Location is always going to be a key feature of any property that you buy. Always look at the locations as if you intended to live there yourself. If you find a bargain in a run-down area that no one wants to live in, then you'll struggle just as hard to sell or rent it.

The exception to this is when you can identify an up-and-coming area. This is an area that borders a really desirable area and property in it hardly ever comes on to the market. You can start to see where investment is going into the neighbouring area by the increase in major builders buying the land, converting old unused 'brownfield' sites (so-called because they are ex-industrial complexes, old factories, industrial and warehouse buildings), and building a number of new properties.

Then there's the 'coffee shop' test for city centre developments. Once the coffee shops and bars start opening, you're probably too late to buy an absolute bargain, because everyone can see that the area is on the up. That's not to suggest that you'll not make money on the property you buy, but you'll not get the bargains or make the same margin as people who got in first.

Long gone are the 'barn conversions' of the eighties, but occasionally you'll come across the odd water mill or derelict substation that comes on to the market. You really do need to know what you're doing with this kind of renovation, conversion and investment.

In cities, there are many brownfield sites which convert into some wonderful loft living type apartments. I'm not suggesting for a moment that you even think of taking on such a redevelopment yourself, definitely leave that for the professionals but by buying one of these apartments off-plan (before it's even built), with a view to selling it as soon as it is finished, you can be looking to make between 10–20% return. This is known as 'flipping' a property, and buyers have been known to make a killing if they get in at the start. Leave it too late, however, and you could buy too high and struggle to sell for some time. Then the investment is good for rental, providing you market it correctly and can make the margin over and above that nice new mortgage you've just taken out. For these types of property, you could see them as costing you money, if you need to 'top up' the rental price you get with your own money. This isn't a bad thing if you're looking at this with a long-term game plan. If you view this as an investment or savings plan, the equity over time will increase as will the rent.

Property prices in the North of England have been historically lower than in the South, and therefore investment requires much less capital. But surprisingly, rental incomes are comparative with the rest of the country, which means you would get a higher return on your investment. The rental market in the North is still extremely buoyant with a good level of demand, unlike some areas in the South, particularly in London, where the market is becoming saturated with too many rental properties available. Property values have more headroom to increase and the market is generally less volatile than in the South. That said, there are large numbers of speculators from the South investing in property in the Midlands, Manchester, Leeds and the North East.

LOCATION TRENDS

As we've seen, location is one of the most important elements in the value of a property.

Let's take that one step further. A good investment buy would be a sound property in a "so-so" area that will increase in value in the future.

Buying into an area that is strongly on the way up is one way to fast track your Property Game winnings. It's like climbing a ladder in a game of snakes and ladders.

Identifying the trend is everything.

The trick is not to get in so early that you are one of the earliest groundbreakers because you may have a long time to wait, but you need to be early enough that there is still plenty of appreciation left.

Being a pioneer is fine, if you are a gambler with a lot of patience. It is much safer to buy into an area *after* the restoration trend is unmistakably established, that way there is no doubt from the start.

A neighbourhood that is a good candidate for restoration must have something positive about it already, such as being in a school catchment area that is high in the league tables or in good proximity to a college or large employer's workplace.

Consider the following:

Transport
If your target tenants/buyers are likely to commute, consider the ease of getting to and from work. Properties near train stations and major road links tend to attract higher prices.

Parking
Investigate where and how easy it is to park if the property does not have a garage or off-street parking.

Education
Moving area may also mean moving children to a different school, consider this if your target tenants/buyers are likely to be families.

Health and social services
Some may consider it important to live near respected health-care amenities such as a hospital with low waiting lists. Also check the council tax charges.

Noise

Noisy neighbours, a busy road, railway line or even an air-craft flight path need to be checked.

Amenities

Are the local shops close enough and have enough variety? The style and quality of shops can give an indication of the area's prosperity.

Conservation Area

There will be restrictions on what you can do if you chose to buy in a conservation area. Ask the council.

INVESTING IN A HOLIDAY LET PROPERTY

Later in the book we'll look at renting out property for profit (See page 148) but there is one sub-section of rental that is very important to discuss in relation to location. Holiday lets, holiday homes and holiday letting businesses are now becoming very popular. Location, location, location is the obvious factor for this type of investment, so it's not for everyone. But providing you have access to a holiday resort, the sea or some other leisure activity – from the rolling countryside of the peak district which attracts thousands of walkers each year, to the Cumbrian lakes, which attracts people just wanting to get away from it all and those who enjoy a water sports holiday, a holiday home investment could be for you.

There are some valuable tax advantages with holiday lets over buy-to-let properties. For example, capital gains tax on profits when you sell is lower with holiday lets and you can claim more of your rent to reduce income tax.

The tax advantages like these can be a real boost when you see that some properties have achieved 25% increases in value in some areas over a 12-month period. However, don't expect rises like this to continue forever – experts are predicting a slowdown.

Don't think that your holiday cottage need be beside the sea: many of the tourist hot spots such as York, Stratford, Bath and Edinburgh can attract rentals of up to £650 per week in the high season, enabling you to cover mortgage costs in just a few months of letting each year and you get the benefit of a 'free' holiday there for your family. Make sure you make your own booking first though, because you might not get in if the property is really busy.

City properties also offer a safe all year-round option, and it's easier to continuously attract occupants off-season, and you can always take advantage of the accommodation yourself, if you want, as an added bonus.

Holiday letting is recognised as a business (generating earned income) by the Inland Revenue, and there are valuable tax incentives for letting your property as a holiday home, but there are some precise Inland Revenue rules which you must follow, which essentially means that when you have the property rented out properly, you get the benefit – sounds fair to me:

- Your accommodation must be available for letting to the public for at least 140 days of the year and actual letting must be at least 70 days.
- Any one occupier (or group) cannot stay for more than 31 days in any period of seven months, but they can for the remaining five months.
- You cannot claim the tax incentives when you use the accommodation yourself, or when the property is not available for letting.
- The property must be fully furnished.
- The letting must be at full market rent, not a reduced peppercorn rent for friends and relatives.
- In addition, if the business makes a loss, which it is likely to do in the early years, you can offset this against any other income you may have and thereby reduce your overall tax bill.
- Married couples can maximise tax allowances by having the property in the name of the lowest earner. This is particularly advantageous if the lowest earner is in the lower rate tax band and the higher earner is in the higher band.
- When you sell your holiday let, you will be subject to capital gains tax as you would if you sold a buy-to-let property,

BUT at a more advantageous business-asset taperrelief rate. (Taper relief reduces the amount of capital gains tax. The longer the asset has been held the greater the relief. The maximum amount of taper relief is available on the sale of the property after owning it for two years. A higher rate taxpayer will achieve an effective tax rate of 10%.)

- You can avoid paying capital gains tax altogether if you invest the proceeds of your sale in another holiday letting property within three years – this is known as roll-over relief.
- Roll-over relief can also be used to avoid paying capital gains tax on sales of other types of businesses, where the proceeds are invested into a holiday lettings business.

(For more information on holiday letting visit: *www.landlord-zone.co.uk/holiday_lets.htm*)

WHERE TO BUY CHECKLIST

- For buy-to-let property, ensure the property is no more than an hour from where you live (unless you're happy to pay for a good property management company).
- Make sure you know the area and what's happening with market forces.
- Buy where you expect demand to increase.
- Location is always important.
- Property that borders soon-to-be 'discovered' neighbourhoods – up-and-coming areas or areas that have not been developed yet but there are plans to be.
- Areas must have potential.
- What are the employment levels like in the area.
- Check the North for investment opportunities.

FINDING THE RIGHT PROPERTY
How do you find a property in the right place, at the right price – before it gets listed?

If you are really serious about finding the right property at the right price, then there are a number of ways you can get to know about it before everyone else.

- Relocation Agents.
- Join a property syndicate.
- Register with a renovation property search service, such as *www.renovatealerts.co.uk*
- Engage a property investment company, such as *www.mrainvestments.co.uk*
- Contact estate agents and ask them to put you on their mailing list to inform you of property before they are listed.
- Visit the myriad of property advertising websites, such as *www.findaproperty.co.uk*
- Contact asset management companies, such as *www.hsh.co.uk*

Thomas Fogarty, of Renovate Alerts, told me: "Many estate agents will add properties to their websites before the advertisements appear in the local newspapers, so searching websites can be a real advantage. But when I first started looking for properties on the internet, it wasn't an easy task – there are hundreds of websites, some with thousands of properties, and it would take me hours to search through just a handful of websites to find properties within a limited area. As more and more estate agents go 'online', this task just got harder." Thomas's company has automated all this, and provides the results with a couple of clicks of the mouse. They search the internet looking for properties for sale that are in need of work. Every few days they email subscribers with a list of links to the latest ones they have found.

In a typical month they expect to find roughly 5,000 suitable links to properties across the UK. Service like this can save you loads of time looking for property.

WHAT TO LOOK OUT FOR

When you first go out viewing properties, write down a checklist of things to look out for (as well as things to ask). Write down how you feel about each point as you go around. Take your time and don't be hurried or afraid to look around again.

THINGS TO LOOK OUT FOR:

- Outside. Look at the walls, windows, paint, roof, gutters, drains and garden. These are good indications of the general overall maintenance of the property and will indicate how well the property has been cared for.
- Inside, check for damp patches and cracks, particularly if you found problems outside.
- Are there sufficient rooms and enough space for your needs?
- Decor. Would you need to redecorate?
- Heating system, water and lighting. Try them all out.
- Check the bath, basin and flush the toilet.
- Inspect the roof and its insulation. Get up into the attic. Many people never go up there, but it can be one of the most costly areas to put right.
- Examine windows, doors and locks for security.
- Check the floors and ceiling for durability and cracks.
- Listen for outside noise.
- View the property at different times of the day and week. Driving around at different times of day can give you an indication of what the road, area location is *really* like.
- Are the neighbouring properties in good condition? If they are all being upgraded with scaffolding up and extensions being built, that is a good sign that the area is up and coming and your getting in to it in good time. If there are lots of properties on the market in the road or the other properties look run-down, it could be a sign that the area is on its way down and that's why it's so cheap!

WHAT TO ASK

When viewing properties; write down a checklist of questions you may wish to ask (as well as things to looking out for). Don't be put off questioning deeper or be taken in by the seller's charm.

Things to ask the seller:

- Why do you want to sell?
- Do you have any other potential buyers?
- How long has the property been for sale?
- How long have you owned the house?
- How old is the house?
- What is included and not included in the sale?
- Are there any structural problems?
- Have you made any alterations?
- Have any surveys been made in the property recently?
- How noisy is it living here, what are the neighbours like?
- What is the car-parking situation?
- Have you found a property; how quickly do you want to sell?

All these questions will help you to determine if this is the property for you, and determine the motivation of the seller and how serious they are.

INSPECTION SPEAKS LOUDER THAN WORDS
Most property investments fail because of the lack of inspection

> **TIP:**
> The £1,000 you spend on a full survey on any property over 10 years old is the best investment you'll ever make.

Always look at an investment property as though you are actually going to live in it. If you wouldn't live there because

of the smell and its proximity to the sewage farm, chances are
your tenants wouldn't want to either.

It's surprising how few first time investors don't have a
full structural survey done on an investment property, but it
is the only true way of knowing what exactly you are taking
on. Too many times have I seen people focusing on the internal décor when the guttering or roof needs replacing! In some
respects it's *more* important on your investment property, otherwise you're buying bruised fruit. At least if you know work
does need to be done, you have a stronger negotiating position, and you need to be able to negotiate if you are looking at
maximising your margin.

THE SEVEN SIGNS THAT TELL TALES

So what are the 'tell-tale signs' to watch out for when you
view a property, and before you spend a chunk of change with
the property surveyor?

When you've viewed as many properties as I have, you
soon get to know what to look for. Let me tell you what to
check for when you find the house you think you want.

Damp patches
Damp patches upstairs could indicate missing tiles or problems with the roof – get up there and check if possible – if not,
at least go up into the attic or roof space.

Patches downstairs could signify poor ventilation or that
the bath has overflowed. If it's not dried out properly it could
damage the wooden joists.

Anywhere else could signify lack of, or no, damp course.
This could cost real money to put right.

DIY
Other people's DIY could mean trouble for you later. Areas to
be avoided are:

- Plumbing
- Electrical
- Gas appliances

Check that all work carried out on the house has been completed by an expert and can be documented.

Always have the boiler, gas appliances and electrics checked if you are buying a house more than 10 years old. Houses less than 10 years old should have a (National Building Certificate) NBC 10-year buildings guarantee.

Panelling on walls and ceilings

Panelling can be a 'red flag'. If you don't like it and are thinking of taking it down, consider why it was put up in the first place. At the very least, you will have to re-plaster.

Ceiling tiles

These are usually made from polystyrene and as such are a fire hazard. If you take them down consider the re-plastering you may need.

Worn carpets

On the stairs this can be a safety hazard. Look at replacement as soon as possible. Always lift carpets and check the quality of the floorboards too. A poorly maintained property can have all sorts of hidden problems.

Poor condition of paintwork and window frames

This is a general 'tell tale sign'. If the exterior hasn't been maintained well it could be a sign that the rest of the house is poorly maintained.

Older Property

Older property can be a great investment – with larger rooms and plot area – but do take the time and investment to inspect the property properly.

NEGOTIATION

Once you've made a thorough inspection of the property yourself, then it's time to get in the surveyor. Make a note of all the concerns you have and get him to check each one – lifting carpets, checking roof tiles, testing for damp and so on, to ensure that the report comes back covering all the areas you want reassurance on – or not.

Armed with the surveyor's report, you have a negotiating tool at the ready. Review the report and identify what areas you are up for negotiation on and which ones you are not.

This is a good time to bring in your friendly builder to give you some ideas on costs for making the property good. Use this information to your benefit.

You may think that as the property doesn't already have double-glazing, you would be putting it in anyway – but the buyer doesn't need to know that. So when the survey comes back with the recommendation that the windows need to be replaced, use that as a lever to get something else done – such as the damp course – and use the windows as a concession.

TIP
BUYER BEWARE – know your local market – be sure you don't pay over the odds for a property that will cost you more money before you get any return.

Be sure to know the market value of properties of similar specification and type in the area. The current asking price of the property might reflect the fact that some upgrading needs to be done, but the margin between what is being asked for and the cost to make-good may mean you need to negotiate downwards. It's no good a seller trying to get more money on the potential value of the property once YOU have done the work; he needs to price it at a level that reflects the fact that HE hasn't! This is the one of the most common reasons that first time investors don't make the margin they should.

So where can you get a good view of properties in a particular area?

NICK FIELD, MARKETING AND CONTENT MANAGER (WWW.HOMETRACK.CO.UK) SAID:

The Hometrack Index is the UK's most up-to-date and independent index of property prices and trends, giving individuals accurate information about prices and trends down to the postcode level. Launched in September 2000, it is gathered monthly from nearly 5000 of the best estate agents, with comparisons based on transactions agreed in the previous month. This compares with Land Registry data or other property indexes, which base their data on completed transactions. In general, it takes two to three months from agreeing a sale, to completing the transaction. Hometrack data, therefore, gives a much more accurate picture of the current market.

It is the first management tool to allow sellers, agents and professionals to interact, communicate and track through the entire sales process.

The process is entirely independent, given that it does not take any revenue from the agents that contribute to the site, nor do we pay them to provide data, nor is there any advertising.

STEPS TO BUYING

So you've found the property – now to buy. Whether you're moving into a 'do me up' or buying to rent it out, the key steps are the same.

1) MAKE AN OFFER

Once you have found the property you like, you need to make an offer.

To do this, tell the estate agent working on behalf of the seller how much you are prepared to pay for it.

Here are a few points to think about at this stage:

- Remember that the asking price is what the person selling the property would like for it – not necessarily its market value or its worth to you.
- Is the price fair in relation to other similar properties in the area of the same condition?
- You need to have considered the cost of making any immediate repairs or renovations. This will affect how much you can afford or are willing to offer.
- Don't offer more than you are comfortable with.
- Don't get into a situation where you have to outbid another offer.

2) FINALISE YOUR MORTGAGE

Once your offer has been accepted on the property you wish to buy, it is time to finalise the mortgage arrangements. If you are financing the property purchase with a mortgage you will need to do this before exchanging contracts.

An Independent Financial Adviser can advise on what mortgage to choose – which may save money in the long run.

To arrange your mortgage smoothly:

- Have ready details of the property you wish to purchase, recent payslips, P60, referees names/addresses, employer details and bank statements. The lender will want to see them.
- Have funds ready to pay your deposit, mortgage arrangement fee, as well as the valuation and survey fee.
- Warn any persons you have given as references that the lender may be contacting them.
- Ask the lender if an independent surveyor can carry out the survey on the property you wish to buy. This way, if you switch lenders you may be able to use the same survey report and save money.
- Arrange buildings insurance on your new property before you exchange contracts.

3) Exchange contracts

Once your offer for the property has been accepted you need to appoint a solicitor or licensed conveyancer. They will do the legal work involved in buying the property. To exchange contracts you will need to have finalised your mortgage arrangements with a lender.

To exchange contracts, your solicitor or conveyancer will:

- Check the property's lease or deeds you wish to buy.
- Arrange a search to check for any road or building planning permissions that would affect the property.
- Ask legal questions about the property to the seller's solicitors to protect you before buying it.
- Prepare the contracts to purchase for your signature.
- Pay the seller's solicitor your deposit. This is normally between 5 – 10% of the purchase price.
- Charge a fee of 0.5% to 1.5% of the property price for his/her services.

IMPORTANT!

Once you have exchanged contracts there is no going back. Both you and the seller will be legally committed to completing the sale. Backing out may incur legal action as well as high costs.

Therefore, before exchanging make sure your mortgage is confirmed, you have the deposit, you have buildings insurance in place and you are happy with the contract.

---

4) Completion

The date for completion (when you finally buy the property) is normally set at the time of exchanging contracts.

It is possible to exchange and complete on the same day.

Normally however, it is a few weeks apart – time for your solicitor to:

- Arrange the signing of the transfer documents.
- Ensure the mortgage monies are available on completion date.
- Pay the Stamp Duty and Land Registry fees.
- Finalise any other legal arrangements.

By now you probably feel like having a holiday, but don't. Between exchanging contracts and completion you need to be available at any time to sign documents or answer your solicitor's questions. Also you need to:

- Arrange the pick-up time and place for the keys to the property.
- Obtain quotes from removal/builders firms.
- Advise all those who should know your change of address.
- With the seller's permission, measure up for curtains and carpets. If not part of the sale, you may wish to negotiate to buy them.

On the completion day your solicitor will:

- Pay the seller's solicitors the agreed price (less the deposit already paid).
- Receive and forward the property 'title deeds' from the seller's solicitor to your mortgage lender.
- Stamp the transfer of ownership.
- Register the new ownership with the Land Registry.

5) MOVE INTO YOUR NEW INVESTMENT

Once you have completed, the property is yours. If you are moving as part of a renovation project, all that's left is to move your belongings in.

Plan the move; it will save time and hopefully make it a little less stressful! Consider the following:

- Arrange for animals to be looked after on the day of the move.
- Advise utility companies (gas, water, phone etc.) the date that you will be moving in.
- Arrange a day off work to move.
- If you have more to move than you can manage yourself, consider a removal company. Ask around for personal recommendations and obtain a few quotes.
- Collect boxes, packing material and a marker pen. It's better to have too many than not enough.
- When packing boxes, use the marker pen to label them with their contents and the room they are to go in.
- Clear out all unwanted items – now is the time to de-clutter.
- Store valuable items, documents and papers safely whilst moving.
- Pack a survival kit: a kettle, tea, coffee, snacks, change of clothes, first aid kit, toiletries and cleaning products.
- Book a plumber, gas engineer or electrician as appropriate to connect appliances.
- Have cash ready for any unexpected costs.

Moving is one of the top three most stressful times in your life, coming in close behind death and divorce. When all around you seems to be going wrong, try to keep a cool head and realistic expectations on what can be done.

Good luck and enjoy your new property – whether you're moving in and doing it up, or renting it out!

IN SCOTLAND...

The process in Scotland is somewhat different. In Scotland a seller would normally ask the estate agent to obtain 'offers over' a specified price and expect to receive offers in excess of 20-30% of the asking price. Once a number of potential buyers have shown an interest in the property, the estate agent will fix a closing date for all offers to be received, in writing. The closing date is usually set ahead far enough to allow the potential buyer to have all the necessary surveys and valuations done in order to secure the mortgage.

Once you have your mortgage offer in place and are satisfied with your survey and want to go ahead, you would then ask your legal advisor to put a formal written offer to the seller's estate agent or solicitor. You must set out the price you want to pay and when you wish to take possession. Any conditions you wish to put on the offer must also be included in this document – for instance, on the condition of seeing the damp course certificate, or on condition of having the central heating boiler serviced.

In most cases it's the highest offer that is accepted. Once the offer is accepted, and all conditions are agreed or negotiated, there is a complete agreement in writing and the contract is legally binding.

There is a leaflet available from The Office of Fair Trading that I would recommend for anyone buying or selling property, called 'Using an Estate Agent to buy or sell your home.'

Call Enquiries on 08457 22 44 99 for your free copy or visit *www.oft.gov.uk* to download a copy.

BUYING AT AUCTION
A great way to get hold of a bargain... but also a great way to lose money! Approach with caution...

You can find some very good buys at auction, with a wide range of properties on offer and usually with no chain involved. But you need to be aware that once the hammer comes down the house is yours and completion usually only takes 28 days.

If you are looking to buy your first investment property from auction, I would strongly advise against it and here's why...

You MUST do your homework before you intend to buy at auction. You must get an inspection carried out on the house or houses you intend to bid on, so you know exactly what you are buying.

You must set the limit on what you can afford to pay for the property and STICK to it!

I can't stress this enough – One of the major reasons property sells at auction is the selling agent wants to get the MOST for the property – not the least and they do rely on 'auction fever' kicking in.

Buying at auction is not for everyone and some people should just NEVER go!

If you are competitive and want to 'win' the property, the chances are that you will keep bidding and not only go over budget, but over what you can realistically afford. You could end up paying well over the odds by buying a property at any price!

The problem for the novice investor buying at auction is that because you have looked around the house, had a survey done (so you've not only made an emotional investment in it but a financial investment too), you think you know what you are buying and become emotionally attached before you even arrive at the auction house. There is an immense desire to go through with the purchase and this can become 'at any cost'.

That's not what property investment is about.

As the hammer falls you will be under a contractual obligation to hand over a 10% deposit immediately.

You must stick with the amount of money you have available. You *can't* overspend. Once the hammer falls you need to pay. No going back.

I would advise that no first time investor ever buys their first property at an auction unless you have a professional working on your behalf. It takes lots of self-control and it is a learnt skill. Observe professional investors and this becomes clear.

Another pitfall is that, because at auction you need to settle your account within 28 days, you may not get your mortgage through in time. Many high street lenders take 6 weeks from arrangement of the mortgage to the transfer of the funds. Buying conventionally will at least allow you some valuable thinking time, and additional inspection time to make absolutely sure that you are making the right 'move' in your game. You can pull out right up to signing of contracts. This is not an option at auction!

Buying through conventional channels means the legwork is more time consuming, but the property game is for the well prepared, well controlled and well focused. If you are still determined to try your hand at auction, however, here's what to do.

HOW TO FIND A PROPERTY AT AUCTION

Keep an eye on local papers where most will be advertised. You'll soon see which Estate Agents run auctions in your area. Get on their mailing list.

Check out *www.propertyauctions.com* for auctions and buying guides.

Sign up for an auction-watch service. Identify the type of property you are looking for and get an email alert when one comes up. *www.eigroup.co.uk*

10 TIPS FOR BUYING AT AUCTION

1) Go to a few auctions to see what happens. You'll be amazed how most properties go for well over the amount listed as the guide price. Calculate the average for your area. This could be anything from 20%–50% of the guide price. Identify the property professionals. They will normally buy more than one property. Interestingly, they KNOW when to stop and let the property go. Study this and learn!

2) Get a solicitor who specialises in investment property and get him to inspect the documentation supplied and get him to make all the pre-contract enquiries.

3) Have a full structural survey on the property and bring in your builder to obtain true estimates for the work to be undertaken. You really do need to know what you are taking on.

4) Make sure you have your 10% deposit available on the day and check how the auctioneer requires this payment.

5) Organise your mortgage and give your lender the time to do their valuation.

6) Check if the auction house charges a 'buyer's premium' on top of the 'hammer price'. This is a fee you need to pay on the day on top of the deposit.

7) If you have any questions the auctioneer will be happy to answer any questions you do have.

8) You will need to have buildings insurance from the moment the property becomes yours, so shop around before you buy.

9) Set a price limit and stick to it! Sounds easy, but you MUST NOT go beyond your reach as there is no backing out.

10) If the property ends up being withdrawn because it didn't reach its reserve price, ask if you can make an offer direct to the seller after the auction.

SO, HOW DO YOU MAKE A BID?

You will need to register with the auction house before the sale. You'll need to provide your name, address and some form of identity. You will be given a number on a card that you use to indicate that you are bidding.

If you cannot attend the auction, you can leave written bids giving the maximum you want to pay. The auction house will bid on your behalf. You may also be able to make a telephone bid, but you will need to book this in advance.

What happens if you change your mind after you 'win' the property?

You can't!

Once the hammer comes down, you own the property and are legally obliged to pay for your purchase.

If you're at all unsure about buying, then don't bid!
Better still don't buy at auction!

FINANCING

SHOW ME THE MONEY
So how do you raise the capital to get into the property game?

If you have to raise capital to enable you to play the property game, then getting the right mortgage product for your needs is vital. Whether you are looking for equity release to modify your existing home, or if you are looking for a second mortgage in order to buy more property, you need to get up to speed on the options available to you.

Banks, building societies and mortgage brokers now have more products available then ever before. Finding your way around the mortgage market can seem overwhelming and even intimidating, especially with the abundance of available mortgage products and mortgage providers.

This chapter goes on to help you navigate your way around them in the quest to help you find the best product for your situation.

Choosing the right mortgage means finding a mortgage tailored to meet *your* needs, taking into consideration *your* lifestyle, *your* age and *your* financial situation.

What might be right for a friend or colleague will not necessarily be right for you. Don't take advice from friends and family; you do need to take professional advice from an Independent Financial Advisor regulated by the FSA (Financial Service Authority). If you don't already have one, you can find one in your local area by visiting *www.ifap.org.uk*.

The information I am going to share with you is information readily available to anyone looking for a mortgage and is designed to give you a quick overview of the mortgage types on offer in simple language. On page 291 I have identified the major providers who specialise in various types of mortgage. But remember, new products are developed all the time, so it's still worth seeing what is available at the time you actually need the finance.

The information in this book should never be used to replace the personalised information your independent financial advisor will give you, but it can help you to understand what on earth he or she is talking about!

If, like many people, you've had the same old mortgage for a number of years, you will find this overview enlightening. Moreover, you may want to review your current situation with your IFA to make sure the money that you are paying out each month is working as hard as possible for you. Many people are choosing to move mortgage and find the better deal elsewhere.

THE MORTGAGE CODE

The Mortgage Code sets the minimum standards of service that borrowers can expect from mortgage lenders and inter-mediaries (brokers, Estate Agents that offer mortgage services and the like) which subscribe to the Code. Visit the Mortgage Code Compliance website at: *www.mortgagecode.org.uk*

The Code has ten key commitments. These specify that lenders and intermediaries will:

- Act fairly and reasonably in all dealings with you;
- Ensure that all services and products comply with this code, even if they have their own terms and conditions;
- Give you information on services and products in plain language, and offer help if there is any aspect which you do not understand;
- Unless you have already decided on your mortgage, help you to choose a mortgage to fit your needs;
- Help you to understand the financial implications of a mortgage;

- Help you to understand how your mortgage account works;
- Ensure that the procedures that sales staff follow reflect the commitments set out in the code;
- Correct errors and handle complaints speedily;
- Consider cases of financial difficulty and mortgage arrears sympathetically and positively;
- Ensure that all services and products comply with relevant laws and regulations.

Choosing a Mortgage

The section in the code that details helping you to choose a mortgage explains that there are three different levels of service which might be given. These are:

- Advice and a recommendation as to which mortgage available from that lender (or via the intermediary) is the most suitable one for you.
- Information only provided on the different types of mortgage product on offer so that you can make your own informed choice of which to go with, or,
- information on a single mortgage product, if you have already made up your mind.

Whichever level of service is provided, you should find that before you finalise your mortgage you have been given information on all the following aspects of the mortgage/s. If you are unclear about any of these, check with the lender or intermediary who is arranging your mortgage for you.

- The repayment method and the repayment period
- The financial implication or redemption penalty of repaying the mortgage early.
- The type of interest rate – variable, fixed, discounted, etc.
- What your future repayments might be after any fixed or discounted period.
- Whether you have to take an insurance with the mortgage, and, if so, whether the insurance must be arranged by the lender/intermediary or if you are free to find your own. I would always recommend, if possible, that you shop

around. I saved over £50 a month by doing this. However, to get a preferable rate, you may be tied in to that lender. I recommend that you do your own calculation to see if the discounted rate is beneficial. It could be that you save £10 per month on your mortgage but it costs you £20 per month extra on your insurance.

- The general costs and fees which are involved with the mortgage – valuation fees, arrangement fees, legal fees, etc.
- Whether your selected mortgage terms can be continued if you move house.
- If/when your account details will be passed to credit reference agencies.
- Whether you are required to pay a high percentage lending fee, and, if so, what this means to you. This will depend on your circumstances and the amount of deposit you have.
- If you are using the services of a mortgage intermediary to arrange the loan, you should also be told if they are receiving a fee from the lender for the introduction of the mortgage, and whether they usually arrange mortgages from a selection of preferred lenders or from the market as a whole.

COMPLIANCE WITH THE CODE

Compliance with the Mortgage Code is monitored independently. In addition, any organisation subscribing to the Code must be a member of a recognised complaints scheme – the Banking Ombudsman, the Building Societies Ombudsman, or the Mortgage Code Arbitration Scheme. Your lender or intermediary will be able to tell you which scheme applies.

Copies of the Mortgage Code are available from your mortgage lender or mortgage intermediary.

TYPES OF MORTGAGES, LOANS AND REPAYMENT OPTIONS

In essence there are now 3 basic ways a mortgage can be paid back. This is how the interest and capital is to be paid back:

- Repayment
- Interest only (endowment)
- Flexible

IN MY EXPERIENCE

If you go back just 15 years, when I had my first mortgage, only "Repayment" and "Interest Only" or "Endowment" mortgages were sold. At the time, an Endowment was always seen as the best bet – oh, how things have changed. Nowadays, the interest only option (tied to an endowment policy) has suffered miserably due to a poor-performing stock market. I have seen my mortgage transfer from Interest Only, to Repayment, and now to Flexible. But remember, that's right for ME – NOW!

REPAYMENT MORTGAGES

A repayment mortgage is structured so that the monthly payment is made up of both an element of the capital AND some of the interest. This allows the original amount borrowed (the capital) as well as the interest accrued over the term of the mortgage to be paid off over time. As time goes by the capital owed reduces.

Points to Note:
Because you are paying off some capital each month, the total amount owed decreases over time and you will pay off the loan, provided all payments are paid on time.

INTEREST ONLY MORTGAGES

So-called because that is all you pay – the accrued interest to the lender each month. The original loan amount remains the same for the term of the loan. Therefore, suitable investments are required in order to repay the loan at the end of the term. These investments are arranged at the beginning of the term and there are a variety of different types to opt for today, including Pension Mortgages, Endowment Mortgages, PEP Mortgages, ISA Mortgages and so on.

The amount originally borrowed on Interest Only Mortgages does not reduce because you only pay off the capital at the end of the term. This is done by contributing towards what is know as the 'repayment vehicle' (i.e. the investment(s)) chosen, which should return a sufficiently large sum to repay the loan at the end of the term.

There has been bad press lately on these types of mortgages and certainly mortgages taken out over 10 years ago are struggling to make their 'repayment vehicle' cover the capital. Lenders will tell you if this is happening with your endowment policy. If you can provide alternative methods to pay it off (maybe like changing mortgage as I did) and keep the endowment policy going, this will give you an independent nest egg when it matures.

PURE INVESTMENT ONLY – There are some lenders who will allow Interest Only payments with no 'repayment vehicle' in place and accept that the loan will be repaid by selling or refinancing the property within the agreed term of the loan. This type of mortgage option can be used if you intend to buy-to-sell, but these mortgages are not very common from the high street.

Points to note

Investments are *not* guaranteed to appreciate (go up), so there is a certain amount of risk involved.

If the investment does not provide as good a return as expected, it may fall short and not make enough to cover the loan. You will then have to look at ways of paying off the loan yourself.

On a more positive note, the investments associated with interest only loans are transferable, which means you can keep the investment and add them to a new mortgage if you move home. You can even separate them from your mortgage if you change the type of mortgage later. That way, it will become a standalone investment plan, where the returns made at the end of the term do not have to go toward paying off your mortgage, but can be used as a nest egg for something else.

FLEXIBLE MORTGAGE

A relatively new type of mortgage originally from Australia. It has only been available in the UK market for a few years. The idea behind it is that, as the name suggests, it is flexible.

The mortgage is structured so that you can make overpayments, underpayments and even take mortgage holidays without incurring penalties. Most flexible mortgages have their interest calculated daily, which has an obvious benefit if you are overpaying. Regular overpayments on a Flexible Mortgage can lead to the mortgage being paid off much sooner and that means you will save thousands of pounds in interest.

You can vary the amount you pay and adjust them to meet your current financial situation and lifestyle.

It has the potential to enable to you to save substantially on interest payments.

It allows you to repay the loan early, before the end of the term, by paying regular overpayments and there is no penalty for the privilege.

This type of mortgage is an excellent place to invest any extra money you may have coming to you; your bonus, a pay rise or tax refund, or if you are self employed you can add in the revenue from a large job, for example. The interest you save on your loan will almost always be more than any interest you would have received from putting it in to a savings account. There are tax benefits too. Money 'paying off' your mortgage debt will not be subject to the tax that it would be if it was in a savings account.

Points to note:
A flexible mortgage will provide you with the option to repay your loan before the end of the term by overpaying without penalty.

As interest is usually calculated daily this gives you the benefit of saving you money when overpayments are made, even if the money is drawn back at a later date.

You can vary the amount you pay depending on your circumstances. Overpayment when you get your bonus, underpayment when the washing machine breaks down and you need to buy another one NOW! And even payment holidays for say, when you're taking time off work to have a baby.

As long as you do not exceed your original mortgage threshold, you can do all that without penalty. There are usually no penalties for redemption of the mortgage either. But it MUST be paid off by your 65th birthday, so you need to keep an eye on the amount you owe overall making sure you 'catch up' on any underpayments or mortgage holidays taken.

FIVE MAIN MORTGAGE INTEREST TYPES

We've looked at how the money is paid back, in this section, we look at how the interest is calculated
- Variable
- Base Rate Trackers
- Discounted
- Fixed
- Capped

1) VARIABLE
Usually known as the standard variable rate offered by a particular lender. This rate normally fluctuates in line with the Bank of England Base Rate. The Base Rate set by the Bank of England is the base rate that all mortgage rates are compared with. You might have a mortgage which is 1.25% over base rate for example.

2) BASE RATE TRACKERS
These schemes 'track' by a set amount above the Bank of England Base Rate. Every time the Base Rate changes, your mortgage repayments will change by the same amount. Lending institutions usually announce their interest rate change within a day or two of the Bank of England announcing the Base Rate change

3) DISCOUNTED
This is a variable rate but set at a fixed amount BELOW the lender's standard variable rate. If you wish to pay back your

loan before the end of the discounted period, you may have to pay an extra charge known as a redemption penalty. In some cases these charges apply for a time after the discount rate has ended. The discount term cannot be extended without re-mortgaging.

4) Fixed

The rate is static for a set period of time, usually between one and three years. Once this time period is over, the rate goes back up to the lender's variable rate and sometimes up to the variable rate plus a percentage point, so you pay more later. That means you get a low start on your mortgage but pay it back later. Again, make sure you are ready for the increase. You can get in a mess if you forget the month the increase will hit your bank account. There is often a redemption penalty on these rates if you wish to pay back the loan before the fixed rate time period is up or change to a more favourable mortgage.

5) Capped

On this mortgage, the interest rates you pay are limited to a maximum so your repayments are set to a maximum rate set for a time period. These can help you manage in the repayments if the market is fluctuating to make sure you can afford any rise. Because it is capped, your payments will never go over the capped rate. But there is another part to the capped mortgage. There is also a minimum rate charged to, so if rates fall below your minimum, you will end up paying more than on a standard variable rate. It can be advantageous to start with but you may lose out later and with the redemption penalty you'll need to pay for early payment of the loan - you could lose out over time.

But Beware – the Interest Rate!

For all types of mortgage, you need to consider the interest rate you are offered.

Interest rates can fluctuate with very little warning. This is another vital factor to take into consideration, due to the dif-

ferent interest rates which apply to different types of mortgage available.

Current mortgage interest rates depend very much on the
current economic climate and financial markets. As these fluctuate, so does the amount you pay each month. You need to
take this into account when you look at the payments you can
actually afford to pay back.

Lenders often put together 'special offers' to entice you to
buy from them, so they are worth keeping an eye out for.
These 'special offers' can include fixed rate and discounted
rates deals. For discounted deals, they usually give you the
first year or two at a discount, but don't forget that at some
point your repayments will go up, sometimes to even more
than the normal rate. This can be a low start for a first time
buyer say, but make sure you can cover the increase. It can be
a huge jump if you're not used to it or if you forget which
month it will hit your bank account. For any 'special offer'
you find, do check the small print carefully to see if there is
any catch.

It's always a good idea to allow for an extra percentage
point rise when you are applying for a mortgage, to see if you
can still afford the repayments. The best way to do this is
when you are with your mortgage advisor, ask them to recal-
culate the payments at 0.25, 0.5, 0.75 & 1% increments and see
if you would be comfortable paying that every month. After
interest rates have been so low of late the only way is up.

IN MY EXPERIENCE
When I took out my last mortgage I calculated that I could still afford the mortgage at 10%. That might seem a bit extreme in today's market but when I took it out interest rates were at 7% and I'd had personal experience of negative equity and interest rates reaching 15%, so my 10% seemed very possible to me. Obviously, I have benefited from the reduction down to 4% as many others have. That means I have more disposable income each month. Now that I have moved to a flexible mortgage, I have paid off more capital in the last year than I ever did in the past 3 years.

If you think interest will go down and you plump for a variable rate when, in fact, the rate goes up, you will end up paying more. On the other hand, you may choose to go for a fixed rate and then lose out if the rate drops again. Fixed rate mortgages can be a good idea if you are planning to invest money in a property investment as a business venture, as it does give you one less variable in what could be a risky operation. Fixed rate buy-to-let mortgages can be a good idea.

CHANGING MORTGAGE

A mortgage is expected to be a long-term commitment but many people find that they can pay off their loans before the term ends. The most common reason for this is when they move house.

You should always check what redemption penalties apply to your mortgage before you agree to it, should you wish to pay it off early. Most lenders will want the total value of any discounts or cash-back of the loan given in the early years, paid back in full if you change mortgage. It's worth asking if your original mortgage can be carried forward to your next property to prevent the penalties kicking in. You might be able to change the mortgage repayment method if you stay with the same lender.

IN MY EXPERIENCE

I managed to transfer my first endowment mortgage to my new property and made up the other 'half' of my new mortgage with a repayment mortgage. That way I didn't lose out on the endowment I had built up over a number of years.

Then, when the endowment started to perform extremely badly, I changed to a full repayment method (and kept my endowment going independently of my mortgage).

I managed to do all this with the same lender.

But I couldn't change lender without incurring a penalty. I had taken a cash-back mortgage on my new house to enable the move – remember we moved in the negative equity days of the 1990's. As I had been paying 0.75% over the standard interest rate for the privilege of having the cash-back at the time, I felt I had already 'paid' for it once already. So I held out until the 5-year lock in had passed.

Then I moved to a flexible mortgage with another lender.

Mortgages that allow you to transfer your existing mortgage amount and terms when you do move, and avoid any redemption penalties, are known as portable. There may be additional requirements and disadvantages if you need to borrow an amount that is more than the original loan amount.

Not all mortgages are portable so look out for those that are.

OTHER MORTGAGE TYPES

We've looked at the main mortgage and interest types, but there are a few alternatives you may want to consider depending on your own circumstances and what you are planning to achieve.

Cash-Back

With a 'cash-back' mortgage, you will receive a lump sum once the loan is taken out or when you have paid the first payment. Most cash-backs are around 3-5% of the mortgage amount. It can be useful if you need a cash injection to your new home. There are, however, redemption penalties if you change your mortgage early. Some lenders can tie you in for up to five years and you will be paying a higher interest rate as well.

I used a cash-back mortgage to help me in the negative equity nineties. How did this help? Well, it enabled me to use the cash-back to cover the moving and legal fees on the next house, as all our savings had got swallowed up to meet the shortfall in the deposit we needed. Let's hope they won't be needed for this reason again.

Note: As property prices vary due to market conditions, the value of your property may depreciate in the short term, as well as appreciate.

This could mean that the mortgage loan may exceed the property's current market value. This is known as **negative equity**. Providing you can continue to make your payments this should be no cause for alarm because, in the long run, property tends to increase in value.

This only becomes a problem if you are forced to sell when you are in 'negative equity', which was a problem faced in the nineties by some people who were made redundant and couldn't keep up with their re-payments.

Current Account Mortgages and Offset

This is a type of flexible mortgage and with offset mortgages all your finances are linked so that your current account, mortgage and savings are all held with the same lender. What this means is that any accounts in credit are offset against the ones in debit, for example your mortgage. So instead of being paid interest on your savings, you avoid interest on the equivalent amount of your debt. Therefore, if you have a mortgage of, say, £100,000, by having £1,000 in your current account and £9,000 of savings, and offsetting these against your mortgage, you only pay interest on the remaining £90,000.

You will also find that the interest is adjusted daily, which means your current account balance and savings balance works at reducing your interest every day. This will in turn, reduce your mortgage term and the amount of capital you owe at any one time.

The main advantage of this type of mortgage is the tax benefits you receive. As you don't receive interest on your savings, you can't be liable to pay any tax on them either. This is particularly useful if you are a higher rate taxpayer.

Current Account Mortgages or CAMs are very similar but rather than having separate accounts with one lender, all your accounts are brought together in to one account. The biggest thing you need to get familiar with is the fact that your account will always show a debit of tens (even hundreds) of thousands of pounds – but don't worry, that's just the money you owe on your mortgage.

The biggest advantage of both these types of mortgage is the fact you can have easy access to borrowing. These mortgages allows you to do all your borrowing at one single mortgage rate, which will always be far lower than a personal loan, credit card or overdraft. This means that you can effectively borrow up to 99% of your property value at any time at a lower rate. This is a great way to raise capital, cheaply; however, borrowing such a large amount of money against the security of your home could lead to serious problems if you get into problems repaying the debts, so make sure you increase your payments accordingly and put in any lump sum monies you have, like your bonus, so you have something in reserve.

BUY-TO-LET (BtL)

The great Buy-to-Let has been the mortgage which has enabled regular folk like you and me to get into property investment for the first time. More and more lenders have been offering options over the last two to three years, which, some might say, have helped to fuel the housing boom of recent times.

Property investment is becoming increasingly popular with many ordinary people deciding it's a better option than the not so well performing pension schemes and the falling stock market. Buying an investment property for your retirement years is a real option with a buy-to-let mortgage and many see it as a form of pension provision.

Buy-to-let mortgages are structured in the same way as the regular residential mortgage; e.g. you pay a deposit (although this is often around 25%). The difference is that most lenders will calculate how much they are willing to lend based on the rental income of the property rather than your ability to pay through your salaried income. However, some lenders do still look at your level of income as well, with borrowers only being considered if they earn £25,000 a year or more.

The achievable rent needs to be between 100% and 150% of the mortgage repayments. For example if your BtL mortgage monthly repayment is £10, then the rental income would need to be £10–£15 per month.

The rentable value will need to be assessed by an independent source to ensure that you can cover the running costs, such as insurance, maintenance, any vacant periods etc.

Generally, you can borrow up to 75% of the value of the property. Deposits are higher for BtL loans because lenders need to be convinced you are a serious investor.

So expect to pay a higher rate on this type of mortgage. Arrangement fees can also be higher than you would normally expect. If you buy a property that is not fit to rent out from day one, not only will you have to pay the mortgage while you do your renovations, but restrictions may be imposed if extensive renovation is required, which may mean there will be a delay in the full loan being paid out.

SELF-CERTIFICATION

I first came across the self-certification mortgage when I started to run my own business. Not surprising, really, as the self-cert mortgage was designed to help people who run their own business, or who are self-employed, who have not got a steady income or have not got three years' of accounts to prove income. Borrowers who fall into this category have found it difficult in the past to obtain a conventional high street mortgage because, traditionally, lenders approve mortgages based on long-term and regular income, usually accompanied by 3 years, of payslips or bank statements.

The net has been cast even wider now and you can consider a self-cert mortgage if you:

- Are self-employed.
- Get a large proportion for your income from commissions or overtime.
- Work on a contractual basis.
- Work part time or irregular hours.
- Have numerous strands of income.
- Rely on bonuses as opposed to just your normal salary.

You will need to make a signed declaration of your income; the amount you borrow will then be based on this. The lender will make extensive credit checks and possibly look at bank, accountant and lender references.

At least that's how they used to operate. But loop holes have emerged that allow borrowers to obtain larger mortgages than perhaps they could afford.

The Money Programme investigation of self certification mortgages

Self-certification mortgages had a severe amount of bad publicity in 2003 as a result of undercover work and the subsequent TV coverage in *the Money Programme* – "Mortgage Madness".

The programme suggested that the misuse of self certification mortgages was having an artificial affect on the increasing house prices and suggested this was how people were managing to meet the soaring cost of housing.

Some major British lenders had changed their lending rules, just slightly, which enabled borrowers to get far bigger mortgages than they were entitled to.

All borrowers had to do was to lie about how much they earned and as the lenders had stopped verifying their income claims, a number of brokers where actively encouraging borrowers to not only lie, but break the law.

If you're thinking of doing the same – think again – lying on a mortgage application form is a criminal offence.

The maximum a borrower could raise on a mortgage has always been set as a multiple of income.

The typical multiple of three-and-a-half times income, means the most someone earning £30,000 would be able raise on a mortgage was £105,000 – that is 3.5 x £30,000.

The income multiple rule is a rough and ready rule of thumb but it does prevent people from borrowing more than they can reasonably afford to pay back And that has always been in the interest of the lender.

This worked because lenders would insist that borrowers proved the incomes they claimed, either by producing pay slips from their employers or, if they were self-employed, profit figures from their accountants.

But some of Britain's largest high street lenders started to change the rules slightly, where proof of income was not required at all.

With these new self-certification mortgages, borrowers simply stated their income and lenders state that they would not check the amount borrowers claimed, and with this lack of income checks, it has made it simple for borrowers to lie about what they earned.

If a borrower lied on their mortgage application about their income, the lender's multiple would be applied to the inflated earnings figure and the maximum mortgage a borrower could get would be increased.

Last year when *The Money Programme* visited Ealing, a house price hot-spot in West London, nine out of ten of the mortgage advisers consulted recommended they should lie about their (imaginary) £30,000 salary, falsely boosting it to over £50,000 on the mortgage application form.

Instead of the £105,000 or so they could have raised on an honest mortgage application, suddenly *The Money Programme* were being offered mortgages of around £185,000.

In Manchester house prices are lower, but nevertheless three out of the seven advisers consulted suggested that they would suggest an applicant lie in order for them to get a bigger mortgage.

The most worrying scenario was when they visited big name high street brands such as Birmingham Midshires, part of Britain's biggest mortgage provider, the Halifax Bank of Scotland group, three out of three of the advisers consulted offered self-cert mortgages of around six times their income for which they would have to have lied.

One of these advisers even boasted about getting a client a mortgage of around ten times income by inflating his salary to over £100,000.

Meanwhile, the Financial Services Authority, which had been investigating self-certification mortgages following the programme, said that self-cert mortgages accounted for only 6% of the market.

Then they came across another kind of mortgage where proof of income is not required.

Mostly designed for people who can put down a 25% deposit or more, typical for second time buyers, these mortgages are called "fast-tracks" because, without proof of income, they are far quicker to process than traditional mortgages.

But, as with self-certs, not asking for proof of income means fast-tracks are also open to abuse.

The lender offering fast-track mortgages is Northern Rock, the seventh biggest provider in Britain.

Northern Rock was quick to point out an important difference between fast-track and self-cert mortgages.

Though neither mortgage requires proof of income, with fast-track mortgages lenders reserve the right to ask for proof of income if they choose.

Lenders do have other checks they make: For example, comparing the amount a borrower claims to earn with the job they say they do.

But brokers have founds ways around that to. A slight change of job title, say from "nurse" to "medical staff", will easily justify a far higher income on the application form.

But the over-riding reason why many lenders seem not to be concerned about rooting out fraudulent applications is down to the size of the deposit a borrower has to put down to qualify for a fast-track or self-cert mortgage.

If everything goes wrong for the borrower and they can no longer meet the payments on a fraudulently obtained outsize mortgage, the lender is unlikely to lose out otherwise they wouldn't loan the money in the first place.

Even if a borrower defaults, a lender can repossess their home and sell it to recover their money.

The deposit gives lenders a comfortable cushion against falling house prices since prices would have to fall by more than the deposit before a lender faced any losses.

Borrowers meanwhile would lose their deposits and their homes.

REMEMBER: Lying on an application form is a criminal offence.

100% MORTGAGE

Aimed at the first time buyer who is struggling to get on to the property ladder and get together the deposit on their first home. You must know that you can easily afford the monthly mortgage repayments, especially if the interest rates go up.

The 100% mortgage is once again commonplace. (The last time they came in to their own was in the 1980s.) They need to be available again, with the high cost of housing today.

Because the risk being taken on by the lender is much higher, both rates and penalties are high.

Note:
Lenders in the 1990s offered 100% mortgages and then borrowers went on to see properties lose value, meaning that many families went into negative equity. Coupled with the huge increase in mortgage interest rates (it went up to a massive 15%) making payments unaffordable for many, this trapped many families in a Catch 22 situation. They could not afford to pay the mortgage and they could not sell to recover their investment.
You have been warned!

ADVERSE CREDIT OR SUB PRIME MORTGAGES

Adverse credit mortgages are a range of specialist products designed to help people with poor credit history to get back onto the property ladder. Once only offered by specialist sub prime companies, more and more high street lenders are starting to get in to the market.

These mortgages are designed for people who have previously incurred mortgage or loan arrears, had a County Court Judgement (CCJ) issued against them for unpaid debts, or for people who have been declared bankrupt. These people will struggle to meet the criteria of a standard mortgage on the high street.

More and more lenders are now offering this option in recognition of the fact that just because you had financial difficulties in the past is no indication of your ability to repay the mortgage today.

These types of mortgages do tend to charge *significantly* higher interest rates than the standard mortgage, as the lender is taking on more risk. But once you have demonstrated that you can manage the mortgage, your credit rating will recover and you will have a much better chance of gaining access to the regular rates of the standard mortgage. Indeed, some lenders are offering a 'credit repair' option where, over a number of years, the high interest charged is gradually reduced, ultimately to the lender's Standard Variable Rate, as long as you have kept up with the payments and you have held down a spotless credit record throughout the period of your mortgage.

THE DEPARTMENT OF TRADE AND INDUSTRY PUBLISHED SOME WORRYING STATISTICS.

Household debt now stands at 134% of income, a record figure.

The number of personal bankruptcies has increased by 30% on a year ago and is now at its highest level since records began.

Most ominously for the housing market, a Financial Services Authority survey published last month found that with a 1% rise in interest rates, 44% of mortgage borrowers said they would be struggling with their borrowings.

Checklists to identify the right mortgage for you:

The following describes the category of lender you might fall into and some options worth considering, depending on the type of borrower you are and what you want to do.

First Time Buyer – with limited funds

No deposit = 10% mortgage
On a tight budget = Fixed mortgage
Want to take advantage of current low rates = Capped mortgage
Previous credit history problems = Adverse credit or sub prime mortgage

Self employed – may not be suited to a conventional mortgage

No regular or standard income = Self-Cert mortgage
Established business but income fluctuates = Flexible mortgage
Large amount of money made from big contracts. Interested in investment = Buy-to-let mortgage

Existing home owners – possibly trading up in property

Want the freedom of being able to under/over-pay according to circumstances = Flexible mortgage
Need extra money initially for furniture, new kitchen and so on = Cash-back mortgage
Want to pay less initially = Discount mortgage

Re-mortgager

Want to benefit from extra funds with initial low rates
= Discount mortgage
Confident that rates will stay low. Looking to save money
= Tracker mortgage.
House increase in value together with income increase, equity release to invest = Buy-to-let mortgage
Want to pay off mortgage securely with set payments = Fixed mortgage.

MORTGAGE FEES

There can be a number of fees associated with mortgages, the amount of which will depend on the options you choose. The following provides a summary of the most common fees charged:

Application Fee
This fee covers the administration expenses incurred whilst processing the application. These include the cost of taking up references, credit checks, electoral roll checks and any valuation fees that apply. This fee is usually deemed non-refundable from the outset.

Existing or previous lender reference charges
If you already have a mortgage and a reference is required from that lender, they will usually charge a fee. This can often be avoided if an annual mortgage statement and bank statement prove satisfactory conduct.

Booking and arrangement fees
These may be charged for specific products and be payable in advance, added to the loan or deducted from the advance on completion.

Mortgage Indemnity Premium
I always think this charge is a rip-off. In essence this is for the insurance the lender takes out to guarantee a percentage of the mortgage in case you default and the property goes in to repossession. Sounds like a good idea – but they make YOU pay the premium. But YOU get NO benefit from it what so ever. (Apart from getting the mortgage because without it they won't lend you the money.) Such cover will not protect you if your property is subsequently repossessed and sold for less than the amount you owe. You will remain liable to pay all sums owing, including arrears, interest and your lender's legal fees. In addition, interest will continue to mount up as long as the mortgage is outstanding. (This is what happened

to so many homes that were repossessed in the nineties.)
Some really nice lenders are choosing not to charge a
Mortgage Indemnity Premium – so keep an eye out for those
products.

OTHER MORTGAGE RELATED PRODUCTS

Repayment Protection

If for any reason you are unable to continue your regular
mortgage repayments, your home is at risk of repossession by
the mortgage lender. This type of protection is an optional
insurance you can choose to take out to cover you. This can be
quite an expensive thing to have, but could be worth it one
day. This can cover accident, sickness or redundancy.
Generally your lender or insurance companies can offer you
insurance to protect you should these circumstances arise,
and it is always strongly recommended that you take out such
protection. Always check the small print because I'll bet that
when you come to need it, you'll not be covered, but isn't that
always the way with insurance?

Life Assurance

For some types of mortgage (interest only, for example) it may
be a requirement to have some form of life assurance to cover
you in case of your death. Your mortgage provider will offer
their own product, but in many cases you are not obliged to
take theirs and it can be cheaper to shop around.

Some mortgage lenders do insist on their own Life
Assurance product in order for you to take advantage of their
best mortgage interest rate.

In some cases this can be worthwhile, but is always worth
shopping around. If you already have life cover from your
employer and it's enough to cover the mortgage, you may be
paying twice.

IN MY EXPERIENCE

I managed to save over £300 per year on my mortgage life assurance by going to a separate company. If you can do this without forfeiting the best rate, then it's worth investing the time in doing more research and finding a better deal. It's worth knowing that this is seen as an 'add on product' by the lender and a commission of the sale of this product will be subject to a commission to the lender. That's why they can push them hard – or even tie you in by only offering a good mortgage rate IF you take their Life Assurance product as well.

Buildings and Contents Insurance

Again, this will be required and the mortgage lender will have their own product to offer you. Shop around for the best deal. Lenders sometimes charge an administration fee if you arrange your own cover, but many insurance companies will pay that for you as an incentive, so don't let that put you off looking for a better deal elsewhere.

Rent Guarantee Insurance

For property that you buy which you intend to rent out, rent guarantee insurance is only available when the tenant passes extremely stringent referencing procedures. In the event of the tenant failing to pay the rent, this policy will cover the full rental payments until vacant possession is obtained (for up to 12 months excluding the first month's lost rent). Additionally, 50% of the rent will be paid for up to three months after vacant possession has been obtained.

Legal expenses incurred if the tenant refuses to leave the property, or damages or removes the contents, can also be covered by such a policy.

One company who provides a Rental Guarantee Scheme is Home Let. They will credit reference your tenant for you and charge you £60-£80 for six months' cover. This is the preferred supplier to most property management companies.

OTHER COSTS

Mortgage Valuation

Lenders require a standard mortgage valuation to be undertaken on a property before even considering a mortgage application. This is to determine the mortgage value of the property being bought or re-mortgaged.

The standard fees are listed below and depend on the property value (which I find quite perplexing, as you need to have a rough idea on its value before you know what the valuation fee will be – which is why you're having the valuation done in the first place).

Valuation/Purchase Price of Property	Valuation Fee	Administration Fee	Total Fee Required
Up to and not including £60,000	£95	£40	£135
Not exceeding £70,000	£115	£40	£145
Not exceeding £90,000	£125	£40	£165
Not exceeding £100,000	£135	£40	£175
Not exceeding £150,000	£170	£40	£210
Not exceeding £200,000	£200	£40	£240
Not exceeding £250,000	£220	£40	£260
Not exceeding £350,000	£235	£40	£275
Not exceeding £500,000	£275	£40	£315

There are two other types of valuation reports, each giving a greater level of information.

The Home Buyers reports and The Full Buildings (or Structural) Survey. These can be used by buyers as negotiating tools for gaining reductions off the purchase price before exchange of contracts.

The Home Buyer's Report

A Home Buyer's report is a property survey report which has more information than a mortgage valuation but is not as detailed as a full structural survey report. This report is used by the lender in place of the mortgage valuation report and gives more information that will enable a borrower to reach a decision on whether or not to purchase.

The Home Buyer's report provides limited information about the general condition of the property, and would be recommended on property under 10 years old (with a current buildings certificate – NHBC or similar – see *www.nhbc.co.uk* for more information).

When you purchase an older property, you may also want to ask a professional to look around the property to give you a second opinion and verify the building is in reasonable order.

A Home Buyer's report inspection should be carried out no more than five days after you instructed it, and some surveyors will do it even faster. The inspection itself takes between one and two hours to complete, and you should receive the results three to five days later. The report comes on a standard report sheet and is normally between about 8 and 20 pages long. The Home Buyer's report fees will vary across the country and for different surveyor services, and may cost from about £250 to £500, depending on the price of the house. For example, a homebuyer's report for a £1,000 home would cost around £330.

Full Building Survey

I would recommend a Full Building Survey (formally known as a structural survey) for all property being purchased that is over 10 years old (which will be outside its National House Building Council (NHBC) Buildmark or equivalent certificate which acts as a 10-year guarantee against serious structural defects), or if you would like to investigate any specific aspect of the building's condition. A full structural survey is money well-spent to give you the required information prior to making any commitment.

This is the most comprehensive – and the most costly – type of survey. It is suitable for any building, but is especially recommended for older buildings, those constructed out of unconventional materials such as timber or thatch, properties which have had lots of alterations or extensions or which you intend to alter or renovate.

The surveyor will check the property thoroughly, looking at everything that is visible or easily accessible to examine the soundness of the structure, its general condition and all major or minor faults. More specialist surveys can also be carried out on aspects such as foundations, damp proofing, or tree roots, either by a specialist within the firm of surveyors or by an independent specialist surveyor. You will have to tell the surveyor to do any specific checks. If floorboards aren't easily accessible, or the flat roof isn't easy to get at, then the inspector is unlikely to give more than a cursory look, so if you are concerned about these things, ask him to check in detail. His recommendations may come back with further recommended checks. It's YOUR responsibility to action them, not the surveyor's.

The report you receive will be extremely thorough and very long as surveyors are legally obliged to inform you of all the findings of the survey. Don't necessarily be put off if it seems that endless defects are listed – every house has some defects and surveyors tend to show the worst case-scenario for anything they discover. You should be provided with a list of prices for repairs and maintenance work, which will also tend to over- rather than under-estimate prices.

A full structural survey normally takes much longer than the one or two hours required for the Home Buyer's report. The survey report can also take a long time to produce so this is a much lengthier process than for a Home Buyer's report. You will probably have to wait up to two weeks after the inspection for the report, for which there is no standardised reporting format. A buildings survey costs anything up to £1,000, again depending on the price of the house.

How Do I Find A Surveyor?

Ask in the first instance for recommendations from your lender, they probably already have relationships in place. Other professionals you can try are your solicitor or estate agent.

Shop around and get plenty of quotes as it costs a lot to get a survey done and prices can vary. The amount you pay normally depends on the cost of the property you are buying. It is important to discuss in advance how much you will have to pay and what kind of survey will be undertaken.

It is possible that you may have to pay more than once for a survey, if the sale falls through or if you decide not to buy the property on the basis of the survey results and carry on looking.

You are advised to check up on the surveyor's credentials if you are unsure that they are a qualified professional. All surveyors should be a member of the Royal Institution of Chartered Surveyors (RICS). *www.rics.co.uk*. Go and check them out. Just because they say they are members doesn't always mean they are.

Always talk to your mortgage lender before instructing a surveyor as it is usually possible to get the basic valuation done at the same time, which will reduce your costs.

Online surveys

The government has been very keen to speed up the whole home selling process and to enable this to happen, a number of online survey and conveyancing sites are now available.

I have come across one such website that enables online conveyancing called Surveys Online – *www.surveysonline.co.uk* – check out their site to get you started. There are further online survey sites listed in the back of the book.

STOP PRESS: PLANS FOR NEW LEGISLATION

The government is planning to speed up the home buying process by introducing a compulsory seller's information pack. This is good news for buyers as it means that every seller will have to provide potential buyers with a surveyor's report, not necessarily as detailed as a full structural report but enough to satisfactorily judge the condition of the property.

It will also greatly speed up the conveyancing process, and save on solicitors/conveyancers' fees thanks to other information in the pack, including:

- replies to local authority searches
- copies of title documents
- copies of any planning, listed building and building regulation consents
- for new properties, copies of warranties and guarantees
- a draft contract

RENOVATING

THE RENOVATION PROJECT

So you've found the perfect "do me up" property, got the mortgage, completed on the sale and you've even set up camp in the property – now it's time to get to work. Here is the lowdown on what to do. There are tips to help you focus your efforts and help you to increase the value when you come to sell, with questions from real people with real renovation challenges.

The abundance of room makeover and DIY programmes on TV are a reflection of the nation's current obsession with home improvements. But it isn't quite so straightforward in real life.

It is all too easy to view an old and un-modernised property and to base all your costs on how much the decorating and curtains and carpets will cost, completely overlooking the essentials. Don't forget the new damp-proof course, the replacement floorboards, a full inspection of the drains, and even the cost of skips to take all the debris away. Once you have found your dream property, always make a detailed calculation of *exactly* how much it is going to cost to put right before you are the proud owner of a new set of front door keys. You did get that full buildings survey, didn't you? So there shouldn't be any surprises.

Contact reputable builders, plumbers, electricians, carpenters, damp-proof experts, decorators, plasterers and get a good structural engineer to find out exactly what you are letting yourself in for, not only in terms of cost, but also time.

If you plan to live in the property while you do it up, but the property is, at some stage of the renovation, uninhabitable, you will need to build the cost of alternative accommodation into your budget. That could be in the form of a caravan in the garden – in which case don't forget the costs of heating it, especially in the winter, and the cost of storage for all your worldly possessions because you can't fit much in a caravan. If you do have a lot of land, you could consider bringing in a container (the type you see on the back of long loader lorries). I know of one couple who did this and saved a fortune in storage fees. Or you may be staying with relatives who can store your goods or renting out another house. Whatever you do, make sure these costs are factored into your project or you'll be on a slippery slope before you start.

Remember that by moving into the property while extensive building work is going on you may actually slow down the project – which could ultimately cost you more.

If you are going to manage the renovations yourself, do remember to book the various tradespeople with time in-between for the inevitable overrun. Getting the sequence of events right will be key to a smooth operation and if you've not done this kind of thing before, then do ask lots of daft questions. It's better to look silly and get it right than be too afraid to ask and watch as it all goes pear-shaped!

Remember that the electrician can't start until the building work has been done, and that the plastering has to be done after the electrics. It all sounds very elementary but if one trade overruns, you may have to postpone another and this can lead to lengthy delays and lots of rewriting of your project plan.

If you do decide to go it alone and do the majority of the work yourself while holding down a day job, consider the following *very* carefully.

Are you really going to feel like knuckling down to four hours a night stripping woodwork after a hard day in the office?

Will your family cope with your 'absence' every weekend for months on end?

Have you got a very understanding boss who will overlook endless phone calls to the builders' merchants during work hours?

Can your family car double up as a works van easily?

Identify Where to Spend your Time and Money

When you are looking to renovate a property there are a few fundamental areas you need to concentrate on:

- The fabric of the building – check for missing roof slates and fix. A new roof or flashings may be required.
- Windows – do they need replacing? Buyers expect double glazed units in a modernised house. But do replace like-for-like rather than replacing with the latest UPVC option. Check the type of windows in the rest of the street and make sure yours don't look out of place.
- Rewiring and boiler – check out when the property was last re-wired and the age of the boiler. You will need to provide safety certificates if you are planning to rent out the property. You need to get quotes for these and get it done before you consider the redecoration.
- Kitchens and bathrooms are the key areas to spend money on – assuming the structure of the property is sound.

A new bathroom suite or updated kitchen units will certainly help you to get the full market value on the property and it doesn't have to cost a fortune.

You can get good white bathroom suites from around £130 from B&Q – then you need the plumbing costs and tiling. Budget about £300-£400 for fittings, suite, shower, tiles etc. plus labour.

For a new kitchen, look at end-of-line ranges to keep your costs low. Don't invest £10,000's if you plan to sell or let. You won't get your money back.

Don't be put off by the thought of re-plastering – you only need a rough coat to put new tiles on, and the extra cost is marginal if you get someone in.

Getting the labour in might take a few months, so be aware of your timescale.

In my experience, think of spending up to £1,000–£3,000 on a new kitchen or bathroom to get an increase of between £5,000 – £10,000 on the initial property value.

A good bathroom and kitchen are the basics that do need to be in place but there are further modernisation features you may want to consider:

- Move the bathroom upstairs – even if it means losing a bedroom – this can be worthwhile.
- Add a power shower – very important for a buy-to-let property.
- Re-model the downstairs to fit in an extra downstairs toilet – this can be particularly important for a family house.
- Add laminate flooring – can be a good move for family spaces in a family home or for upgrading the living space of a buy-to-let property.
- Convert the loft space – providing you have good access for a full staircase, adding an extra bedroom in the loft space can be a good investment for most property types.
- Always check with your local estate agent before embarking on any major projects, to check if there is a market in your area. You will need to know your likely buyer or tenant before you invest another penny.

Renovation Advice
I get asked hundreds of property-related questions each year and these are the top four topics of concern

This section shares some of the real life advice I have given to my clients over the years. Some questions arrive by email, some by letter, and we always try to respond with free advice in our online forums at *www.homestagers.net*. I have selected just a few samples from the most frequently asked questions, which may help you if you should need ideas of your own renovation priorities.

Kitchens and Bathrooms

Kitchens and bathrooms truly make a sale. Maybe that's why we have more questions on these two critical rooms in the house than any others:

Kitchen renovations – where does Jo start?

We have a Victorian terraced property with a downstairs bathroom at the back of a galley kitchen. We want to move the bathroom upstairs and extend the kitchen. We would like to put a glass roof over the kitchen 'extension' (i.e. where the bathroom was) and remove the kitchen door, put in under-floor heating, move the boiler upstairs and install new cabinets and appliances. Where do we start? With a builder, architect or kitchen design team? Will we need planning permission?

Our Advice:

Well, it sounds like you know exactly what you want which is always a good start.

Begin with an architect: that way, when your plans are drawn up, you can get like for like quotes and submit the plans to the council should you need permission. The architect is the best person to advise at the early stages.

Go to RIBA – Royal Institute of British Architects *www.architecture.com/go/RIBA/* to find one near you.

HOW CAN MICHAEL LIGHTEN HIS CUPBOARD DOORS?

I would like to lighten the cupboard doors in my kitchen. They are currently in a dark oak stain and I am under the impression that I can remove this and lighten them by lime washing, can you advise?

Our Advice:

Yes, you can lighten them by lime washing. You need to rub them down first with fine grade sandpaper to get a key and to remove the existing finish.

Then use a sugar soap – you can now get it in a spray from B&Q. This is a great product to use before applying any wax, paint or a wash (which is just thinned downed emulsion) as it removes all the dust and grease from a surface. Then use paint on the lime wash. Work it in the same direction of the grain. You retain the feel of wood but with a much lighter effect.

Replace the knobs for a chrome alternative and it'll look like you've spent thousands on a new kitchen for a fraction of the investment.

HOW CAN I PROMOTE THE BENEFITS OF A SMALL KITCHEN?

Unfortunately the kitchen in my property is relatively small (8' x 6') and this seems to be the main negative comment on any feedback we have had from viewers. We've been here for 12 years and haven't found it to be a problem other than when we have been cooking dinner for 6+ people. It is semi-open plan into the dining room (which is 13' x 11') so when we've needed more work-top space we've pulled the dining room table over to the kitchen and used that.

Any ideas on how to persuade viewers, other than waiting for somebody who's looking for a small kitchen?

Our Advice:

Small kitchens can be a problem...

I would suggest the following:

- Clear all surfaces completely – leave only the kettle on display.
- If you have dark flooring, replace it with a pale alternative.
- Use a butcher's block for more work top space – not the kitchen table, don't say that to your viewers either.
- Make sure you have enough light coming in – clean windows, fit white roller blinds and turn on any under unit lighting – make sure all the bulbs work.
- If the work surfaces are in a dark colour, consider replacing with a lighter alternative.
- If the unit doors are dark oak, consider using a lime wax to lighten.
- Consider painting the open plan dining room the same neutral colour as the kitchen to make the kitchen area an extension of the dining room, to make both look bigger.

WILL OPENING UP MY GALLEY KITCHEN AFFECT THE VALUE OF MY FLAT?

I have recently bought a 2 bed flat and would like to make various improvements, but want to be sure not to make changes that either decrease the value or make future resale harder.

The flat has a good-sized (for London) reception room (4m x 4m). However, the kitchen is a long galley (4m x 1.8m) which runs the length of the reception room. I am debating the pros/cons of removing the partition wall between the two rooms. I would include some form of breakfast bar as a partial divider between the rooms.

My worry is whether such a change will add/detract from the value of the property when it comes to resale.

Our Advice:

As having a more open space would be more appealing, I expect that you would make the space more saleable and by adding a breakfast bar you would be gaining a feature which doesn't exist at the moment.

Making money on the modification will depend on a couple of things though – how much it costs and when do you think you will come to sell. Providing you intend to stay put for a year, you'll get your money back and then some too.

My advice would be, if it improves the living space for you, do it and it will be appreciated by your buyers when you come to sell.

IS IT WORTH REPLACING OUR YELLOW BATHROOM BEFORE WE SELL?

We have a 3-bedroom turn-of-the-century terraced house, which we wish to sell. The bathroom is tiny and the suite is yellow, also badly lime scaled. Although the rooms are freshly painted the tiles are ugly and will at the minimum need the grout freshening/bath re-sealing. Taking the tiles off will almost certainly mean re-plastering. Should we bite the bullet and have the whole room re-done (actually 2 rooms, as the lavatory is separate) or would it be more cost-effective to clean, clean, clean as much as possible, replace the carpets and then "dress" the bathroom as well as possible, leaving the replacement of the suite to a buyer? I should add that my husband and I are both hopeless at DIY, and could do almost none of it ourselves, other than wield a paintbrush.

Our Advice:

I suppose the question should be – do you want to make the most money on your property as possible?

A new suite will certainly help you to get the full market value on the property and it doesn't have to cost a fortune.

You can get good white suites from around £130 from B&Q – then you need the plumbing costs and tiling. Budget about £300-£400 for fittings, suite, shower, tiles, etc. plus labour.

Don't be put off by the thought of replastering – you only need a rough coat to put new tiles on and the extra cost is marginal if you get someone in.

Getting the labour in might take a few months, so be aware of your timescales. In my experience, think of spending up to £1000 on a new bathroom to get around £5000 back when you sell.

If that's too much investment and time when you want to sell, then use a tile primer and tile paint to make the tiles more up to date, seal around the bath and sink.

To 'work' with your yellow suite, use softer shades of yellow to complement what you have (never use contrasting colours), buy a new shower curtain in white. White and yellow look really clean. Buy new towels and completely de-clutter all the bottles and personal items from the bathroom. You still might find it a problem, but it should stop people being completely put off or offering silly money.

HOW CAN JOHN TREAT HIS PINE CLADDING?

I have just finished half-panelling my bathroom in pine cladding, now I don't know what to treat the wood with.

Would I be better using varnish, oil, or a stain? I wanted to keep the natural pine colour. I've been told varnish will crack and make the wood go black. Would oil protect the wood sufficiently? I will still need to put a silicone seal around the bath, would it stick to oiled wood?

Our Advice:

An interesting question. Cladding can be a good choice for a bathroom.

Using a wood stain should be fine as you are right, varnish

can get flaky in a bathroom.

You should have no problem with the silicon as that will adhere to your bath and tiles as well.

We had a cladded bath panel in our last property and it lasted a good few years.

HOW DO I PAINT MELAMINE KITCHEN UNITS?

I am selling my flat, and need to re-paint the kitchen units. The cabinet doors are solid wood and painted white, the cabinets themselves are white melamine.

Please can you tell me how best to go about painting the melamine so it doesn't look obvious, and what paint is best for the doors, as I don't want a gloss finish as I think a chalky effect would blend better and hide imperfections that I am sure re-painting a kitchen will show up? I am sugar soaping the units and doors now ready to go, so any help would be most appreciated...

Our Advice:

Here are a couple of thoughts:

- If you had unpainted wooden doors you could consider a lime wash, to give you that chalky look, but as they are painted white already I would suggest a silk finish. Choose a pale green or yellow and keep it quite neutral.
- Depending on the type of update you are looking for, one idea would be to spray with a silver paint and varnish over. Another good tip is to use a textured 'hammerite' paint – that would conceal any imperfections. You can get some good colour options – slate grey would look good if you keep the rest of the kitchen very light.
- Use a melamine primer – available at good DIY stores, to ensure a good 'fix' as your base, then the sky really is the limit!
- Add trendy replacement handles and you'll get that new look you've been wanting without blowing your budget.
- Don't forget your tiles – tile paint them if they won't match

your new scheme and use a grouting pen to update the look of the grout. Other people's grime is such a turn off when you do come to sell, so don't forget to clean, clean, clean.

WILL KNOCKING TWO SMALL ROOMS INTO ONE BIG ONE AFFECT OUR PROPERTY'S VALUE?

I live with my husband in a tiny 1-bed ground floor garden flat – a bog-standard Edwardian conversion. We share a front door and hall with the upstairs flat. 'Our' front door leads into a tiny, long, dark and very narrow hallway. Our kitchen (also small but lighter) runs parallel to the hall and we are considering knocking down the wall between them (not a load bearing wall) to open up the kitchen and make it big enough to eat in and light enough to like! This would mean we'd walk straight from our shared hallway into our kitchen and lose 2 small rooms to make one larger, even though the hall doesn't really count as a room (it's so narrow we have to have 'passing spaces'!) We can't bear it as it is, but want to sell up in a couple of years, so I'm wondering if doing this will devalue the property. HELP! Thanks in advance!

Our Advice:

If this is causing you so much grief I would suggest you do knock through even if it means losing the hall.

I would suggest that you can still keep a walk way though and the use of a breakfast bar – with the bottom blanked at the back (where your hall wall would have been – but not the entire length) could be a successful compromise.

At eye level you would see into the kitchen, but you would gain so much more light and space.

Use a light wood such as beech and laminate flooring throughout to open up the space.

SHOULD I REPLACE THE BATHROOM AND KITCHEN BEFORE I SELL?

I am selling a one bedroom flat in a sheltered accommodation block so I am aiming at a specific market – a buyer would have to be over 55 to live there. Prospective buyers so far have commented that the property is in need of modernisation. I thought that purchasers would prefer to put in their own kitchen and bathroom and so have left these as they are – they are both in reasonable condition. The flat could also benefit from a fresh coat of paint and having the carpets cleaned or possibly replaced. Do you think that would be adequate to give a better impression or should I have the bathroom and kitchen replaced as well?

Our Advice:

It's true that kitchens and bathrooms can make or break a sale. It really does depend if you are looking to maximise your property's potential or are looking for a quick sale.

I would recommend that you do freshen up the decor with that coat of paint and do something with the carpets as this can be a real turn-off to buyers.

I would also suggest that if your target buyer base is the over 55s, they are likely not to want to 'modernise' and would prefer to purchase sheltered accommodation that was ready to move in to.

I NEED A KITCHEN MAKEOVER ON A BUDGET OF £500 – HELP!

This summer I'm putting my flat on the market. I have managed to decorate all the rooms apart from the rear kitchen diner and it needs a good makeover. My budget is £500 – can you help!

Our Advice:

Don't panic, it can be done! In fact, I did one kitchen makeover for under £500 that was featured in *Perfect Home* magazine.

Think bright, clean and neutral for the kitchen, here's what to concentrate on:

- Matching units that are well fitted (nothing worse than the viewer opening a cupboard to find the handle comes off in their hand!). Replacing units need not be expensive. Try the high street stores such as Wickes, Homebase or B&Q. Ask about end-of-line ranges or special offers. Keep the style simple and avoid dark wood. Painting the units yourself is an option but this really depends on what they are made of and doesn't always look as good as you hope for.
- A clean floor. A brand new floor is a good investment. White with a regular pattern such as a diamond insert, tends to look very fresh.
- Wall tiles are usually best in white. Just use a tile paint that can be purchased in your high street DIY store.
- Clear the work surfaces and clean until everything sparkles! Only leave a few of the essentials out such as the kettle and some co-ordinating accessories. Add finishing touches of colour such as a bowl of fruit and a couple of healthy plants.
- And finally… As yours is a kitchen diner, be sure to define the dining space (even if it is small) with an appropriately sized table and chairs.
- I just helped a client sell within 2 weeks of a makeover plus he got nearly £10,000 more than the Estate Agents' appraisal.

FLOORS AND CEILINGS

These are notorious problem areas, especially in the realms of the inherited polystyrene tile or dreaded Artex… the answer here is to make sure you have a reasonable budget for re-plastering.

HOW CAN DANNY FINISH HIS UNSIGHTLY CEILING?

I have recently fitted a new kitchen. In doing so I changed it from a partitioned kitchen and dining area to a large kitchen.

However this has left me with a very unsightly ceiling. The main problem is that it has been Artexed using two completely different styles, with a smooth band in the middle where the partition wall was. Obviously polystyrene tiles are no longer an alternative, so what are my options other then replastering or sanding? Is there an acceptable type of tile?

Our Advice:

I can only think of a few of options:

- Have the ceilings skimmed by a professional plasterer.
- Have a false ceiling fitted – more expensive than the first option.
- Clad with tongue and groove and wax to keep it light – not ideal and more expensive.
- Go on a plastering night class and learn to do it yourself.

I still think having it skimmed would be the best option though.

HOW CAN DONNA FILL A HOLE IN HER FLOOR?

How would I go about filling a hole which is just exposed concrete then applying my new lino to the area?

Our Advice:

What you need to do is use a concrete mix to fill in – make sure any dust is removed from the area first. A self-levelling compound can be used on larger areas to level off the entire floor if required.

How can Helen fix her floor grout?

Unfortunately I tried cleaning terracotta floor tiles with diluted caustic soda and the black grouting has now gone patchy grey – how can I blacken the grouting without having to re-grout the whole area?

Our Advice:

The black grout is due to years of build-up.

Try using a permanent marker pen to fill in the greyer areas. If the grout is missing in places, try a grouting pen to replace the missing grout and then 'colour in'.

How can Dave cover his wooden ceiling?

I have wooden ceilings downstairs, without removing them what can I do to cover them up? Could I plaster over them?

Our Advice:

When you say 'wooden' I am assuming you mean cladded in wood. I also assume that the colour would be orange/honey pine? Well, you wanted options so here goes:

- If you want to plaster you will need to board with plaster board first (I'm assuming here that you have ridges in the cladding).
- Or rub down and wax to leave the look of the wood.
- Or paint with satin finish to lighten but keep the wood grain.
- Or remove them and skim with plaster.

Is it difficult to get rid of Artex?

Is it very difficult to get rid of Artex? What would the cost be approximately per square metre?

Our Advice:

Unless the Artex is especially deep and really ugly, I wouldn't even think about removing it, you may be opening up a can or worms you didn't bargain for.

However, if you really can't live with it any more, then you should take into account the following before going ahead:

- If it's thin Artex, then you will need to have the whole area re-plastered.
- If it's thick and you have it removed, it means having it sanded down – very dusty and time consuming.
- You also have be careful if the Artex is pre-50s as some types do contain asbestos and that could cost you thousands.
- My advice, is don't do anything until you have consulted a recommended plasterer to advise for your specific requirements, and they will give you a quote for the job.

WILL LAMINATE FLOORING PUT OFF BUYERS?

I live in a two-bedroom bungalow and intend moving in the next couple of years. I am considering replacing all the carpets with laminate flooring.

I expect most potential buyers for the property will be older people. Is laminate flooring likely to put them off?

Our Advice:

Laminate flooring sounds like a good idea. Don't assume just because you live in a bungalow, that your buyers will be older people. Many younger people buy bungalows too.

Older people I have recommended it to have been very pleased with laminate and wood floors. As well as the aesthetics, they have also been pleased to find it easier to keep clean than carpet. And don't forget the health benefits and dust reduction of a carpet free home.

You should ensure rugs have non-slip grippers to save you skidding around.

I think having good quality flooring throughout can only be a bonus. Make sure it is good quality though. Some laminate can start to split at the joints after a couple of years.

When laying lino or floorboards – how do you cut around awkward edges?

When laying lino or floorboards – how do you cut around awkward edges? Can you provide a step-by-step guide?

Our Advice:

Tiles and planks of laminate are much easier to lay than full 'off the roll' vinyl but you can always use a cardboard template for the tricky areas. If you are not a DIY kind of person and the area you are covering is large, I would recommend that you pay the extra £20/£30 to get a professional in.

However, if you want to have a go yourself try the following tips.

- When cutting into a skirting, lay the plank, vinyl or tile to be cut directly on to the floor. Press its edge against the skirting. Using a pencil or biro, mark the other edge of tile or plank.
- Place the area to be cut on a scrap piece of board and, using a sharp knife pressed against a steel straight-edge, cut firmly through the tile. It will fit perfectly into the space left for it.
- Awkward shapes around sink pedestals, door architrave's etc, are best overcome by first making a cardboard pattern of the precise shape and transferring this to the area of the plank, vinyl or tile.
- Where there is a radiator pipe, cut a slit from the back edge to the pipe position and then cut a circle out for the pipe. When the plank, vinyl or tile is laid, the slit will not be visible.

PAINTING A GARAGE FLOOR – CAN YOU HELP?

I have a question. We have a dry garage floor. We have painted it twice and neither time has the paint stuck to the floor. We live in N.Y. state and they use road salt. We would like to know if there is a paint out there that will stick to the floor. We know that it will not last a long time, but we are now painting it once a year. We do not drive on it for two days after it has been painted and we paint when it is warm and dry out.

Our Advice:

You can buy concrete floor paint that is very hard wearing.

Preparation is everything when it comes to painting! I would suggest that you make sure the surface is cleaned thoroughly prior to painting. Use detergent and a wire brush to remove any oily residues. Rinse and allow it to dry.

I would suggest that you use two coats of paint, allowing each to dry before applying the next.

ATTIC CEILING HAS 25-YEAR-OLD WHITE POLYSTYRENE TILES – PLEASE ADVISE

I've just taken over my parent's old house, which is a Victorian terrace with a large attic room, that I intend to use as an office/study.

The problem is the ceiling, which has old white polystyrene tiles on it, which must have been put up about 25 years ago. The tiles are looking decidedly weathered with grey and yellowing stains. Some of the tiles have disappeared.

I'm concerned that removing the tiles will cause two problems; one we may lose valuable heat though the roof, and two I'm not sure of the state of the original ceiling, which may look pretty awful.

Question is, is there anything you'd recommend to improve the ambience of the room – at the moment we have a natural light source from a Dorma window, and a bright strip light – while also replacing the thermal benefits of the tiles.

I intend to work from home, so would naturally like the room to be comfortable as well as attractive.

Cost is also an issue, so any cheapish options you can recommend would be appreciated.

Our Advice:

I must agree, you need to take down those tiles. They are a potential fire hazard you know!

You will probably find that when you take them off they will leave behind a little of the glue. Use a wallpaper scrapper to lift it of gently.

You could use a textured paint to cover minor imperfections, which is a cheap option at £12 per 5Ltr tub.

You could try covering the surface with a thin linen. This can have some good heat retention qualities. The cheapest way to do this is to add some 2x1 inch batons running the length of the room and using a staple gun, fix the cloth in place. You can get large dustsheets for a few pounds each, which look remarkable good!

You could use wooden tongue and groove again fixed on to batons, but this is a slightly more expensive solution, but perhaps the best for heat retention. You could use a lime wash to keep the whole area as light as possible.

LAYING LINO ON OLD FLOORBOARDS?

I want to lay lino rather than carpet on my kitchen. It is an old flat with floorboards, is this a good enough surface to lay lino onto or should I lay plywood first?

Our Advice:

Good question.

If the boards are old they are more than likely to be uneven. For the best results use marine ply otherwise the boards can leave an impression in the lino.

That said, it can be done, but they just doesn't look as good over time.

BUILDING WORK AND EXTENSIONS

It's not just about looking after the space you already have, but what about extending upwards and outwards...

Here are our top questions and answers for those extensions and loft conversions

DOES KEITH NEED PLANNING PERMISSION?

I am looking to build a new garage 18 feet in front of an existing one. The new garage will not protrude further forward than the building line but will be 2m closer to a boundary fence. The new garage will be 1.8m from the fence once complete.

The garage will be the same height. Do I need planning permission?

Our Advice:

Always check any kind of extension out with a qualified architect. Go to RIBA – Royal Institute of British Architects to find one near you. *www.architecture.com/go/RIBA/*

Depending on exactly where the garage will be positioned will determine whether you will need planning permission. Often extensions can be built without planning permission under what is known as permitted development. So it is worth checking out what the conditions of this clause are.

Some Local Authority Planning Departments run 'surgeries' where you can visit a Duty Planning Officer to discuss an outline proposal and their possible response to a planning application. Because these sessions are free to the public it is a good value way of tapping into expertise. In addition, the Planning Officers can also offer some useful tips and direction about the type of application that would be most likely to receive approval. This could save you time, money and effort if you need to have plans drawn up. Check with your local Planning Department to see if they offer such a scheme or any other form of free advice.

Which is better an over the garage extension or a loft conversion?

Should we add a bedroom and en suite extended out the side of our house over the garage? The width is around 92 inches and the length is 185 inches, so basically long narrow rooms. Or would it be better to do the same but as a loft conversion, giving more of a square room. Which is more cost effective and gives better return for value?

Our Advice:

For both options you need to look at the access points – you must ensure room for a full staircase on the loft conversion and access through existing rooms/corridor for the extension.

Extensions are generally the best option, although you may need to reinforce the garage if the foundations will only support a single level.

However, in your case it sounds like the extension may be a bit slim and the proportion of the loft conversion may be your best choice.

I would suggest you get in a buildings surveyor or architect to get some idea of feasibility and get drawings done. Then you can get quotes and decide from there.

Can you advise the best way forward for a loft conversion?

I have a semi-detached property and want a loft conversion. Can you please advise me on the cost and the best way forward for this.

Our Advice:

Contact a reputable builder and discuss the practical aspects. You need to ensure that you do have the room to do this properly or you could end up losing money on your investment.

You need to ensure you have good access for a full staircase if you intend using the conversion as a bedroom space.

You also need to check that the joists would be strong enough. Getting them strengthened adds to the cost.

Try the following links to find a reputable builder in your area:

- *www.findabuilder.co.uk* – Search the Federation of Master Builder's database, containing more than 12,500 members.
- *www.homepro.com* – Find a quality recommended professional in your area. You agree the quote with the trade professional of your choice. Insurance Backed Guarantees are also available.
- Quote Checkers – Independent consultants online, with the potential to help you save a small fortune for a "small fee".

SHOULD I EXTEND DOWNSTAIRS OR ADD A BEDROOM IN THE LOFT?

Am I better to extend downstairs, i.e. dining room and bigger sitting room, or extend into my loft, bedroom plus en suite?

Our Advice:

Adding an extra bedroom and en suite, if done correctly, can add a significant value to a property because you are adding to the number of actual rooms. You must make sure you have the room for a full staircase for this option to work.

Extending the downstairs as a single story extension does have its drawbacks. Flat roof extensions can make a property look unattractive. You could compromise the remaining grounds of the property.

My advice would be to only do what you actually need as a homeowner, with intentions of staying in the property for a period of time, rather than looking at the added value the extension would have.

I'M PLANNING IMPROVEMENTS: WHAT WOULD YOU RECOMMEND THAT WILL HAVE THE GREATEST EFFECT ON VALUE?

I'm looking to make some improvements to my 1935 3-bed semi. Which would you recommend to have the greatest effect on value; large kitchen, reasonable size kitchen + utility, or loft conversion to add a bedroom. I'd welcome your views/advice. Thanks

Our Advice:

It depends on how much you want to spend. If your kitchen is particularly small, an extension to it would be beneficial.

Separate utilities can add a bit more value.

Adding a fourth bedroom will add the most but not if the kitchen is then proportionally too small for a 4 bedroom house.

It all depends if you need the space or are looking to make money.

Remember that you should limit the amount of work you do based on the location and the fact that it will always be a semi. Most people looking for 4 bedroom homes are looking for a detached too – so don't expect to make as much as a detached.

I would go for the larger kitchen and cost effective units if you are thinking of selling. Don't spend £20k on a new refurbished kitchen when you could spend a fraction of that. Again, if you plan to move, keep the style as simple and neutral as possible.

WHEN TO CASH-IN

I see many common problems when people come to sell... Here are my top questions and answers for those who are selling:

WE NEED TO SELL, AND GET THE BEST PRICE POSSIBLE

We need to sell our bungalow and move down market before retirement. We have a detached bungalow in a good area with a large garden and the property will sell, but we need to achieve as much as possible.

We have 3 bedrooms: two with fitted mirror wardrobes, one with Artex walls, light coloured walls and skirting, light carpeting, dark wooden doors, one with sink. During the 70s we attached beams to the lounge and kitchen ceilings. All the doors are wood stained medium oak with brass fittings as is the skirting board in the living areas.

The kitchen is American oak doors (honey coloured) built under double oven, tiled worktops, spotlights, vinyl flooring, white walls.

Should we put new flooring down? I was thinking of a light wooden floor.

Do you think we should do something about the Artex ceiling and beams?

Should we leave the beams and Artex ceiling in the lounge?

I have two medium oak settees with beige covers and an oak corner dresser. We have metal patio doors in the lounge. The house is decorated in mostly neutral colours but I have a plain red carpet in the lounge, hall and dining room, would you replace this?

The dining room has a pine table, chairs and dresser, and a beech wood settee. My husband thinks it's a waste of money upgrading and we'd still sell without doing anything but I'm not sure if we would achieve as much.

Our Advice:

Your house sounds as if it could do with a bit of money spending on it to bring it up to date.

Dark wooden false beams are not in fashion as they were in the 70s and the Artex will certainly put people off buying.

I recently made over a house in Nottingham who had some of the same 'features' as you describe and they really did struggle to sell before they called us in to tackle the problem.

It sounds like you know exactly what needs doing and I think these case study anecdotes may be of help to persuade your hubby to take note:

One of my clients had been on the market for 3 years before we discussed ways of updating the interior and staging it to sell – it got an offer that same week!

Another was advised by the selling agent to reduce the price by £35,000! – we spent £2,000 to update the interior, and the property sold for the asking price.

And another, who had a very limited budget but a weekend to spare, took our advice and spent £100 and the whole weekend doing all the necessary jobs himself – not only did he get TWO offers the next week, but ended up getting £10,000 more than the valuation!

So, my advice is to keep the replacement carpet to a cost-effective option – go for a neutral Berber in light beige.

Go for a pale lino in the kitchen and take up any carpet you have in the bathroom too and replace with cushion flooring.

SHOULD I CONVERT MY EXTRA KITCHEN BACK INTO A BEDROOM BEFORE I SELL?

I have a three-bed terrace, in which I converted the small room into a kitchen some years ago to rent. I'm now planning to sell, do I leave the kitchen in or do I return the property to its original three beds? I would appreciate your advice.

Our Advice:

It really depends if you have converted the property into two discreet flats or not (with two bathrooms). If you sell it as it stands, who would be your prospective buyer? Would you only be targeting some one looking to buy-to-let or to 'share'? Is there a sitting tenant? This would limit your buyer base.

More bedrooms will return a higher valuation as larger

spaces are more sort after and the mid market is VERY buoyant right now.

If it's not two discrete flats, having a bedroom as a kitchen would look very odd if it was left as is. Odd is a negative you need to remove.

My advice would be to return the room to a bedroom before you put it on the market and push it toward people wanting to move out of one bedroom flats.

WE ARE TRYING TO SELL OUR EMPTY COTTAGE, SHOULD WE "STAGE" THE ROOMS OR LEAVE EMPTY?

We have moved out of the cottage we are trying to sell. It has no furniture only bits and pieces, like dried flowers and wicker baskets etc. What can I do to make it look more attractive and cosy? Is it better, in your opinion, to stage the rooms as if they are still lived in, or leave all rooms empty, so they look larger?

Our Advice:

This is a good question, which we get asked a lot.

It's often not possible to leave a property furnished, but try to ensure that the place is warm well before any viewers arrive (especially in winter months). Replace dried flowers with paper/fabric flowers. There are some good choices from garden centres. Choose cream lilies with large green leaves for best effect and a touch of opulence.

Make sure you leave a gilt-framed mirror over the mantle to keep a focal point to the room. If you have a couple of large candlesticks, use them to balance the mantle.

Leave scented candles in staged places. This can add a welcoming smell rather than that unwelcoming empty smell you can get. Use Vanilla, as it is a rich odour reminiscent of chocolate rather than any strong air freshener that can smell like you are masking something unpleasant.

Empty or staged? Well a staged room will 'win' over an empty one any day – you just have to think of those lovely show homes you see.

You can either buy or rent full furniture packs to stage your home. Although renting is not necessarily cheaper than buying, at least you don't have the additional problem of disposing of the furniture once the property has sold. Look for furniture rental packs for up to 4 month periods.

Hope this gives you some ideas on helping you sell.

I WANT TO SELL MY SMALL FLAT IN BATTERSEA. IT'S CURRENTLY IN A PRETTY AWFUL CONDITION – SHOULD I DO IT UP OR SELL AS IS?

My small flat in Battersea is currently in a pretty awful condition, and if I were buying it, I think I would want to gut it, re-plaster, re-wire and re-plumb. Is the cost of doing this likely to be covered by the increased price I would get, or would I be better off just selling it as is?

Our Advice:

If you sell a property with that amount of work needed you may end up 'giving' it away. It's worth getting quotes for the work you think needs to be done. Then get a valuation from 3 local estate agents and ask them what it would be worth 'as is' and then if all the work was done. But tell them you ARE doing the work or they will convince you not to do it. Generally, they want to sell your house as it is to meet their sales targets so won't care about what you want to do.

My feeling would be that you would get your money back (and some) as I expect the area you are in is still a buoyant market, but you will need to get a local, expert view on this.

Make sure you have enough funds left to redecorate, add a power shower and do up the kitchen. These areas really DO help you sell.

HOW DO I GET MORE VIEWERS?

Our house has been on the market for 10 weeks now with a local estate agent but we have only had 2 viewings. Any ideas how we can generate more interest? The estate agent has advertised the property 4 times in the local press.

Our Advice:

There are 3 things you need to ensure are right to maximise the viewings for your house...

1. Is the price right for your property type in your area – Many estate agents give you a high valuation just to get your business (so beware)! Check prices of similar properties in your area.

2. Advertising – It's good to see that your agent has advertised your property 4 times. Ensure that the pictures you get really show off your house to its full potential. If you don't like the pictures, get them to do them again, until you're happy! Internal shots can help make your house stand out.

3. Presentation – We all know first impressions count, so make sure you maximise your "drive-by desirability"! Many viewers 'drive by' before committing themselves to a viewing. SO MAKE THE MOST OF IT!

TINA'S TOP TEN IMPROVEMENT TIPS AND SEVEN REMODELLING SECRETS

Top ten improvement projects that will add the most value to your property, and seven secrets for a successful remodelling project.

Many property owners will look at remodelling their home at some point. Sometimes it is so you don't have to move, at least for a while. Some will buy a property that hasn't quite met their wish list and buy with a view to making a few structural changes. But as many people do move, usually between five and seven years, you will need to be sure that you will get your money back on the improvements you make when it is time to sell.

But when should you decide to stop sinking money into a home and buy a bigger place? And how much work is too much when it comes time to recovering re-modelling costs through a home sale?

With these concerns in mind, here are few tips for those of you who are struggling to decide what projects to do to add the most value to your property.

TOP TEN IMPROVEMENT TIPS:

1) Always protect the character of your home when you look to replace the windows. Nothing sticks out more than a new addition in a completely different architectural style. Be consistent. Recognise your home's character and stay within its framework.

2) The most financially rewarding areas to remodel are usually the kitchen and the bathroom. New cooking appliances and cabinets can attract more buyers and may command a slightly higher price for the home than a comparable, unmodernised one on the market. Simple repairs that are made to last will bring you the biggest returns upon sale.

3) If you've just spent £5,000 re-modelling your living room but didn't extend your small kitchen, the chances of increasing the number of interested buyers are slim.

4) If you have a downstairs bathroom, do look to move it upstairs, even if that means losing a bedroom. Properties with downstairs bathrooms are very unpopular and will always reach much lower prices. The value you lose on the bedroom will be more than recovered by a new bathroom upstairs.

5) Converting the garage to an additional living space and building above it could be a better option than investing in an expensive loft conversion and a one-storey extension, especially if your loft conversion doesn't conform to building regulations. To comply, you must have a full staircase and

enough natural light coming in through the windows. Not converting a loft to building regulations means you can't include the additional space as a bedroom when you come to sell. If you do convert, do it properly!

6) Adding a downstairs cloakroom or additional toilet is especially good for property targeted at families.

7) Power showers and wet rooms are desirable for professionals in executive houses or apartments.

8) En suite, with his and hers basins, are the new trend in apartments.

9) Under-floor heating in kitchens and bathrooms for family and professional property is always a great investment.

10) An extra room which can be used as a home office or playroom is increasingly desirable for all property types.

SEVEN REMODELLING SUCCESS SECRETS

1) Be sure to install modest, solid fixtures rather than top of the range options. It's easy to quickly over-spend and not get your money back.

2) Replacing worn or dated carpeting or tiles and laying wooden floors can give your home an immediate advantage over similar properties in the area.

3) Updating paint colours in all areas of your home can be of great benefit without costing a fortune.

4) Use lighter, neutral colours, such as cream, beige and off-white when adding new flooring and wall colours. Fewer buyers will turn away because their tastes are different to yours.

5) Keep it simple when you remodel.

6) Look at your home as though you are the buyer. If you find the room at the back could be brightened by a larger window or french doors then a potential buyer will probably feel the same.

7) Don't go overboard. Concentrate on improving two or three deficiencies in your home. More than likely, the time and money you spend adding to the quality of your home will be rewarded with greater profit at selling time.

REALISING YOUR INVESTMENT

Once you've purchased your property, and done the necessary updating or remodelling, you need to decide whether to rent the property out, or turn it around and sell for a profit.

This will depend very much on what your initial game plan was at the very beginning.

You will either have planned to:

- rent out the property, to gain an income and cover your mortgage payment, whichwill cover your investment over a long period of time;
- sell immediately on completion of your renovation project in the hope of making a profit on the purchase price immediately.

The following chapters look at renting and selling your property.

RENTING

GETTING SOMEONE ELSE TO PAY YOUR MORTGAGE

Getting someone else to pay is exactly what you do when you rent out your investment property

If you are considering renting out a property for the first time there are a few things you need to know. Here we look at the types of tenant you can get for your type of investment – from student lets and social services tenants, which means a steady, guaranteed monthly income, to the young professional let and the corporate tenant which can return very good capital growth.

WHAT IS A TENANCY?

Here we delve into the legalities of renting property. Understand this and you shouldn't go far wrong.

According to the *www.landzone.co.uk*, a tenancy is an "estate in land", granted for a determined period of time (term of years or fixed term – six months, one year, 21 years, 99 years etc.) or a specific period (a periodic tenancy – yearly, monthly, weekly, even daily).

In return for the "time limited" but exclusive use and possession of the land (and any building/s on the land) the tenant pays the landlord a rent.

The landlord may be the freeholder (owner for life – life tenant) or a tenant herself.

For example:

Freeholder (owner) Landlord grants tenancy to:

Tenant A (Head lease holder)

Tenant A grants a tenancy to "B" (sublease holder)

Tenant B grants a tenancy to "C" etc.

So long as each subsequent sublease is shorter than the previous one there is no problem.

To all intents and purposes, whilst a tenancy is in force, the tenant occupier is the owner of the land and can act as any other owner would, so long as it's within the terms of his lease agreement and current statutory requirements (Acts of Parliament).

WHAT IS A LICENCE?

A tenancy gives the tenant a legal interest in the land – in effect, legal ownership for the period of the tenancy. The tenancy can even be sold (assigned) to another tenant.

Conversely, the grant of a license does **not** create an estate in land and the licensee does not gain an interest in the property, purely permission to occupy it. Hotel guests, hostel residents, employees of a business residing on the premises, and holiday-renters are all on licence agreements, not leases.

LONG TENANCIES OR LEASES

Residential landlords are mainly concerned with letting on short tenancies (up to seven years) but if they let out flats they may themselves only have bought a long lease on the flat – usually up to 99 years.

A long lease involves the purchase or payment of a premium (purchase price of the lease) along with a small annual rent and service charges. See Long Leases.

MULTIPLE TENANTS

When more than one residential tenant occupies a property it is common to have all the individuals sign the lease

agreement so that all have **joint and several** liability. If one
tenant absconds, all the others, or if the landlord can find only
one, just one of the others, is responsible for all the rent and
expenses.

Tenants should ensure that their sharers in a joint tenancy
are responsible people, or they may find themselves footing
the bill!

CREATING A TENANCY

A tenancy can be created by the conduct of the parties and
does not need to have a written agreement to be legally binding. Once a person is given possession of land or property
(usually by possession of the keys) and the owner accepts rent
payments, a tenancy comes into legal existence.

Creating tenancies on a casual basis such as this (even for
friends; in fact, especially for friends) is not the sort of thing
any sensible landlord would do! A written agreement or lease
is absolutely crucial to any successful tenant–landlord relationship.

Any landlord (or tenant) without a written agreement is
trusting to fate or, more specifically, the civil courts. The relationship is then governed entirely by whatever statutory rules
exist.

Modern agreements aim to strike a fair balance between
the interests of both the tenant and the landlord and should be
in plain English.

It's good practice for landlords to make sure that tenants
understand their agreements (obligations) at the signing of
the agreement, by discussing the terms.

Tenants in any doubt should seek legal advice, though reputable "standard" residential tenancy agreements often afford
some reassurance.

TENANCY AGREEMENT OR LEASE?

Ordinary written residential tenancy agreements can be
bought "off the shelf" from various sources.

So long as these agreements have been well drafted they often suffice quite nicely for residential tenancies. Experienced landlords and agents often like to include specific clauses of their own, and may have them prepared by a solicitor.

An ordinary written agreement cannot be used for a tenancy exceeding **three years in length.** Tenancies for longer periods need a lease by deed.

Anyone can draw up a **tenancy agreement**, but a **lease** by deed requires a solicitor or licensed conveyancer.

What kind of Residential Tenancy?

There are currently 3 kinds of residential tenancies:

- The **Rent Act Tenancy** – tenancies entered into before 15 January 1989.
- The **Assured Tenancy** – introduced by the Housing Act 1988.
- The **Assured Shorthold Tenancy** – introduced in 1988 but modified by the 1996 Housing Act.

The Rent Act Tenancy

These tenancies give the residential tenant considerable security of tenure and they also regulate the level of rent payable by the tenant.

Basically, these are uneconomic to operate and landlords need to exercise caution when purchasing properties with existing tenants, in case there are any Rent Act tenants.

As a general guide, a property with a sitting Rent Act tenant is worth 50% of its vacant possession value.

The Assured Tenancy

The modern assured tenancy still gives tenants security of tenure, but it does enable the landlord to charge a market rent and to regain possession on certain grounds, as detailed in the

Housing Act 1988. For example, if the tenant falls behind in his rent payments by more than two months, the landlord can apply to the courts for a possession order.

THE ASSURED SHORTHOLD TENANCY

A special kind of Assured Tenancy is the Assured Shorthold, which has one additional special ground for possession – it is a guaranteed granting of a possession order after an initial agreed period (the shorthold period) of usually six months.

All new tenancies since 28 February 1997 are automatically Assured Shortholds, unless the agreement has specified an Assured Tenancy.

Shorthold Tenancies granted after 15 January 1989 and before 28 February 1997 are only enforceable by the landlord if the correct notice is served at the start. A prescribed form Section 20 Notice is needed.

DOCUMENTATION

You need to prepare yourself with lots of documentation:

Lodger Application Form Get applicants to complete a form, then take time out to review the application. Make sure you get third party contact details, bank details, NI number.

House Share/Lodger Agreement Get a legal agreement that spells out what they can and can't do, when they pay, deposits etc.

Smoke Alarm Release form Check the alarm in the presence of the lodger/tenants; get them to sign the form to say that it was tested in their presence.

Gas Certificate Get your system checked out by a Corgi Registered Gas Engineer.

Rent Book Get one month's deposit, plus one month's rent in advance, to ensure you get at least one month's notice.

Standing Order Form Preferably get your tenant to complete a standing order form so money is transferred automatically to your account and you don't have to chase tenants for cash.

INSURANCE

In these days of higher risks and a litigious public, adequate insurance cover is vital. The types of cover you need to consider are:

Buildings cover – your mortgage company will insist on this.
Contents cover – your own contents should be adequately covered, whilst your tenants should cover their own contents as well as accidental damage to your property.
Public liability – covers you for civil actions brought by tenants who may sustain injury on your property.
Loss of rental income cover – this can be had for a small percentage of the annual rental income.

NEW LANDLORDS – POINTS TO WATCH

- Once a tenancy has been created it cannot be changed to another type of tenancy on renewal.
- Rent Act Tenancies can seriously damage your wealth, and perhaps your health as well!
- Beware when buying properties with sitting tenants. Are there any Rent Act tenants?
- If there are early Shorthold tenants, has a Section 20 Notice been properly served and does a proper Shorthold agreement exist?
- Never, ever create a tenancy on a casual basis – always have a substantial written agreement which is properly witnessed on signing.
- Make sure that all occupants in your property are documented tenants, having signed an agreement. New arrivals should be put on the agreement as soon as possible.
- Never try to force a tenant to leave – a court possession order must always be obtained if the landlord wishes to end a tenancy.
- If in doubt about the financial security of the tenant or for younger tenants, always try to obtain a surety agreement (guarantee) from parents or another homeowner willing to

stand surety in case of default or damage.
- *Landlordzone.co.uk* – is an informative website that I would recommend to all new landlords.

A QUICK GUIDE TO BECOMING A LANDLORD

With rising interest rates, becoming a landlord is *not* a get rich quick option. You need to be in it for the long term in order to see a growth in the value of your property in approximately ten years. During the investment period, you need to be able to cover the cost of any mortgage (including increasing interest rates), periods when the property is empty, the costs of maintenance and repairs, as well as any management costs.

MANAGING THE RENTAL

There are two options: manage the rental yourself, or contract a lettings company to manage it for you.

The very best rule of thumb to remember if you choose to manage a rental property yourself is 'proximity'. It will need to be very local to your main residence, so that you can be called out in case of an emergency. That's much more difficult if you live a hundred miles away! Because called out you will be. Every time there is a problem with the electricity, the boiler, the roof, the leaky taps, the bin collection, you will receive a call and be expected to sort it out.

It's not to say it can't be done, but having all the responsibility of a landlord does mean that you can't just sit back and let the money roll in. You need to give your tenants a good level of service.

You need to make sure you have a good relationship with good tradesmen. This will be your 'A' team and will include a:

- Plumber
- Electrician
- Carpenter
- Handyman
- And all the contacts you may need at the local council too!

Below, I've taken a look at the costs and the benefits of having someone else manage your properties for you, so that you can make an informed decision about what's best for you.

> **Property Management Checklist**
> 1) How long have they been in operation?
> 2) Can you talk to an existing investor who uses them?
> 3) Check the small print in the contract.
> 4) Review their Investment Property Examples.
> 5) Review high yield property vs yield plus property growth (in plain English this means look at the types of property they have on their books – 'high monthly rent against high increase in value').

Look for a well-established company with a solid background in estate agency and property management.

Many companies have dealt with the large mortgage lenders to refurbish, sell or rent repossession and relocation properties.

Most first time investors don't have the required knowledge themselves or lack time to build a portfolio of property themselves and manage it. That is where property investment and management companies, who can take on the whole thing for you, can come into their own.

The obvious downside is that you will have to pay them a percentage of your rental income, but they will provide you with many of the safeguards you'll not get if you try to do it all yourself.

Typical lettings management costs include:

- A set-up fee of around £100 for each tenancy. This cost includes initial inspection, property itinerary, promotion (advertising and lettings board).
- Then another £100 for each tenancy agreed. This will usually be charged again each time the tenancy is renewed, and you will pay this on each tenant, which is an important factor for you to consider in multiple occupancy tenancies like bed-sits or student house shares.

- Ongoing, you will pay around 10% of the gross rent collected on your behalf; this is usually deducted before the remainder is passed to you.
- In addition, you will usually authorise them to spend around £200 for urgent maintenance work, anything in excess of that they will need to seek further approval from you.
- Property management companies can also source the property for you initially, usually at a very low, or under market value price (especially when they are selling repossession property). The property is usually refurbished, decorated, carpeted and furnished, and some companies have packages available to do all that.
- Then they find a tenant and provide the full management service with the investor receiving monthly rent in arrears. That way the tenant can achieve all the benefits of investing in the property, but with none of the associated work. All at a price, obviously.
- These companies have made extensive contacts over the years with estate agencies, lenders and asset management companies and are continually seeking out suitable property for acquisition, to ensure the investor receives the best value for money. This enables the investor to choose between either low cost high yield properties with little capital growth, or higher value properties with both a good yield and attractive capital growth. As the portfolio is built up, often you will see a mixture of both.

GETTING THE RIGHT TENANTS

Knowing your target tenant and pandering to their every need might not seem the right thing for a landlord to be doing – but just watch the rental value rocket if you do!

With increasing interest rates, you must ensure your rental income covers any increase in your mortgage payments.

Gone are the Days of the *Rising Damp*-style of Landlord!
In the 21st Century things have changed – tenants demand
so much more...
   The best way to make a success at 'Playing the Property
Game' and find and keep good tenants is to take good care
of the building and take good care of the tenants too. If
they like you they will stay with you, which is important,
because a tenant that renews every 6 months will save you
time and money finding a new tenant.

STUDENT LETTINGS

Student homes and student lettings are a sound choice for
anyone looking to play the property game. Student lets are
usually paid for, either a term at a time in advance, or monthly
via direct debit, and there is always demand each year. You do
need to buy your property in a town or city where there is a
university or college and the property needs to be within easy
reach of the facility, either by foot or by bus. Parking is becoming an increasingly sort-after requirement as well.

HOUSING BENEFIT TENANTS?

When considering tenants in receipt of housing benefits you
should not be under the illusion that the council is responsible to you for the rent. Although the council provides help to
tenants, the payment of rent remains the responsibility of the
tenant.
   You should also ensure you get a deposit and around two
months' rental upfront. As housing benefit payments can take
up to 12 weeks to come through.
   Tenants that move from one property to another will have
to make a fresh housing benefit claim, and therefore may not
be entitled to the same level of benefit claimed previously.
This even includes moving from one bedsit to another in the
same house!

HOLIDAY RENTALS

Holiday lets demand a different type of tenant again. The marketing to this type of tenant will be very different. You may want to invest in your own website and have a number of pictures available as it's unlikely that people will visit the property prior to booking. You will also need to allow for on-line transactions or at least to do telephone bookings and credit card transactions, to make booking easy. The AA is one good website to be listed on but there are numerous sites available to cover different areas. A clear cancellation policy needs to be included in your terms of business.

WHO THE INVESTOR DOES NOT RENT OUT TO ...
Typically, they do NOT rent out to housing benefit tenants and here's why...
They are paid four weeks in arrears – not in advance.
There is no increase in rent.
When there is a change in the tenant's circumstances their benefit stops.
These types of properties often have a lower rental return.

WHO THE INVESTOR DOES RENT OUT TO ...
Corporate lets, which usually hold the greatest rental return.
Student lets.
Young professionals.

WHO WOULD RENT YOUR PROPERTY?

The property needs to be both practical and affordable and there is a type tenant you should be aiming your property at.

- 19–35-year-olds.
- Singles/partners or a share.
- Average wage is £18,000.

WHAT PROPERTY IS BEST FOR RENTAL?

A two bed terraced house is better than a flat or apartment as
you have fewer disputes over communal areas, services and
parking.

- These properties are freehold.
- You own the whole property.
- You only have neighbours to the side, not above and below.
- They are ultimately the easiest to sell, attracting the first
  time buyer. Who, incidentally, now averages 37 years old!

OVERCOMING PROBLEMS

It doesn't always go to plan. So what can you do?

If you are unhappy with the way your property is performing then there could be a number of reasons:

- The managing agent is not adequately carrying out his
  duties.
- The rent may be set too high for the local demand for similar properties.
- The actual location of your property maybe deterring
  potential tenants.
- Perhaps the property needs some minor improvements or
  re-decoration to improve tenancy.

The solutions to these problems could include:

- Change the letting agent to one who is more proficient.
- Reduce the rent according to local demand to improve
  occupancy.
- Sell the property if it is deemed unsuitable for you.
- Carry out minor repairs and re-decoration.

Change Your Letting Agent

This can be the simplest way to improve the occupancy of your property. Changing to a pro-active and efficient agent with good local knowledge and experience should improve your occupancy and, therefore, your income. It may also be possible to change to an agent whose fees are lower but who provides the same level of service, thus increasing your margin.

Rental Refresh

As time goes by, a property will start to date and the only way you can keep on getting top rent for the property is to keep it

a) well maintained
b) keep the fixtures and fittings up to date.

In my experience, the kitchen and bathroom need to be replaced every six to 10 years, depending on wear and tear. Do not fit the most expensive kitchen or bathroom, because even if the fittings last, they will still date, so do plan to update these fixtures at a regular interval.

Handles, light fitting, carpets and curtains will also need updating every few years.

Staging to Rent

Attract a better calibre of tenant by staging to rent. This is especially important in an over-saturated market as we are starting to see in London. Professional tenants are demanding much more from property today and many corporate lets (temporary accommodation provided to employees who are working away from home for long periods) are required to be fully furnished and accessorised for immediate occupation.

Some management companies are already tying in with furniture rental agencies and home staging services to ensure the 'whole package' is not only offered for rent, but the lifestyle is also available, just as a show home is presented to give you the impression of lifestyle – so you can just move in and everything you'll need will be there for your use, from cutlery in the drawers to sheets on the bed.

To compete in this market and get a good price, you will need to offer 'everything', but it can be well worth it as rental value will increase accordingly.

REDUCE THE RENT

If the rental market takes a tumble, you may be forced to reduce the rent. This can also happen if the market is flooded with rental property. The better-looking properties will return a better rental value and be let for more months of the year, but if you don't have the budget to update, then a short-term solution is to reduce the rent.

BUT, be warned, this is a slippery path; you will attract a lower calibre of tenant, who may not care for the property, which in the end may cause you even more problems.

SELL YOUR PROPERTY

You may wish to sell a property to release some capital, to downsize your portfolio or just to cut your losses in an under-performing area, where properties with rent arrears should be sold to reduce the impact on your capital.

This is a good time to refresh your property before you put it on to the market as it will gain a better price if it is presented at its best. Often, after a property has been rented out for a few years, the carpets will need cleaning if not replacing altogether, the walls will need a fresh coat of paint and even the kitchen or bathroom could do with some work. You must do this before you get an estate agent to value it and you will be able to put it on the market at a higher price, certainly achieving more than the initial investment required to do the work. Bringing in a professional home staging company at this stage will help you to identify where to spend your budget wisely and give you the value of their experience in knowing what works in your market.

SELLING

Whether it is six months or ten years on, you may want to release your equity capital to allow you to move on to the next stage of the game

ESTABLISHING THE PRICE

Knowing the right price to put your property on at is a bit hit and miss. This is where an experienced estate agent comes in very handy. Always, always get at least three **independent** valuations. By this I mean that you bring in the estate agent to value and DO NOT tell him what figure the other agents have given you as a selling price. If you do, you might find that you get into a bidding competition for the business, with the valuation being artificially high, just to get the instruction.

When you have got the three valuations, unless they are all in the same ballpark, I would always recommend you go with the middle price – not the highest, unless the agent can give you a local example of a similar property he has SOLD at that price (rather than one he has on his books currently).

If you do use an estate agent to market your property, do make sure you look at the quality of the marketing materials and the frequency of the advertising. Don't get drawn into a contract that means you have to stay for 12 weeks or more. If they said they could sell it, it shouldn't be around after 12 weeks! I would always recommend no tie-in period. You can negotiate on the terms of doing business. If they won't budge, take your business elsewhere.

WAYS TO SELL

In this section, I will look at the pros and cons of selling via an estate agent, through a sales management company or doing it yourself, and ways to get the best from whichever method you choose.

CHOOSING YOUR ESTATE AGENT WISELY

Typically it's the estate agent who will market your property and get prospective buyers to your door – get this wrong and you'll have a long wait!

IN MY EXPERIENCE:
When I sold my previous property, I went into my local agent's branch and caught one of the advisors talking down a nearby area.

That could have been my property she was talking about. How would she get viewers to my door if she talked to potential buyers like that?

Needless to say I went elsewhere with my instruction.

You need to review a number of things before settling with an estate agent who is going to represent you and your little palace:

- Check their location. Is it in the high street or back street?
- Look in their window at their display. Does it look inviting, clear, and draw you in?
- Speak to the staff and make sure you think of them as helpful and friendly. If not, prospective buyers could well be put off going in to that office in the first place or ever going back if they do have some interest in your property.
- Look at the quality of the details they hand out. There is NO excuse for not having good quality photos on every set of details. Gone are the days when a black and white photocopy will do.

- Check how often the agent advertises each property. Once per month in their own newspaper isn't good enough. You need to ensure that YOUR property goes in to the local property guide every fortnight. Property guides are either free newspapers delivered to all doors in your area, or in the local evening newspaper once a week. If people don't know about your house, you can't expect to sell. Check the print quality of the newspaper is up to scratch. I've seen some awful reprint quality in some newspapers and the advert is just wasted. That means it will take much longer for you to sell.

Only then, would I recommend that you book a valuation.

Don't go with the cheapest commission rate. In my experience 'cheap' commission rate means little work in return and you could be on sale for months, not get people through the door, and not even get your property advertised as often as with other agents. These are all areas worth considering.

Don't automatically put your property on with the agent who has given you the highest valuation. Hard I know, but it can sometimes be a ploy.

The Ombudsman for Estate Agents, the industry's voluntary complaints scheme, issued figures in 2002 stating that complaints about estate agents rose from 4,466 in 2000 to 5,730 in 2001 – that's a massive 25% increase and a new record, not to be proud of.

The Ombudsman is there to protect you and mediate when problems arise. They can award compensation of up to £25,000, although last year's highest award was £5,000.

Complaints included excessive fees, disputes about property particulars, conflicts of interest, and sales boards going up too soon, or not being taken down.

However, it's not all bad news! Just under 1.5 million properties were sold in the UK in 2002 and if you work out the maths (or math, for you American readers) for complaints it's actually less than 0.05%.

Any industry is subject to complaints; however. you can avoid some of the common mistakes by being prepared.

Do estate agents really overvalue properties? Do they overvalue to get the instruction, expecting a sale due to high demand or thinking that they can always reduce it later if it doesn't sell? Does this thinking actually give a good level of service to their clients or is it a no-win scenario?

With an increase in complaints and the housing market going crazy – what are estate agents doing to help?

I seem to meet the absolute extremes – from the one who valued a property at £220,000 and when it didn't sell suggested the price was dropped by £30,000, yes £30,000! And they said that it was down to "location". Well shouldn't that have been taken into account when the property was valued in the first place – after all the house hasn't moved! What is the homeowner to think? Does this company know what they are doing or are they just trying to exploit the market?

The estate agent went on to tell the owner that no matter what they did, the property wouldn't fetch the asking price. Then we were called in. We worked with the client to help maximise their property value, and with £1,000 spent and two weeks of redecorating and staging – and after an American style open day – we finally acheived the full asking price.

The other extreme – well, I have met estate agents out there who do care, although an awful lot say that with the market being so buoyant, anything sells and it's easy money, but better not tell that to their clients … in the latest review of estate agents, sellers want to know what they are doing with their extra 20% commission. As house prices have increased by approx 20% over the last year and as most agencies are paid on a commission of sale basis, there are now complaints asking what extra services the agent is offering for this astronomical increase in their fees. Easy money indeed!

When property is not selling in a buoyant market, it's all to do with ensuring the property does meet expectations. Most estate agents will tell the seller to 'do nothing' to it, because they want your sale on their books. Some agents will even disagree with the high price the owner wants to put on the property, but goes along with it anyway, so they don't lose the sale. They are 'salesmen': they can sell anything to anyone. But if you want to get the maximum from your property, it takes work. So if you think your house needs some work doing, chances are it will. That's why getting a number of viewpoints is so essential.

What a Nice Man!

I did meet the nicest man. Not surprising, you might think; after all there are many of them about. The surprising difference about this nice man is that HE IS AN ESTATE AGENT!

Now I know the words "nice man" and "estate agent" do not usually feature in the same sentence, given the reputation estate agents can have, but bear with me.

The man in question is James Richards of Richards & Co – a specialist estate agent dealing with property in the tiny Wharfedale villages in Yorkshire. James's career in estate agency began in 1984.

He aims to bring together the best of what he has seen whilst working around the country, together with a number of new ideas to provide quality, integrity and service in an industry where these have often been lacking.

His estate agency is very successful and the key behind his success is simple – service. Not really a radical idea, but James uses it to his advantage.

He believes that no matter when a potential seller might want to sell their property he's happy to go and see them at any time and, even if they don't want to sell in the short term, he would never think of them as time-wasters.

He offers all potential clients a free guide on how to choose an estate agent, which gives them the opportunity to weigh up using his services versus other estate agents. It's the fact that this guide is so helpful and points out exactly what to expect from an estate agent that makes sellers want to sell their properties with James, because it shows the level of service he can provide.

He is also of the opinion, that if a property needs a bit of work, he'd rather be honest with the client and if by spending a bit they can add to the value, he'll say so.

James uses the internet to full advantage by putting all his properties' details on his website – and his commitment is that they are never out of date, unlike so many.

What I admire about James is that he makes no apologies for his fees; yes he charges a higher percentage than most other estate agents. But when you add in the level of service and the fact that the properties he sells are usually sold at a higher value than other estate agencies have suggested, the slightly higher fee is well worth it. A very satisfied client recently paid the bill promptly and sent a box of chocolates as well.

James is well aware that things do not always go smoothly. One of his very few clauses in his contract is that if a client is unhappy at any time and wishes to change estate agents, he will happily let them go and even give them £50. The only stipulation being that the client has to call in the office to collect it, or he will take it round. The purpose of this is so that James can enquire about the problem to make sure that it never occurs for any future clients. It must be said that in his two years of trading not one client has taken him up on his offer. (An estate agent that pays you – now that is different.)

On his part, he is reluctantly expanding into other areas. The reluctance is because he doesn't want to lose any of the high level of customer service he currently offers. But not surprisingly "word of mouth" has earmarked him as the best estate agent to have in the area and he is inundated with requests from people to sell their houses in other areas.

James still prefers old-fashioned customer service. He deals directly with his clients and enjoys every minute of it, and his success proves it works.

Hopefully, one day this will be the minimum standard for all estate agents and the words nice man (or woman) and estate agent in the same sentence won't be so alien.

The Office of Fair Trading provides a free booklet called – 'Using an Estate Agent to buy or sell your home'. Call Enquiries on 08457 22 44 99 for your free copy or visit *www.oft.gov.uk*

Five-Step Checklist For Selling Via An Estate Agent

1) Always get three independent valuations and go for the middle one - not the highest.
2) Get an idea of the value by looking at similar properties on the market which have sold.
3) If you are getting viewings but not offers, chances are the price is right, but the presentation needs work. The expectation is set higher than the viewers can visualise.
4) Make sure you have the right marketing strategy to maximise the exposure of your property.
5) To enable you to afford your next property, consider spending a little time and money to realise the house's full potential and stage it as a show home.

For Sale by Owner

With the advent of internet marketing, property portals and Sale by Owner websites – do you still need an estate agent to sell your house?

Even under a "sole agency" agreement, there is nothing to prevent a homeowner from advertising and selling the property privately... with no liability to pay commission if he/she ultimately finds a buyer without the help of their agent.

Since the introduction of the Unfair Contract Terms Act, it is very rare now to find the term "sole selling rights" in an estate agent's consumer contract, meaning that individuals are still free to market the property themselves – even where they have appointed a sole agent.

The internet offers the perfect tool for the DIY home seller to advertise their home at very low cost. Recent surveys by the Halifax have shown that more buyers than ever (over 65%) are using the internet to search for properties for sale.

You don't have to have a computer to get your home on the internet, as there are many services that offer the private seller a complete access package. But just being 'on the internet' by no means guarantees that the property advertised will actually be 'visible' to the many-thousands of buyers now surfing the net for homes.

There are dozens, if not hundreds of sites that promote themselves as allowing a vendor to sell their home privately for little or no cost... but, before choosing a free to advertise internet property service, homeowners need to consider carefully what they are likely to get 'for nothing'. It can work – it is theoretically possible to connect to the right potential buyer – but the fact is that this remains a remote possibility with many of the sites available. You have to be careful your property doesn't stay 'a billboard in the desert'.

The problem is, that most 'free' sites are poorly marketed usually due to inadequate budgets, and rely either on advertising for their profit – which gets in the way of the message and can be off-putting to buyers – or worse, selling-on registered users' e-mail addresses for junk purposes. Again, this is likely to put off the majority of homebuyers searching from using such sites – the very target audience you need.

The biggest, most well-known free to advertise property service, until recently, was *easier.co.uk*, which relied upon selling its customer mailing list for profit. Despite substantial backing which allowed it a multi-million pound advertising budget, it was forced to withdraw its free service, because it was unable to make a profit on that basis!

Many sites offer to list homes for the do-it-yourself seller, with photographs of the property, 'for sale' boards and other bells and whistles supplied, in return for various fees – so how do you choose?

Look for a site that firstly offers a nationwide service to sellers anywhere in the UK and, most importantly, is able to attract buyers in all areas of the UK. Then ask these simple questions:

- How are the property particulars presented and what do your photos look like?

- How easy is it to find and search the website database?
- Is telephone assistance provided?
- How are buyer enquiries handled?
- Is the website easy and attractive to use, so that it will naturally draw in buyers (like bees to a honeypot)?
- How well-connected is the site to the property market in general?

The internet property world is an extremely crowded one and search-engine /directories may not find and categorise a new website for months (if at all), so chances are that few buyers will ever get to see your dedicated website. Better to piggyback on the multi-million pound marketing budgets of the industry's biggest players by using an established property service. But people still need to know the name of the site to be able to find it.

Most internet buyers are now being channelled by massive TV and press marketing campaigns to a handful of household names: high-profile property-search services such as **Assertahome**, **Rightmove** and **Fish4Homes**. These are 'portal' databases of properties held by estate agents; normally the only way to get your property listed with these major players is by signing up to an agent's commission contract.

However, one independent service, quaintly named "The Little House Company", has negotiated arrangements to publish their customers' properties on these and many other portals and charges just £89. They can be found at *www.thelittlehousecompany.co.uk*. Compared to one-off advertising (say, in a local paper), this offers huge ongoing exposure in the mainstream market at low relative cost.

An interesting point revealed by recent market surveys is the fact that buyers actually prefer to deal with the seller direct, rather than through an agent – the Halifax survey found that buyers have greater confidence in what a seller tells them about the property than what an agent says. Honesty, it appears, is alive and well. So when preparing details, it is important to offer an honest and accurate, rather than an exaggerated, description, as this is likely to be better appreciated by buyers and saves wasting everybody's time.

There is no rocket science involved in writing a property description, but when using the internet, it is better to think in terms of "marketing" and highlight the features of the property details and why it is so nice to live there. Rather than bland details, try and sum up the whole property from the buyer's perspective 'in a nutshell' – preferably in the first two sentences. Once hooked, buyers will then read the detail.

Then there's the photography. A 'surf stopper' photo is vitally important when advertising on the internet – whether you are selling DIY or through an agent. There's no point having your property's portrait up there if it looks like a tired old hag, taken in bad lighting, with the neighbourhood traffic in the foreground. The photographs you use can really help to reel people in OR make them move on without a second glance. Remember, on the net, you're "only one click away from the next property", so you really need to draw people in.

The internet is a great resource 'toolkit' for the private home seller and is virtually unlimited. You can find anything from a mortgage and conveyancing to a builder or plumber; all the services you could possibly need to get that sale moving swiftly and inexpensively. One of the best single location compendiums of internet property services and free information is *www.themovechannel.com*, which lists and reviews some 5,000 property-related websites and is a great place to start.

SALES MANAGEMENT COMPANY

Managing the estate agent – of course you want to sell your home without all the hassle of calling, chasing, chasing and calling all the people who will be involved. Unfortunately that sounds all too familiar, doesn't it? Well, I found a company who will instruct and manage the estate agent, solicitor and removal company for you and charges no more than an agent would, and even pays the agent out of their fee.

Corporate Asset Management Company, HSH, has developed SmoothMove, which takes away the aggravation of selling your biggest asset. They have been selling homes for corporate clients for years, and recently made this service available to regular homeowners.

OK so I'm biased; my company Home Stagers, is partnered with HSH to deliver staging services as part of their SmoothMove package, and together we develop the right promotional strategy for homeowners to sell property, ensuring the best possible price without the hassle you normally get when selling a home – and all for less than 2% of the final sale price.

PROPERTY PROMOTION

Get this right and make more on your property. Today, the internet is often the first stop in the quest for buying a new house! You need your property to become a surf stopper – otherwise the next property is just one click away.

PHOTO STAGING

Make YOUR property stand out on the web – otherwise the next property is just one click away.

A recent Home Stagers study concluded that people will only make an appointment to view a property once they have driven through the neighbourhood and seen the exterior of the property for themselves, even if they use the internet to find a property in the first place. Our impressions also show that people don't actually buy homes over the internet – they eliminate them!

In photos or virtual tours, most homes appear cluttered, small and unattractive. Only by staging your home can you prepare your home to show it at its best. It is vital that the photos used to promote your property on the web are the very best possible.

Don't settle for poor lighting, interior shots taken in the dark with the curtains closed, or pictures of rooms you've not prepared yet. You really will be wasting your time and hard-earned money with your agent.

You must stage your home before your estate agent prepares your listings to ensure a faster, more profitable sale. Market your home using the art of "model" or "show home" target marketing, while tailoring each property to look irresistible to all.

STAGING TO SELL

When a property is valued, the high price that is now being placed on property in the UK actually creates 'buyer expectation'. If the presentation then doesn't live up to this 'buyer expectation', the buyer will feel extremely let down and move on to the next, more aesthetically pleasing, property.

The process of staging creates just enough theatre to meet buyer expectation, the first step to a home sale. You will need to identify and highlight the home's most desirable features, edit out memorabilia and personal items, and rearrange furniture for the most dramatic impact possible with the space you have available.

You will need to evaluate and position lighting to create that special mood and ambience, add plants or accessories for increased 'lifestyle aspiration' ... and, when necessary, bring in outside services for professional cleaning, redecorating or storage.

Only 10% of people can visualise the untapped potential in a house! Make sure your home's potential is 'seen' by the other 90%.

This is the secret weapon of estate agents and their savvy clients. It is the service that will more than pay for itself with less than 1% of the sale price yielding anywhere from 10% to 100% return on the staging for sale investment.

£10 spent on a tin of paint is worth £1,000 on the wall

Judith Healey, 20 years as a Real Estate Agent in Toronto, Canada and now a Home Staging Consultant in Somerset.

**If a property is not dressed to sell quickly – for the top price –
IT PROBABLY WON'T!**

Whether it's a new build or a renovation project, if you don't dress your property, you could be missing out on a lot of its value potential.

I see a growing number of properties that are not reaching their ceiling price potential purely due to poor presentation. Just a small investment (as low as 1% of market value) and a little focused time can make all the difference.

The key is to ensure that you transform all of your 'wasted' space into 'value space'. An empty granny annex or a cluttered box room with no bed in it is seen by the majority as wasted space and wasted space has a lower 'perceived' value than well-defined 'value' space.

To drive real value out of your property you must ensure you have defined rooms or living zones, and that they are shown to best effect in the house.

Properties that have well-defined living zones sell 30% quicker or realise 20% more than properties that are ill-defined.

WHY?

Only 10% of the population has adequate visualisation skills, so the more you can stage, the more you can show just how the property can be utilised to maximise the space available.

That does not mean having too much furniture in a property, but it does mean having furniture in each room and defining each room with one function.

I have seen many houses where the owners believe that by pushing the furniture up against the wall, the room will look bigger. This is just not true. All this does is make the room look odd, like a corridor or waiting room, and it loses its function.

Dining rooms should have the table centred with the chairs put around, as if for dining. Setting the table can also help make the buyer aspire towards entertaining.

Oversized tables should have their extra leaves removed to allow access around them from the door to the window.

If you have room, you should consider adding a dresser, table and lamp, or standard lamp in the corner. Make sure you have either a picture or a mirror along one wall that can be seen from the door.

If you only have room for a table and chairs, then make them work for you, and remove all other items.

If you have your computer in the lounge or dining room, find a reasonable space for it. Define it; add uncluttered shelving above it, to make it the computer zone of the room.

Use a simple wooden screen with fabric stretched over it to hide any unsightly area or a prominent TV.

Consider packing items away if you don't need them. They'll have to be packed at some point, why not now?

Make sure that any third reception room is well-defined. It might be your playroom but you must stage it with seating – a room with no seating is just a corridor to another area, or, worse still, it's seen as wasted space. Stage it as a sitting room, or casual family room, leaving your lounge for best.

If you have a dining kitchen or a breakfast kitchen, don't confuse the space by adding a sofa – centre the table and stage as a full breakfast space. Clear any breakfast bars of clutter and set it up with settings of breakfast crockery for two, three or four people, depending on the space available.

Ensure that all bedrooms do have made up beds in each area, making features of the bed with new bed linen, scatter cushions, and matching bedside lamps. Make a feature of the window too if you can.

Ensure that bedrooms are staged to cater for one to two people. I have been in several properties where three children sleep in one room, and the "spare" bedroom is left unoccupied. Much better to utilise all the rooms available to balance out the belongings. Three beds in one room always looks cluttered as well as odd.

The one item I often have to remove from the lounge is the over-sized coffee table. I've not seen many lounges large enough to take one. The table just gets in the way and, in some cases, viewers have hit their shins on it, making the room feel quite literally, painfully small. Not a great first impression!

To stage or not to stage? That is the question: The power of staging and how it works

That was certainly the question asked by Mr H. from Yorkshire when he was looking to sell.

After being on the market for several months, he knew he had to do something to start to get the offers in. After two hours with a Home Stagers consultant, he knew exactly what he needed to do over the course of that weekend to get the house staged before his next viewers arrived on the Tuesday.

The property was a detached bungalow, which had remained relatively untouched since it was built in the mid 80s, and it was starting to look very dated. Rag-roll paint effects in the kitchen in grey looked more like mould was growing up the walls rather than the marble effect it was suppose to represent. The sealant around the sink had seen better days too. That had gone black with mould and age.

The bathroom also looked tired and unloved with the tiles in desperate need of re-grouting and the sealant around the bath looking disgusting. The problem with bathrooms which have not been touched for a while is that grey/black mould is actually other people's dead skin. A horrible thought, isn't it?

The consultant worked with Mr H. in prioritising the jobs that he should do first (such as taking down the net curtains which hadn't been washed in 7 years), and agreeing what was practical for him to do over the weekend.

Two days later he received two offers on the property. One for the full asking price and the second for £7,500 *over* the asking price – he had only spent £100 on materials and a weekend of his time!

To stage or not to stage? Is it worth it? people ask. Too right it's worth it, I say!

Top Five Tips To Help You To Sell

1) Tidy the frontage, mow the lawn, re-hang that broken gate. Then add such features as hanging baskets and a clear house

name or number to increase drive-by desirability.

2) Clear out clutter as this is the first thing that people notice. Clear it – then clear it again! Be ruthless! Reduce before you move and it will save time and money later. Start to pack up the things you will be taking with you and create more value by showing off the space you have. Don't forget to dress it back with a few choice accessories, though – you don't want 'bland and bare'.

3) Clean carpets and curtains or replace with economical alternatives. Consider using rugs or stripping down to the floorboards and adding in new blinds to refresh the look of a tired room.

4) Kitchens and bathrooms are the biggest selling points: replace (economically) the flooring, worktops and cupboard doors if necessary; re-grout the tiles and reseal around the bath; clear surfaces (including children's artwork from the fridge) and ensure both rooms are spotlessly clean.

5) Stage the garden as an extra room by adding table and chairs, put up the umbrella and add some flowers in pots. Even add lighting for those darker winter days. And take down that washing line! Buyers expect a lot from property today – both inside and out.

INCREASING THE STAKES

Once the property game is starting to work for you, you need to start thinking ahead

> To achieve total financial independence, you need to have a portfolio of rental properties

BUILDING A PORTFOLIO

In this section on Portfolio Planning, we look at:

* When to sell
* When to re-mortgage and grow your portfolio
* What property to buy next

Once you own property, you will start to build equity over time. After a few years, you can look at using that equity to release funds to help you afford the next property.

By re-mortgaging on an existing property and using that collateral as the deposit on the next property, you can soon have a portfolio under your belt and start to reach financial independence.

You can then look to sell off your portfolio, either individually or as a complete portfolio. That would then enable you to retire, sell up and buy the property of your dreams outright or move abroad to a property in the sun. All this is possible once you've started on the property ladder.

Many investors simply purchase a number of properties outright to create an instant portfolio. However, a process of raising a new mortgage to fund subsequent purchases, which is known as 'gearing', means that once your first property is purchased, refurbished and let, you can begin to build your portfolio with minimal further capital investment. The first property is valued and a buy-to-let mortgage, subject to status, is arranged. The mortgage commitment is covered by the rental income, with the difference representing the investor profit. In theory, the size of the portfolio created could be limitless as the process is repeated with each property. It must be stressed that this is a *high risk* strategy and will plunge you in to hundreds of thousands of pounds worth of mortgage debt, which you will only survive if you manage your properties effectively and can keep the tenants paying in each one.

INVESTMENT PROPERTY EXAMPLES

(All the following examples have been provided by MRA Property Investment Ltd, 2002.)

EXAMPLE – HIGH YIELD PROPERTY

A £35,000 cash investment is used to purchase, refurbish, furnish and let a modern or traditional terraced flat. The rental income provides a gross yield on capital of 12% per annum, i.e. £350 per month. Growth on capital of 5% per annum is also anticipated. The 5% management fee plus all costs associated with funding, purchasing and refurbishing the property are included in the original £35,000 investment. Solicitor's fee for the purchase of the property along with all the relevant insurance premiums for the first year are also included. The aim after refurbishment is to produce an asset that would be initially valued at circa £35,000.

The property is valued at £35,000 and an 85% buy-to-let mortgage is obtained on the property – i.e. £29,750. These funds along with a further cash investment of £5,250 are used to fund property two at £35,000.

This process is repeated until property five is mortgaged to release £29,750 of the total capital invested. You therefore hold a portfolio of five properties for a total cash investment of £26,250 producing a rental income of £11,460 per annum net of

mortgage repayments and management fees. Realistic anticipated capital growth of 5% per annum would increase the initial value of your portfolio by £8,750 in the first year alone.

1A) HIGH YIELD PROPERTY

	Cash Invested after mort-gaging	Value of property after refur-bish-ment motort-gaging	85% Mort-gage	Rent Received after mort-gaging	Monthly Mort-gage pay-ment	Cleared profit per month
Property 1	£5,250	£35,000	£29,750	£375	£124	£191
Property 2	£5,250	£35,000	£29,750	£375	£124	£191
Property 3	£5,250	£35,000	£29,750	£375	£124	£191
Property 4	£5,250	£35,000	£29,750	£375	£124	£191
Property 5	£5,250	£35,000	£29,750	£375	£124	£191
Totals	£26,250	£175,000	£148,750	£1,575	£620	£955

Note: In the example given, the net yield will reduce in year
two onwards to 38% or £9,950 per annum due to a premium
of approximately £300 per property for buildings and contents insurance.

That's a net yield on your investment in year one of 44% –
sounds tempting on paper, doesn't it? No wonder first time
buyers are being forced to rent when investors are making
money like this.

But will the market become over-saturated, even in the
North where property prices are still this low?

How long will they stay this low for?

What happens when there is an interest rate increase?

Would you be happy to be the proud owner of up to six
mortgages – most of us get the heebie-geebies about having
just one.

Mortgages are subject to status. Remember, properties are

at risk if mortgage payments are not maintained. As with any investment yields and capital investments, values can go down as well as up. – Funny how that bit is always in the small print... Can you afford to pay an additional £620 per month on top of your current mortgage if things don't work out as the management company says?

Example – Yield plus growth property

A £60,000 cash investment is used to purchase, refurbish, furnish and let a small modern or traditional terraced house in a popular residential area. The rental provides a gross yield on capital of 10% per annum, i.e. £500 per calendar month. Growth on capital of 7.5% per annum is also anticipated. The 5% management fee plus all costs associated with funding, purchasing and refurbishing the property are included in the original £60,000 investment. Solicitor's fee for the purchase of the property along with all the relevant insurance premiums for the first year are also included. The aim after refurbishment is to produce an asset that would be initially valued at circa £60,000.

The property is valued at £60,000 and an 85% buy-to-let mortgage is obtained, i.e. £51,000. These funds along with further cash investment of £9,000 are used to fund property two at £60,000.

This process is repeated until property five is mortgaged to release £51,000 of the total capital invested. You therefore hold a portfolio of five properties for a total cash investment of £45,000, producing a rental income of £14,220 per annum net of mortgage repayments and management fees. Realistic anticipated capital growth of 7.5% per annum would increase the initial value of your portfolio by £22,500 in the first year alone. See figure 1b.

1B) Yield and growth property

	Cash Invested after mortgaging	Value of property after refurbishment	85% Mortgage	Rent Received after mortgaging	Monthly Mortgage payment	Cleared profit per month
Property 1	£9,000	£60,000	£51,000	£450	£213	£237
Property 2	£9,000	£60,000	£51,000	£450	£213	£237
Property 3	£9,000	£60,000	£51,000	£450	£213	£237
Property 4	£9,000	£60,000	£51,000	£450	£213	£237
Property 5	£9,000	£60,000	£51,000	£4505	£213	£237
Totals	£45,000	£300,000	£255,000	£2,250	£1065	£1187

That's a combined annual yield plus capital growth return on your investment in year one of £36,720, or 81%.

All these figures are for illustrative purposes only; actual prices and achievable rents will, of course, vary from property to property. The figures are net of a 10% management fee and figures are based on an interest only current interest rate of 5% (Oct 2003). Let's see how long they stay that low!

With a realistic annual growth rate of 7.5%, the value in 20 years time could be over £1.25 million and that's why these schemes are being seen as replacing the good old pension plan. But it is not for the faint hearted and it is NOT without RISK.

I don't know of many people who would be comfortable holding down six mortgages, being liable to pay over £1,000 in additional mortgage payments and all the responsibility of owning that many properties.

What's the annual maintenance bill going to be like in 10 years?

EXAMPLE – HIGHER VALUE YIELD PLUS GROWTH PROPERTIES

An investor wishes to purchase a substantial three bedroom semi-detached house in a popular residential area. A suitable property is identified by the management company and an offer of £85,000 is accepted. The property requires some light refurbishment, redecoration and furnishings. An 85% buy-to-let mortgage is arranged for the investor, i.e. £72,250.

Therefore, the investor must have a cash deposit of £12,750. Further cash expenses of £3,000 are required for the refurbishment and furnishings.

The 5% management fee of the purchase price and approximately £2,500 for solicitor's fees, stamp duty and insurance are also required.

Therefore the total cash outlay is circa £22,750. The property is let at £600 per month based on an interest only mortgage at 5%, therefore the investor's gross monthly profit is £250. This is £22,880 per annum, a 12.65% yield on the investor's initial cash investment of £22,750. The aim after refurbishment is to produce an asset that would be valued at circa £90,000.

The anticipated average growth is 7.5% per annum, giving a projected value for the investment of £185,000 in 10 years. The gross return on investment in year one would be £9090 or 40%.

All well and good if you can bring in rent every month and interest rates stay affordable.

LOWER VALUE, HIGH YIELD PROPERTIES

These types of properties often require a full cash payment up front for two main reasons:

Good quality investment properties are in strong demand. If there is cash waiting you are far more likely to be successful in your purchase of a property at an attractive price because you are a much more appealing proposition for the buyer.

Some of these properties would not pass mortgage survey

without having a part of the mortgage retained, as they are by definition, refurbishment properties. Obviously, once the property is refurbished and let, it is a much more attractive proposition for your lender to secure funds on.

Buying To Let – An Investment

Property is best viewed as a long-term investment. This is because house prices can go down as well as up, and if you had to sell in the short term you might lose money.

There is no fixed term to this sort of investment. You can sell the property at any time. Alternatively you could clear the mortgage and retain the property as a source of income.

If you buy or own a property outright then the net rental income will be the return on your investment.

How To Calculate Your Net Rate Of Return On Your Investment

Net profit or rental income minus operating expenses x 100% net rate of return on the purchase price.

Or look at your total annual rental income – your expenses in managing the property x initial property value = net rate of return. This should be somewhere around or higher than 7% (the national average).

This compares favourably with interest-bearing accounts, although remember that there is a low risk to your capital with interest-bearing accounts. The rates of return in your selected area may differ and you should make your own calculation.

Few people will have the resources to buy outright. Most people will opt to borrow the majority of the purchase price.

If you buy a property for £100,000 with a £20,000 deposit, and the capital value increases to £110,000 after two years, you could sell up and redeem your mortgage of £80,000, leaving you with £30,000. Your initial investment of £20,000 has increased to £30,000 – an increase of 50% over two years, or 25% p.a. (ignoring the costs of buying and selling).

The above example demonstrates how your investment of £20,000 benefits from price rises in the full value of the property.

PLANNING AN EXIT STRATEGY

Remember that the economy, interest rates, employment and construction trends impact every investor. Watch the trends and speak with brokers, appraisers, investors, and property solicitors.

An investor always needs an exit strategy, preferably more than one, when they buy property. You need to have a vision showing when you will sell, whether you will take the money and pay taxes. Is your plan to have enough money for retirement? Are you going to pay off the property or refinance it and use the proceeds to buy another investment?

If you live in a depressed marketplace you need to decide if the weak economy will last a long time, or if the area will pull out of it. This information is critical to your exit strategy. If you cannot find a buyer when you're ready to sell, then what? Structure your mortgage without prepayment penalties so you can change to a better mortgage without having to pay thousands to get out of your term.

Remember, banks structure loans to benefit their bottom line, and financing shouldn't be taken for granted. It pays to research financing options before you make a final decision, and interest rates should not be your only focus.

You have to think ahead and be prepared for a range of possible events. For example, you invest with your best friend and her husband, but she gets divorced and needs the funds out of the investment to pay off her husband; what do you do? Another variable is your health or your family's health: Will you have to liquidate the property investment to pay bills?

Your exit strategy will help you make a better decision as you invest into the future. Plan your goals ahead. No one is forcing you to buy. Pick your time, and pick a property you can live with into eternity. Worst case, if the market does not move the direction you expect and the value does not go up, at least your tenants are paying off the loan.

As a property investor you have different needs than an owner-occupier who is selling the home that he lives in. You have cash-flow to worry about. You have capital gains (or losses!) that factor into your decision as to when to sell.

That's why most investors NEVER sell unless they have to!

INVESTMENT CASE STUDIES
We spoke to three very different investors to see just what they did and what worked for them

CASE STUDY 1 – BUY-TO-SELL

Sharon bought her house in May 2002 for £64,000. It was on the market for £75,000 but she managed to get the price down based on the survey. She planned to live in it and hold down a full time job whilst the work was being done, budgeting £30,000 for the development work. The house is expected to achieve £130,000 on the market, giving her a grand profit of £30,000.

"I reconsidered the additional work I thought needed doing from what I had initially thought on the basis of the full survey. It cost a bit more, but then I had a very strong negotiating tool.

"Houses in a good state in the area were selling for between £100,000 and £110,000, so I thought that I had got a reasonable deal.

"I figured I needed around £30,000 to do it up and add value. The house needed the roof relaying, all the damp proofing doing and some serious work on the kitchen. I also decided to add a bedroom in the loft while the roof was being done. This didn't need planning permission, as it did not extend outside of the existing structure.

"While the damp-proofing was underway I decided to remove a concrete floor in the dining room and replace with more traditional floorboards. This was the only time that the house was uninhabitable, and a friend kindly put me up for a month!

"When the kitchen extension was underway my living room was made into a makeshift kitchen with a camping stove, fridge and microwave (with all my washing up being done in the bath!).

"I was in the process of re-decorating (two bedrooms and the bathroom to go plus little bits and bobs) when I had the house re-valued before any re-decorating was done and it was valued at £115,000. A 2 bedroom house just round the corner is currently on the market for £124,000 so if the property market stays the same in the next couple of months I would expect to put mine on the market for about £125,000 to £130,000.

"So I'm looking to make around £30,000. I'm a good project manager and have just about kept within my initial £30,000 budget. I've currently got £2,500 to finish off the decorating, which I'm now doing myself to keep the costs down.

"Would I do it again? Well, it has taken 4 months longer than I expected but as I'm living in the house anyway, it's not actually costing me more money to take my time. It is tough though, when you're working full time and some evenings you want to slob and not paint. Yes, I would do it again, but not just yet. I think I'll rent for a few months and take the whole of the winter off, before I start on my next project."

CASE STUDY 2 – BUY-TO-SELL

Graham was moving from East Yorkshire because of work opportunities for his partner, and sold his 3 bedroom country cottage for £55,000; a good price for the area at the time. They bought their investment property for £170,000 with a mortgage of £160,000. Graham is on target to make a profit of £100,000:

"We found a three bed detached chalet bungalow in High Wycombe. The owners had been in the property for 20 years, were heavy smokers and liked dark colours and complete privacy. All the rooms were dark green and purple, and were thick with nicotine. The few light fittings had 40-watt bulbs and, as we moved, in December, there was little natural light. We got the keys and stood in the kitchen (wall to ceiling dark brown tiles) tearful at having paid £170,000 for this 'hole'.

"We knew in our hearts that it had potential but in the dark grey cold of the day, all optimism seemed to leave us.

"We had no choice but live in it while we made alterations and improvements – including moving a staircase, adding another, taking out ceilings and floors to replace joists and having the whole house re-wired. The builder started before Christmas and was wonderful, but we still spent the weekend between Christmas and New Year with no heating or hot water, nipping to neighbours across the road for showers.

"Eight months on, we are about to have the last of the carpets laid and we have a light, airy property on which we have spent approx £30,000 but should be worth around £300,000 in today's market.

"The property comprises a lounge, galleried dining room, breakfast kitchen, study, master suite with galleried bedroom with vaulted ceiling, ensuite bathroom and dressing room / bedroom five, guest suite comprising bedroom and sitting area, overlooking rear gardens with private access and ensuite WC, two further double bedrooms and large shower room.

"It is on a double width plot with over 100ft rear gardens, double garage, drive, and additional parking and full planning permission for a single-storey extension with first floor roof garden.

"The purchase was on a whopping mortgage of £160,000 and the work funded on £10,000 legacy from my late father, a £10,000 bank loan and a B&Q Home buyers card. My partner took a part-time job at B&Q just for discounts and it saved us a fortune.

"Living in rubble whilst working full-time certainly is the most stressful thing to do, but, needs must!"

CASE STUDY 3 – RENTAL INVESTMENT

In the East Midlands, when David and Julia got married they each had a property of their own. Rather than sell both properties and consolidate their assets to buy one bigger property, they decided to keep both properties. They moved into one, and kept the other as an investment, with the mortgage being paid by rental income.

A shrewd move. At the time they married, the properties were worth £40,000 and £35,000 each. Now only three years later, those same properties are valued at £89,000 and £79,000 respectively. The mortgages are paid by the rental income, and they have just invested in a third larger property, which they have moved to. They now rent out both smaller properties, which covers the cost of upkeep and maintenance, and they anticipate their asset value to continue to increase even more over the longer term.

Said David, "At first it was a bit of a struggle, especially when we stretched to accommodate the third property, but it's amazing how easily you adapt to live on a certain income. We are hoping to buy a holiday home in Spain at some point too, and have even started taking Spanish lessons. But we're hoping that the UK will enter the Euro, and hope that, as with decimalisation, this will trigger a rise in British prices which will also push up property values, and make our Spanish dream more affordable too."

INSIDER TIPS

By listening to what the professionals have to say you can save yourself months of leg work and cut short your research time. By learning from them you can avoid those costly mistakes – I asked a number of insiders for their tips to help you Play the Property Game. Some give a national view and some have personal experiences to share.

THE INDUSTRY ADVICE

SHORT FALL IN NEW HOME SUPPLY & DEMAND

Hometrack advises: think tank Nationwatch UK estimates that 800,000 new homes will be needed in the UK over the next 30 years and the latest government review states that 2.4 million homes may be needed in the next 10.

According to these reviews there is currently a shortfall of 39,000 homes each year in relation to current new building figures. This could mean ever increasing prices, overcrowding and a negative impact on the nation's economic outlook, if the situation does not improve. This will certainly hit first time buyers who are already suffering by not being able to afford to get on to the property ladder, in the first place. That will have the knock on effect of an increased demand for rental accommodation. Not so good for young people wanting to leave home, but perhaps more encouraging for buy-to-let property investors, because people will always need some-where to live.

BUY-TO-LET IS LOCKING OUT THE FIRST TIME BUYER

Affordability is the key issue for the first time buyer in 2004. According to the Council of Mortgage Lenders, only 29% of mortgages taken out in 2003 a long-term average of close to 50%

In their most recent survey, the Council of Mortgage Lenders (CML) reported a continuing growth in the buy-to-let market, with many existing landlords taking advantage of their current property increase in value and re-mortgaging their existing properties to release capital and reinvest in further property, enabling them to enlarge their portfolios.

Between the end of 2002 and 2003 the total number of buy-to-let mortgages had increased by nearly 50%.

While experienced landlords take account of the property yield, property price expectations, anticipated void periods (when the property will be empty), the impact of taxation and maintenance costs, the inexperienced landlord may see this investment opportunity as a quick win option. That is one fear in the market at least with the BtL increase. People should only be entering the buy-to-let sector if they intend to hold their property portfolio for a long period of time.

CAPITAL GROWTH & RETURNS

The Association of Residential Lettings Agents (ARLA) reported an appreciation in value of buy-to-let properties of 10% in the final quarter of 2003. The rate of return is now averaging just over 9% (9.07%), on the cash purchase of buy-to-let investment, (including both the rental yield and capital appreciation) The failure to keep properties in good order, buying the wrong property for the local market or asking rents which are too high appear to be the common reasons for long void periods.

Contact:

- CML *www.cml.org.uk*
- ARLA *www.arla.co.uk*

IS INVESTING IN PROPERTY AN ALTERNATIVE RETIREMENT INVESTMENT?

The consumer research company Mintel is one of the UK's best known producers of market intelligence. In a recent report it confirmed the growing trend for people in the UK to regard property ownership as a better alternative to investing in a pension scheme.

The pensions market in Britain has been failing for some time. Following the dramatic decrease in the value of the stock market, many pension companies have had to reduce the amount of the final value of the schemes that they run.

This is particularly relevant to people who, like me, had an endowment policy attached to a mortgage and who are now facing large shortfalls when their policy matures.

A senior Finance Analyst from Mintel, Paul Davies, states, "Low interest rates and the recent poor performance of the stock market, as well as a fall in pension scheme funds, has meant that property has never been so attractive as a way to save for retirement.

"Indeed, people today think that they cannot lose out by investing in property. But investing in property can catch homeowners out if fortunes change and interest rates continue to rise. On top of which there are no guarantees of selling a property."

Such a note of caution is appropriate, but in the present climate it is not hard to understand why people are placing their faith in 'bricks and mortar' rather than in the traditional stocks and shares. Is this the new way we will be running our financial affairs in the future or is it just a flash in the pan? I suspect that the way we handle our affairs will change and property investment becomes just another option open to us. Likewise, I am sure that over time, high profile losses will be reported and the general public will start to become less confident. But at this moment in time, I think normal, everyday people are starting to view property as a sound investment.

HOUSE PRICES REACH 10 TIMES LOCAL EARNINGS

It looks like house prices are now 10 times the average local earnings of the workforce, according to analysis by the wealth management arm of Barclays.

- The highest ratio is in Kensington and Chelsea where property prices are now 18 times (£663,506) local earnings despite the borough having the highest incomes in the country (£36,493).
- Kensington is followed by Westminster and Camden in London at 13.5 and 12.8 respectively, with Elmbridge in Surrey at 12.8. The average across England and Wales is 5.98.
— And it's not just in London and the Southeast. Other high ratio areas:
- Cotswold in Gloucestershire 9.9.
- East Dorset 9.6.
- Purbeck in Dorset 9.2.
- South Hams in Devon 9.0.
- East Devon 8.7.
- Malvern Hills in Worcestershire 8.8.

The most affordable property in the country is in Burnley, Lancashire, where the average income is £20,467 and average property prices are £34,860, giving it an income/property index of 1.7 and that's a massive difference across the north south divide.

The data is from the Land Registry and was for property prices in England and Wales for June to September 2002. The average incomes are for 2002 and calculated on information from Barclays data warehouse with over five million incomes surveyed. The index is a simple calculation of property price divided by local annual income to give the index.

LANDLORDS TO SWELL PORTFOLIOS BY 18% IN YEAR

Recent findings from a major study of buy-to-let investors, conducted by flexible buy-to-let lending specialist Mortgage Trust, has revealed overwhelming market confidence in the sector with landlords expecting to grow their portfolios by an average of 18% in the next 12 months.

The typical landlord's portfolio contains 3-4 properties and has an average value of £763,400. They expect to boost their portfolios by at least one property within 12 months with optimism running high among large and small landlords alike.

Despite critics' claims that supply of rental property is outstripping tenant demand, the average vacancy period per year is less than 3 weeks, with the vast majority (78%) experiencing vacancy periods of less than 4 weeks. This low vacancy rate shows no signs of deterioration, being broadly the same over the past 2.5 years. This demonstrates that the strong growth in buy-to-let investment supports continuing strong tenant demand. See Figure 1.

Adding further support to the view that buy-to-let is still growing robustly, the findings reveal that landlords' gearing is at comfortable levels.

Almost 50% of investors have borrowings of less than half the value of their portfolios, which not only debunks the doom-mongers' claims that the buy-to-let market is vulnerable to house price declines and an increase in the cost of finance, but also demonstrates that landlords have plenty of equity for further expansion.

Austin Jelfs, Head of Sales & Marketing at Mortgage Trust observes, "The buy-to-let market is still strong and growing and it looks set to stay that way for at least the next 12 months with investor confidence as buoyant as ever. This has been reflected by the number of new products being launched across the sector, offering investors a wider range of choice and rates."

PENT-UP DEMAND PUSHES HOUSE PRICES UP AGAIN

The Hometrack March survey of the housing market reports a 0.7% increase in house prices across the country. This follows last month's 0.9% rise, the strongest recorded increase since October 2002. This year's monthly rises have been significantly above typical month changes recorded last year.

As a result of the strong rises seen so far this year and also ongoing pent-up demand in the market, Hometrack has upgraded its house price forecast to 8% (previously 4%).

Strong price rises were spread across the whole country. All 52 county areas reported price rises, the highest increases being in the North: Teeside (1.5%), Northumberland (1.2%), Tyne and Wear (1.2%), Cumbria (1.1%) and North Yorkshire (1.1%). London – North also recorded a rise of 1.1%. Oxfordshire was the slowest moving county, with a rise of only 0.1%.

Among the country's major cities, Bath compounded its status as fastest moving city for the second month running with increases of 2.4% (2.2% in the February survey). Other cities with high price rises included Middlesborough (2.1%), Cardiff (1.7%), Milton Keynes (1.7%) and Taunton (1.6%). No city experienced falling values this month although Cambridge, Winchester and Hull remained static with no recorded rises.

KEY HOUSING MARKET STATISTICS (MARCH 2004)	
National House Prices: Rise over the month	0.7%
National House Prices: Rise for this year to date	1.9%
Hometrack National house price inflation forecast for 2004	8.0%
Consensus estimate for National (UK) House price rises for 2004	8.5%

The overall average price of a house has now increased to £149,800 (last month £148,500).

Hometrack's unique national demand index shows how both the number of properties for sale and the number of buyers registered has increased. However, the number of new buyers registered has increased by 6.5% while the number of properties listed has risen by 4.2%, implying demand outweighing supply. This pent-up demand suggests further strong house price rises in coming months.

Average sales price achieved as a percentage of asking price continued to rise to 96.2%. This is over 2% up from the low of 94.2% recorded in last year's June survey. This is the highest percentage recorded since November 2002, and again provides evidence that demand is strengthening in relation to supply.

The average length of time taken to sell a property has fallen to 4.3 weeks (4.6 weeks in February's survey). There is currently an average of 10.4 viewings before a sale is achieved.

John Wriglesworth, Hometrack's Housing Economist, comments: "The housing market this month has strengthened, with strong house price rises across the whole country.

"Demand by new buyers is outweighing supply and the upward pressure on house prices continues. Low interest rates remain, and despite prospects of rises this year, buyers are not being deterred from borrowing even higher multiples of their income to afford their desired homes.

"Income growth and employment prospects remain strong, particularly so in London where City jobs and bonuses are on the increase. The current market is very much a sellers' market, with buyers having to accept very close to asking prices.

"Due to all these factors, we have raised our house price inflation forecast for 2004 to 8%, previously 4%."

Hometrack's UK HOT spots and NOT spots (March 24)

Top 5

Borough	Weighted Overall Average Price Change
Teeside	1.5%
Northumberland	1.2%
Tyne and Wear	1.2%
Cumbria	1.1%
London – North	1.1%

Bottom 5

Borough	Weighted Overall Average Price Change
Oxfordshire	0.1%
East Riding of Yorkshire	0.2%
South Lincolnshire	0.3%
Staffordshire	0.3%
Suffolk	0.3%

The Wealth Coach

Nicola Cairncross – *www.nicolacairncross.com*

Nicola Cairncross is a Wealth Coach who works with bright, successful people to enhance their financial intelligence, help them make (and keep) more money, and create passive income flows.

Nicola polled visitors to her website and asked:
What has the most effect on success in building financial freedom?

Support of family / friends	15 (12.61%)
Ongoing learning / personal development	12 (10.08%)
Positive mental attitude	18 (15.13%)
Taking action	74 (62.18%)

What 10 things would you say investors would need to look out for, to help them to identify future 'hot spots'?

1) Properties not hanging around on the market for more than a month

2) Lots of skips and scaffolding in the area. Are there any big luxury apartment developments planned?

3) Are the three or four bed properties selling at just under £250k? This is the next stamp duty threshold (1% jumps to 3% so it holds prices under that artificially). If so, they are probably worth £10-20k more already and you are within a year of a major leap in prices. It will only take one property to sell at over the £250k mark and the prices will jump immediately and keep rising to the next threshold which is £500k.

4) Call the local schools (first and middle) and see how many places in each of a couple of age groups they have left – if not many, then it's popular with young families.

5) Is there a Costa Coffee, Café Nero or Starbucks in the area?

6) Who is buying the ugly, unkempt houses in the area? Is it property developers / investors?

7) Is there a Tesco Metro or any other big supermarket chain's smaller version?

8) Are there great direct train links to the local big town or city (ideally within 1.5 hours travelling time)

9) Is there a "trendy" wine bar/restaurant in addition to all the local restaurants? Is there a Pizza Express?

10) What is the local Boots the Chemist like? Does it sell only essentials or does it sell luxury ranges / perfumes too? If so, do they have concession stands with sales ladies, or is it just on the shelves?

What would you say are the 10 property Hot Spots in the UK in your experience and why?

I like to buy based on sound figures and don't get caught up in looking for the next hot spots. I think you can find great bargains in any area. Having said that, I have just bought a house in Shoreham Beach, West Sussex, for all of the above reasons. Shoreham Town is also good. Doncaster is supposed to be excellent right now because a little airport locally has just been given permission to develop as a commercial airport. I still think there is growth in Manchester, Leeds, Glasgow, Liverpool and Cardiff.

What would you say are the indicators of when to sell an investment property and when to stick with it.

When to sell:
There are only a couple of reasons to consider selling.
1) If you need the money to get into a deal with a better return-on-investment. I base all my business decisions on the ROI (return on investment)
2) If it's not "feeding you" (putting money into your pocket) anymore but "eating you" (taking money out of your pocket).
When to keep:
If you don't need to sell (see above). Why would you sell if it's a great return on investment? There's no better deal around at the moment and it's putting money into your pocket!

THE SELF-BUILDER

BEVERLEY NORTH, SELF-BUILDER

Beverley saved money by building her own house.

Many people dream about designing and building their own home. In 1999 this became a reality for Darryl and Beverley North. Now, four and half years on, Beverley, Darryl and ten-year-old daughter Rebecca are enjoying living in their dream home at Thurgarton in Nottinghamshire.

Why did you do it?
"We had seen many programmes on the television about building your own house and we attended two self-build exhibitions at the NEC in Birmingham. We also read and digested a lot of advice given in the *Individual Homes Magazine*. We felt that building the style of home that we desired would be more cost-effective than buying one.

"Darryl's sister introduced us to Ray, who has completed a number of self-builds over the years. After discussing the pros and cons of self-build, we decided to go ahead and Ray agreed to be our project manager."

When did you do it?
"We started the design process in late 1997. Thurgarton is within a conservation area, so the planning process took longer than expected. Ray used a local builder to build the shell of the house and we hired local tradesmen to complete the finishing jobs. We started the build in July 1998 and we moved into the house in June 1999."

What is the size of the house and plot of land?
"The total size of the house is approximately 20 square feet. The living accommodation comprises: lounge, dining room, sitting room, kitchen and downstairs toilet. Four bedrooms (master bedroom with dressing room and ensuite bathroom), family bathroom and separate shower room.

"The total plot size is approx. 1.5 acres."

What did you learn?
"Employing a project manager proved invaluable. We were living in Huddersfield at the time, so we were unable to keep an eye on the build during the week.

"Ray was on-site during the initial stages of the build and he introduced us to his builder and tradespeople, none of whom let us down on quality of work, and they all turned up when they said they would. Ray also told us which building suppliers to use and we obtained trade discounts for many of the required materials."

What would you have done differently?
"The roof of the house was built using roof trusses, which do not enable the loft space to be converted into additional rooms. Next time we would use attic trusses so that we can make more effective use of the loft space. The same principal applies to the double garage – it would be extremely useful to have a playroom or workroom above the garage."

What advice would you give to someone doing the same?
"Be totally realistic in the initial stages about how much money you will need to build your own house. Small over-runs can add up to a significant amount over the full length of the project.

"Don't underestimate the time it takes to build a new house. Building is a very labour-intensive operation, so if you are planning to do some of the work yourself, then you probably need to double the length of time it will take.

"Plan how you want each room to look and feel during the planning stages. This will save time, disappointment and frustration later when it comes to installing items such as light fittings, doors, kitchen cupboards, appliances, fireplaces, wardrobes (and other storage space), bathroom suites, radiators, windows, and so on.

"It is a fantastic opportunity to buy lots of new items for your dream home but when you are buying them all at the same time the choice is even more daunting than, for instance, just buying a new kitchen. Do your homework first. Homeware catalogues are very useful and the internet is a good source, especially for ideas and suppliers."

How did you find the land?
"We were very fortunate in obtaining a large plot of land, which had been in Darryl's family for many years."

How much did it cost?
"The total cost of the build, including design and project management, was approximately £115,000. The house is now worth over £600,000."

What did you do yourself?
"As an experienced soft furnishings designer, I made all of the curtains, cushions, swags, tails and accessories and completed most of the smaller upholstery jobs myself.

"Darryl and I chose the colours for each room and decorated the interior of the house ourselves.

"When we moved into the house in 1999, the back garden looked like a building site. The job of designing this large garden felt quite daunting, so I attended a full-time garden design course at Brackenhurst College. We then sat down and designed the garden on paper. Darryl has put in many spare hours landscaping and developing the garden."

Would you do it again?
"Yes, definitely. It was a thoroughly enjoyable project. There were times when we wondered what we had taken on, but we can now honestly say it was well worth the effort."

What would your next house be?
"I would like to renovate an unusual property such as an old chapel or a barn conversion."

THE NEGATIVE EQUITY SUCCESS STORY
Michele – Founder of Letalife.com – From Negative Equity To Letalife – *http://www.letalife.com*

"In the mid-nineties I got caught, along with thousands of other homeowners, in the trap that was negative equity. Living in Nottingham and needing to move to Fareham in Hampshire, our family was left with no choice but to rent out our property, hope for an upturn in the market and to become tenants ourselves.

The experience was pretty grim at the time.

"The only way to find tenants was to engage a letting agent and fork out mega-bucks for the privilege. What's more, the only way to find a place to rent was to throw ourselves on the mercy of letting agents in southern England.

"Smelling desperation, they showed us the dregs of their

books. Pressed for time and with a low budget we picked the best of a bad bunch (houses not agents). We ended up in a property without central heating and with a manifestation in the bathroom of an unearthly odour produced by a combination of damp-heat and distemper paint which our son named the 'Pongster'.

"All this as an end result of days of travelling expense and stress. Plus the tenants the agent found us in Nottingham left the place in need of serious repair, devaluing the property even further! Four moves later in as many years and finally in our own home again, I had time to mull over the problems involved. There had to be a better and cheaper way of doing things.

"So I decided to put together a website that someone like me could use. One that was clear, logical and easy to use. One that would be free to use. In fact, the site I would have fallen on my knees and thanked providence for – if it had existed in those dark days of yore. I decided to call it Letalife, in the premature ambition that it would make a great slogan for marketing one day – 'Get a Life – Use LetaLife'.

"Today LetaLife has over 150,000 people using it every month. Landlords, tenants and even the dreaded agents can find the town or village relevant to them and place a free 'wanted' or 'to let' advert completely free of charge. There is no boring and intrusive registration, there is no longwinded form asking you how many light fittings you want, or what category of tenant you are seeking. Just a text box to write in your own words exactly what you seek in a tenant or property. All we need is an email to send you your link to remove the advert once it has done its job.

"Oh yes, and your phone number. That's the clever bit. LetaLife provides every advertiser with a 'virtual' telephone number which is published online with the advert. When a call is made in response to the advert it is redirected to the advertiser's own phone and the two parties get to talk to each other. LetaLife makes a small premium on the call and the advertiser never has to publish personal contact details online. So a spamless experience. Once the advert is expired the calls stop as the virtual number is discontinued. This feature is particularly appreciated by single landladies. We even added a housing exchange section this year for social housing tenants. You can even use it to find a local letting agent – we have over 6,000 listed across the UK – just choose them carefully!"

Michele's advice on choosing the right agent.

Make sure they give you a real bricks and mortar address you can find them at. Even if they are working from home; if they are on the level they should give you an address, which you should check out before you sign with them. If they can find you then you should be able to find them. Important if things go wrong. Check they are on the voters' roll for that address.

Speak to your local trading standards office at your council – have they got a bad track record?

Are they a member of a recognised organisation? ARLA, NAFAE? Check this out with the organisation concerned – don't take their word for it.

If your gut instinct is against them – trust it.

Do they give you clear answers to your questions or are they evasive/jargon users?

Get everything checked by a good lawyer before you sign anything.

Don't assume because you found them on a 'good' website that they will necessarily be 'goodies'. But do tell the website involved if an agent listed turns out to be a 'baddie'.

None of these things are guarantees in any way, but if any of them check out badly then they are a definite no-no to take a chance on. You will probably have problems with any agent at some point, but the bigger the company, the more money behind them and the more likely you are to get compensation if things do go wrong. You can also write to managing directors who can sort out individual branch failings.

THE FIRST-TIME BUYER
Naomi Crosby – First Time Property Investor And Life Coach - www.meta-physical.co.uk

Why did you think you needed to invest?
"Other people where doing it and it seemed to be within the realms of possibility that I could do it too.

"My husband was also looking for an 'escape route' from his government job, so we needed to look at the options."

Why did you decide to play the property game?
"It seemed the kind of investment you could get your head around. Property is very tangible and you can see how, over time, you can make money from it.

"Unlike shares as an option, you feel like you're more in control."

What steps did you personally need to go through?
"I needed to know it was an okay thing to do. Being a bit of a socialist and thinking about becoming a private landlord did not sit easy with me at first.

"I went on my first Property Investment Seminar with Simon Zutshi – founder of The Property Investors Network, where I met lots of other investors who shared his view.

"It has taken a couple of years to get up to speed with the information I needed to get started and a couple of years to convince my husband it's the way to go.

"My own wealth coach had her own view of building up a portfolio called the 'up north strategy', where you buy property in the north of England very cheaply with sitting tenants which assures a rental income. There were two things I didn't like about that strategy.

"It didn't sit well with my values as these tenants are amongst some of the most vunerable in society."

"I really didn't want to take on a older property with too much maintenance.

"I had links with the housing association through my previous job and I knew how difficult it could be to manage the upkeep of an older property and keep it fit for tenancy."

What were the most important things you learnt?
"That there are different strategies you can use and to find one
that is right for you.

"You're not alone having doubts about investing money in
property.

"You can do it if you learn about it. I think this book will
be a good starting place for ordinary people to find out some
options. The research I did helped me to decide that I wanted
help with some parts of the process rather than doing it all on
my own.

"I also learnt that I had to look at property from a different
perspective. Not one I liked personally, but one which people
would want to rent.

"There was a change in thinking I had to deal with before
I could start. The paradigm shift from 'pay your mortgage off
early and have no debt' – to 'it's okay to owe money that's
invested in a capital asset'."

What would you have done differently?
"I felt rushed in to adopting someone else's strategy. You need
to find the right decision for you. You need to surround yourself with the right people and be in the right place mentally."

*If you were to give one piece of advice to others, based on your own
experience, what would that be?*
"Find someone who has done it before, take all the help and
advice you can get and don't think you can do everything
yourself."

Naomi has just invested in an off plan two bedroom, duplex
apartment in Leeds. She is hoping to secure a three-year company letting contract when the property is completed in a few
months time.

She managed to keep below the £250,000 stamp duty
threshold by buying the 2 car parking spaces under a separate
transaction.

Her five-year plan and how the numbers worked for
Naomi:

She has a £30,000 mortgage on her family home worth

£200,000. So by re-mortgaging she has managed to put a deposit down on a buy-to-let mortgage.

She intends to grow her portfolio over the next four to five years and aims to receive a passive investment income of £1,500/mth to allow her husband to retire.

She is aiming to invest in five properties of this type and she is also looking at a two-bedroom house locally, to rent out.

When her existing property is completed, she intends to use a property investment company to help find a tenant as well as using local rental agents. She intends to rent the property furnished and would bring in someone to do that for her.

She is looking for her second property and has decided that she wants to take on no renovation. She tells me she is no good at 'playing house'.

THE PROFESSIONAL RELOCATOR
Tim Richens Managing Director Of HSH Property Consultants, Offering Relocation, Asset Management, Property Management, & Move Management Services

Tim has many years of experience in relocation and property disposal. He gave this advice:
"One thing we know about making money from property is buying it at the right price or even below market value is something to aim for."

So how would people get hold of property below market value?
"The official line is that there is no such thing as repossession properties, but the reality is that they do still exist. There is always a danger of litigation and it has happened in the past."

Where would you hear about them?
"Well, no estate agent ever lists them. They do turn up at auction along with probate property. These are both types of property where a quick sale is paramount and a bargain can be picked up."

What's the best source?
"The best source of finding property offered at below market value would be relocation property, especially when a company has provided bridging funding. Essentially, a company will have a budget to fund its relocation activity and the company buys the property from the employee, enabling the employee to be a cash buyer.

"As the company then owns the asset until the property can be sold, a quick sale is often required. The company only has so much money in the fund and can only offer more relocation packages once the existing housing stock is sold. For the top end of the market, say, £500k plus, the interest payable will erode the capital if left for too long. In these cases it's not unlikely for a below market value offer to be accepted. A reduction of say £20,000 could be accepted if the property hasn't sold within 6 months."

What type of property falls in to this category?
"Properties which require a particular style of living or are unique in some way. Barn conversions are a common example of a type of property which appeals to a specific type of buyer. To find the right market value for a property you do need 'comparable evidence' of a similar type of property selling in the area at about the same time. A low offer might not be accepted early, but if you could gain access to the portfolio lists that are over-subscribed, you could find a good deal."

How could you do this?
"Well, a lot of property investment companies do go out to key Blue Chip companies who have corporate relocation schemes and then offer these properties to their investors."

What's your view on property investment?
"I do see it as gambling, because there are outside forces that can impact on your investment. The government can always change policy which you never accounted for.

"If you do go ahead and do it, you need to stay in the game for the long term. Money has been made in the short term by people who are incredibly lucky with their timing and who have researched hard. You must have some form of insider knowledge to make it work."

What advice would you give others?
"Don't over-stretch yourself.
Take the wide view.
Don't put all your eggs in one basket.
Realise that there is no easy way to make big money overnight.
Realise it takes loads of leg work.
It's not an either/or – keep your options open.
Get to know, like and trust the right people who can help you"

What's your take on property syndicates?
"I have a couple of friends from a shares club who started their own syndicate. They see it as a gamble and operate more as speculators than long-term investors at the moment, where they have bought and sold property quickly. They eventually want to move into long-term property investment.

"It's all about mindset. You only owe a percentage of the debt and think of your second mortgage as a long-term savings plan. Many people do it instead of paying into a pension.

"In my experience, top up mortgages are on the increase with people raising the funding by releasing equity on the main property to invest in another. Buy-to-let mortgages allows the borrower to count the regular money coming in."

Three ways to buy a property below market value are:
"Auction: Look for repossession and probate property. Some will be in need of cosmetic work. As more and more property developers are interested in the land they have deeper pockets than you or I and push up the price in some areas.

"Self build: A great way of getting what you want at below market value IF you can find a plot!

"Syndicates buying off-plan and achieving a discount against the full market value on behalf of their members."

THE PROFESSIONAL INVESTOR
Simon Zutshi, Professional Property Investor, Investment Coach And Speaker – Founder Of The Property Investors Network – *www.propertyinvestorsnetwork.co.uk*

I asked Simon, who has been investing in property for over eight years, to share some of his experience and insights in to property investing.

What are the three rules you would give to anyone who is thinking of investing in property?
1) Decide why you want to get involved in property.

"Are you looking for a passive income and a return straight away? Are you looking for a long-term investment where capital growth is important, maybe to replace or subsidise a pension plan?

"If you are looking for a short-term passive income you are best to go with a 'HMO'." A House with Multiple Occupancy. The best type of property is terraced property where you can rent out each room to a different person. Student accommodation comes in to this category but it's not exclusive to this group.

"If you are looking for long-term capital growth, then new build city centre apartments let as company lets are your best bet."

The answer to this question will help them to determine their investment strategy.

2) When you are buying a property, make sure you don't just buy the first one that comes along. Do the sums and make sure it 'stacks up' before you commit to anything. You need to make sure the price – rental return ratio works. There is a simple ratio you can use to help you see at a glance if it will work. All buy-to-let mortgages on the high street use this ratio to calculate if they can lend you the money. REMEMBER: a buy-to-let mortgage is NOT based on your own income; it's based on the rent you will get for letting out the property.

The ratio is 1:1.3.

You will need 15% or more as your deposit.

The biggest mistake people make: is to just buy a second property rather than thinking about it as a source of income. You have to make sure that there is enough rental potential for the property type you choose and for the location you buy in.

An example of the 1:1.3 ratio:

You buy a property with a mortgage of £120,000. For an interest only mortgage (which is always the type of mortgage you should use for buy-to-let) the interest you pay is £6,000 per year, which equates to £500 per month.

£500 monthly interest x 1.3 = £650.

Therefore: on a mortgage of £120k you would be looking for a monthly rental fee of £650.

The 1.3 ratio includes any void periods you might have and gives you some headroom.

If you can achieve more than this it's a good investment. Employing property staging can even provide extra rental value.

Off set some of your portfolio

If the rental value doesn't work for your property, you still might decide to go ahead. Paying into a property, say the income is only £625 – the additional £25 per month you need to pay from your own pocket could be seen as a savings plan, especially if your strategy is to have a long term capital gain you may be willing to take a short term loss.

3) Never sell a property.

Re-mortgage to get money out.

There are new mortgages called 'let-to-buy' which allows you to let out your own home so you can get more of the equity out than you could purely based on your own income. Then you use your income to buy the next property, plus your 'let-to-buy' mortgage.

There are just three exceptions to this rule;
• You need the money and have to sell.
• House prices go up but not the rental income. The amount you can re-mortgage is capped based on the rental income, but you have greater equity in the property. Sell up and

move into a better investment property.
- A change in the rental market in that area and you are not achieving the capital growth you wanted.

Simon's top five clever tricks
1) Always minimise the amount of your own money you put into a property.
2) Buy under market value from:
Motivated sellers
Auction
Discounted property off-plan
Renovation property
3) Buy off-plan:
Put 10% down before it's built, complete months later when it's built and if the market has increased you can double your investment money BUT BE WARNED:
i) Do your research to check that the discount is genuine.
ii) Check who else is buying the property; if it's all investors then it could be no good, as everyone will be looking to rent and the return might not be so good – then they all decide to sell and the price drops
4) Check out the Hot spots
Where you live is the best place to buy because YOU know what's good and what's bad, it's easy to do the research based on local knowledge and you can manage the property your-self if it's nearby.
5) Buy one at a time.
Make sure you can cope with one before you start building up your portfolio. Don't rush out and buy lots at once until you've tried it out first and checked it is for you.

Property investing is something to do over a number of years It's a long-term strategy although it can be done in the short term, you'll want to keep doing it.

Should I use a managing agent?
"If they only collect the rent for you, I wouldn't bother. Set up a standing order and the rent will find its way into your bank account. If there are any late/non payments you will be much

more on the ball to chase it than any agent. I have heard some horror stories where the managing agent didn't collect, and didn't chase for three months. I've also heard of agents that collect but then don't transfer the money to the landlord for a couple of months, losing the landlord a heap of interest.

"If it's in need of regular maintenance and your agent will call out the services for you, then it can be worth it. It depends how 'hands on' you want to be. In my experience the best landlords are the ones who get involved and actually know their tenants. They seem to get more extensions to their leases with the same tenant and that reduces the void periods and saves you loads of hassle finding new trustworthy people."

What one lesson have you learnt?
"One good lesson is that there are loads of good deals out there and if you miss one there is another just around the corner, it is an active game! Property investing is like a partic- ipation sport – you have to DO something to stay in the game. That's the real key to playing the property game!"

HOT SPOTS

A number of factors will determine a property 'hot spot'. The Move Channel (*www.movechannel.com*) gave me these general rules to identifying property hot spots

HOW TO IDENTIFY PROPERTY HOT SPOTS

There are a number of factors to consider when choosing the right area to live or invest in property which will fully maximise your capital investment. These factors are important when trying to predict hot spots, as they contribute to the overall appeal of an area and will therefore have an impact on demand for property.

If you choose well when you are buying for the first time, you can be set up for life, making massive gains in just a few years for relatively little capital outlay.

But how exactly, can you predict which areas are going to be hot, and which are not? The following pages serve to illustrate that picking property hot spots takes a mixture of thorough research, analysis, timing, good judgement and a large dose of luck...

For an area to become a hot spot, it must improve in such a way that makes it more appealing than competing locations. The area must be perceived as offering better value for money than an alternative, in order to pull in the demand that will eventually lead to prices rising. Hot spots can exist on a very local level, with different parts of a town, or certain streets even, becoming hugely sought-after, or it can work on a wider geographical scale, for instance amongst the many towns and villages from which people commute into London.

Certain factors have historically shown themselves to be underlying causes of surging property prices.

Transport Improvements

New transport links can hugely change the nature of an area. There are many examples of how this can impact property prices. New tube lines, tram systems, motorway bypasses, train line improvements – all of these things generally end up improving the value of the properties situated along their routes. Better transport makes it much easier to reach nearby urban areas or centres of employment, something that people will generally pay a premium for. Examples of this are the new tram systems in Sheffield, Manchester and Nottingham.

Find out what new transport is planned by scanning civil engineering trade publications, to find out when new projects are proposed and confirmed. Make sure that you don't buy before confirmation – you don't want the planners to revise the proposals and change the route, or you could find yourself with a noisy new train line at the end of the garden rather than the convenient five minutes walk away that you thought it was going to be.

New Jobs

Local employment markets have a big impact on the demand for properties. A re-locating government department or a big national headquarters of a large corporation could bring thousands of new employees with it – and they'll be looking to buy or rent as close to work as possible.

Ideally, you should target areas which are becoming popular with companies whose employees earn well above the local average. If there is a growing local population and a rising level of affluence, then it can usually only have a positive influence on prices. More people, with more money to pay for property, means more competition and higher prices. Examples of this in recent years are Reading and Cambridge, where numerous major technology companies have moved over the last few years.

The main thing to be beware of when taking this into account is an area solely dependent on a single employer.

These days, global companies move their operations around so much that there is no guarantee that the massive new headquarters building will still be operational in five years time.

With a bit of prying you should be able to find out who your local council is trying to tempt to the area, where they might locate themselves and which out of town sites are being primed for commercial development.

INVESTMENT IN AN AREA

When you look at an area with the view to living there, it is clear that not all areas are equal. One may have too narrow a range of amenities, problems with social exclusion, or be generally run down. As many a management guru would say – look for opportunity in a problem. With billions of pounds available in EU and government redevelopment grants, many of the most deprived areas are set to benefit from large levels of inward investment, particularly if they are located in the shadow of a far more affluent area. Shopping centres, park landscaping, new public works, retail, leisure, public-private initiatives – the whole of the UK is buzzing with development at the moment.

Fortunately, finding out where public money is going to be spent is easy, as the government is so media aware these days, and keen to get maximum exposure for all the positive things that it does. Don't forget though, that miracles don't happen overnight, and you have to be prepared to wait for the changes to take effect. Getting in really early means you will probably end up with the biggest gains, but it also invariably means you will have to wait a significant time to maximise your returns – and you may not enjoy living there in the interim.

PROXIMITY TO OTHER 'HOT SPOTS'

Last, but not least, don't forget the ripple effect. If all else fails, consider buying in an area that is near to a former hot spot, but which hasn't had the same growth yet. Areas that people are looking to move into when they can't quite afford the current hot spot often give you an indication of which areas are next in line for a surge in popularity.

Fashion is one of the biggest causes of property price increases. It is also the most volatile and the most difficult to predict.

POPULAR PROPERTY TYPES

Much of the popularity of some areas can be put down to the make-up of the building stock and the availability of certain types of property. One of the most popular trends at the moment is for loft-style warehouse apartments. A high concentration of this type of property or lifestyle opportunity is likely to attract developers keen to convert the buildings and cash in on the demand for this type of home.

The evidence of this is fairly stark: riverside property in London, former industrial buildings in Manchester, Leeds, Liverpool and Birmingham – all these have been converted in line with this growing trend. There are many other cities that have numerous old mills, warehouses and other buildings that have not yet seen this trend and if the fashion spreads to those areas, then they could prompt an upsurge in local demand. Nottingham could be a future beneficiary of this effect.

Beware of changing fashions. Buying a fashionable style property is risky. Trends never really stay the same for long, and by choosing a popular property type you are probably paying something of a premium. When fashions change demand will fade, so buying a fashionable property may not be that good a proposition in the long term.

Don't assume things will be universally popular. Just because a certain type of home is all the rage in one place, it is not always correct to anticipate that the trend will spread to all corners of the country. For example, I know that riverside developments are taking place in Derby, but you have to ask the question, who would buy these? With many of the local employers moving to out of town industrial parks (Pride Park), who would want to buy a city centre apartment with no parking? Just because it works in Nottingham, doesn't mean it will work in Derby because the employment profile is very different.

PREFERRED SCHOOLS

This is one area in particular that will increase the value of a family property. The modern phenomenon of public service performance assessment has driven a huge amount of interest in government-issued school league tables.

For years, anecdotal evidence indicated that properties within catchment areas of good schools fetched higher prices than those outside. Following several pieces of research, there is now scientific evidence to back this up. Parents, it seems, are prepared to pay a premium to get their children into the best schools.

It is fairly easy to identify what parents consider to be a good school, by looking at how successful their candidates are in GCSE and A level exams. However, from a rising property price perspective, it is no use buying with recent past performance in mind, as this will already have affected prices. And unfortunately, there is no easy way to tell which schools are going to have drastically improved their performance in five years' time. You could do worse than looking out for new schools that are to be built, or existing ones that are set to receive additional funding. Failing that, buying a run down property to do up in a school catchment area or refurbishing a property to appeal to buyers with school age children, will pay dividends.

SOCIAL HOT SPOTS

Another factor that can swell or hit prices depending on the direction of the trend is the popularity of a place as a social venue. If a street, suburb or area of a city suddenly becomes a popular nightspot, then unknowingly influential affluent young professionals can contribute to dramatically rising prices, by trying to move nearer to their favourite evening entertainments.

When you're thinking about which area to buy in, it can be tempting to go for an area that is being touted as a hot spot. This is a dangerous tactic. Once an area is being regarded in this way, you will probably have already missed out on the biggest gains in the price value of properties.

One of the more common ways in which investors try to pre-empt the market is by spotting the early signs of gentrification. This is the process by which an area's reputation and social makeup moves upmarket.

According to Ludlow Thompson, the residential buy-to-let agency, there are a number of key indicators which point to a neighbourhood in the early or late stages of gentrification. If the majority of these features are already in place, then the chances are that you are too late. As Dan McLoed, Residential Investment Manager of Ludlow Thompson said: "Once an area has its own branch of Starbucks, All Bar One or Pizza Express much of the explosive period of capital growth is largely over."

Here are the main things to look for:

• **High percentage of period properties**
Gentrification tends not to occur where there are a large number of 1960s tower blocks or other "characterless" buildings.

• **A number of small independent restaurants/cafes**
Look out for the appearance of Tapas bars, Thai restaurants and coffee shops, which hint at an influx of a new young clientele. New pine furniture/kitchen shops and estate agents are also a good indicator.

• **Changing social makeup of an area**
Firstly, it helps if there is no single dominant ethnic group in the area. Such communities tend to be more insular and therefore resistant to the influx of changes that are necessary to gentrify an area. Areas that becomes popular with young "arty" types are often in the throes of gentrification. Their arrival in an area suggests that prices per square foot are still

relatively cheap. They also help establish an areas reputation and encourage an influx of fashionable bars and restaurants that are soon seen as local amenities that attract other residents to the area. The movement of the gay community into an area also has a similar affect. Their higher than average level of disposable income allows them more money for renovating properties and also for spending on a fashionable nightlife.

- **Early signs of property developer interest**
New build developments, or the conversion of disused buildings can help to strengthen an area's reputation and signs of small scale redevelopment such as skips outside properties are another sign of investment that will help to improve an areas look.

The general consensus is that you should avoid following fashion and focus instead on taking advantage of the rather more tangible things discussed on the previous pages, before they have a widespread impact on prices.

It rarely does much harm to get the objective view of estate or lettings agents in an area, as they should have their finger on the pulse. That doesn't mean they always will, however. Estate agencies in many areas simply don't have the time to read all that they should about developments and changes in their catchment area. And don't forget that they are probably trying to sell you their service...

If you are adamant that you want to buy somewhere specifically to enjoy capital gains, then make sure you enter the venture with realistic timescales. Property is not a liquid asset and there will be serious cost implications if you want to bail out before your investment comes to fruition.

Even when the signs appear to be right, things can still go wrong. Some areas may never attract the anticipated demand and consequently will be left with a surplus of property. By getting in early, you are usually buying at a price that is undervaluing the property should the planned change take place in the area. The chances are that you won't be the only person to have taken the decision, meaning that the market could have already risen by the time you buy. If the thing you are banking on fails to materialise, you could be left with a property that is difficult to let, is overpriced, difficult to sell and in an area you don't really want to live in.

My own personal advice would always be to pick somewhere you'll be happy to live. Even if those prices don't rise, at least you'll be somewhere you want to be – which may well be the most important thing in the final analysis.

Halifax Hot Spots

Here we can see what Halifax Estate Agents, part of the Halifax Bank of Scotland, the UK's largest mortgage provider, has to say about looking forward to the 2004 market and looking back over 2003.

> The HBOS Economic forecast focuses on the prospects for the UK housing, mortgages and savings markets in 2004. The forecast incorporates a range of official statistics as well as information from the Halifax House Price Index.
>
> HBOS is the UK's largest mortgage and savings provider and also publishes the longest running monthly housing index in the UK.
>
> Halifax Note concerning the data contained in the report: The Halifax House Price Index is prepared from information that we believe is collated with care, but we do not make any statement as to its accuracy or completeness. We reserve the right to vary our methodology and to edit or discontinue the indices at any time for regulatory or other reasons. Persons seeking to place reliance on the indices for their own or third party commercial purposes do so at their own risk.

Halifax Economic Forecast For 2004

Shane O'Riordain, General Manager, HBOS Group Economics, commented:

The annual rate of house price inflation in 2004 is expected to be 8%, close to the longer-term average over the past 20 years. If anything, the risk to our forecast is actually on the upside, as the three pillars that have underpinned the housing market during the last two years – low interest rates, good employment and good affordability – continue into 2004. Following two years of exceptional house price growth, house prices will continue to ease as the impact of higher interest rates coupled with the increasing problems facing first time buyers combine to put a gradual brake on house price inflation.

2004 will once again be the 'Year of the North'. Although house prices in the north have risen by almost 60% in total during the last two years, prices are expected to ease quite significantly from these very high levels during the coming 12 months. Following this years, estimated 33% increase in house prices in the north, we forecast house price growth of 17% in the region during 2004. We anticipate that house prices will also continue to be strong in Scotland and in Wales during 2004 – we are expecting double digit house price growth in both countries during 2004.

North/South divide narrows. The traditional north/south divide, which narrowed significantly during 2003, will continue to narrow during 2004, before re-establishing itself during 2005. Our figures show that at the end of 2002, the average property in the south cost 3 times as much as in the north. The gap has now narrowed and the average property in the south is around 2.3 times more expensive than in the north. This narrowing of the north/south divide is likely to continue in 2004, albeit at a gentler pace as prices moderate in the north and gently increase in the south.

House prices in London and the South East will increase modestly during 2004. Following a period when the capital 'paused for breath', house prices in the London 'mainstream market' (properties up to £250,000) are expected to grow by approximately 8% during 2004 – around the same level seen in 2003, but still below the long term regional average (10%).

High levels of employment, low inflation and a strengthening UK economy will continue to underpin the housing market. Mortgage payments remain low in relation to earnings and currently represent around 14% of gross earnings for a typical homeowner. We anticipate that UK bank base rates will increase during 2004 and end the year at around 4.50%. Assuming a base rate of 4.50%, mortgage payments will represent approximately 16% of gross earnings – very good affordability levels.

The cost of owning and running a home continues to significantly increase. Even though mortgage rates have been at 50-year lows, the cost of running a home has risen very significantly. Separate research by the Halifax to be released next week shows that between 2001 and 2002, the cost of owning and running a house has risen four times faster than the rate of inflation. During this period, the figures show that the average homeowner spent, including mortgage payments, £5,604 on owning and running their home. We forecast that the true cost of owning and running a home will continue to rise quite significantly during 2004 as large council tax increases, coupled with hefty rises in utility bills, impact homeowners right across the UK.

First time buyers will continue to face difficulties getting a foothold on the housing ladder. Traditionally the problems first time buyers have experienced trying to get onto the housing ladder have been confined to London and the South East. We are predicting that due to the very significant house price growth experienced in the Midlands and the North over the last 12 months, the first time buyer problem will extend over significant areas of the UK by the end of 2004. As a result, the number of first time buyers entering the housing market during 2003 is expected to be at the lowest levels since records began in 1974. As house prices continue to increase above the rate of earnings, the number of first time buyers entering the market is expected to continue falling during 2004.

3A) Regional House Price Growth

	% year on year			
	2001 Q4 Actual	2002 Q4 Actual	2003 Q4 Estimate	2004 Q4 Estimate
North	12	26	33	17
Yorks/Humber	12	26	24	12
North West	8	25	20	11
East Midlands	12	42	13	6
West Midlands	7	36	16	8
East Anglia	20	20	15	8
South West	16	33	6	3
South East	15	26	6	3
Grt London	17	19	8	8
Wales	7	28	31	14
N. Ireland	7	6	15	8
Scotland	5	12	16	12
UK	12	26	15	8

(Source Halifax House Price Index)

Mortgages and Consumer Credit

The rate of growth in mortgage lending in 2004 is likely to ease. The fundamental drivers in the mortgage market – low interest rates, good employment levels and good affordability – continue to underpin the market as a whole. We expect the mortgage market to grow from around £270 billion in 2003 to around £280 billion in 2004. With net lending volumes finishing 2003 at around £98 billion, we forecast that net lending next year is likely to be in the range of £90-£100 billion. Transaction volumes are expected to slow in 2004 as the impact of interest rate increases, as well as the reduction in the numbers of first time buyers entering the market begins to take effect.

Consumer credit is set to remain strong. We expect consumers' appetite for credit to dampen slightly during 2004 as projected interest rate increases begin to take effect. We expect net consumer credit lending to moderate from an estimated £19 billion in 2003 (down from £20.8 billion in 2002), to around £18 billion in 2004.

Savings

The saving ratio, which represents the proportion of post-tax income that households save rather than spending, is recovering from the historic low it reached in 2000. In the 40 year period that the savings ratio has been published, it has varied from a high of 12.4% in 1980, to a low of 4.3% in 2000. During 2003, the savings ratio, at 4.7% was above its historical low, but was still significantly below the 8% average for the 40 year period. As UK interest rates start to rise and house price inflation continues to slow down, we expect to see the savings ratio to also begin to creep upwards over the next couple of years – with the ratio breaking the 6% barrier again by the end of 2005.

UK households are getting wealthier. The rapid rise in house prices in the past few years has significantly increased the majority of homeowners' wealth, which has reduced the incentive to save as the value of most people's biggest asset has appreciated, making many feel more financially secure. The prospect of more house price growth and a rising stock market means that the UK household balance sheet will continue to strengthen during 2004.

REVIEW OF THE HOUSING MARKET IN 2003

The UK housing market remained strong throughout 2003:

- The annual rate of house price inflation for 2003 was recorded as 14.1% in the most recent Halifax House Price Index of the year (published Wednesday December 3rd, 2003).

- House price inflation has remained strong throughout the year – supported by historically low interest rates, good affordability and strong levels of employment.
- The average house price currently stands at £139, 492.
- The Monetary Policy Committee (MPC) increased rates for the first time in nearly four years in November – however mortgage rates remain at historically low levels.
- The continuing low interest rate environment has ensured that affordability for borrowers remains good. Mortgage payments continue to remain low in relation to earnings and currently represent around 14% of gross earnings for a typical homeowner.
- The lack of good quality, affordable new housing in the UK is set to continue:
- There continues to be a chronic shortage of new homes in the UK and this is contributing to the upward pressure on house prices. New house building peaked at over 414,000 in 1968. In 22 only 170,000 new homes were built in Britain, slightly above the 2001 figure, which itself was the lowest total of new homes built in any year since 1947.
- Halifax conducted its own extensive research in 2003 looking at the number and type of new homes which are currently being built to see if they are actually meeting the needs of prospective homeowners. Even though the size of the average household in the UK is getting smaller, 3- and 4-bedroomed detached properties are the most common type of property being built.
- Halifax estimates that if the current low level of new house-build continues, there will be a major shortage of homes in the UK by the year 2020.
- Although house price inflation is slowing, first time buyers are still struggling:
- First time buyers will continue to face difficulties during 2004 getting a foothold on the housing ladder. On a regional level it is a mixed picture for first time buyers, but affordability is constraining demand for the majority. There is already strong evidence to say that this is a major factor in the gradual brake in house price inflation.

House Price Changes in Major University Towns and Cities

Hundreds of thousands of A-level students will be eagerly awaiting the arrival of their exam results in August to enable them to confirm their university places and finalise arrangements for their accommodation. Most new students usually spend their first year living in the university's halls of residence but other students will be moving into rented shared houses with friends.

Halifax Estate Agents has examined the changes in average property prices for the country's top 20 university towns and cities as well as those of the universities offering the most popular courses. Increasingly parents are considering buying investment properties for their sons and daughters to live in whilst they are at university. The figures in table A.A show the increase in property prices that parents could have benefited from over the past four years, the typical length of an undergraduate course.

The average increase in property prices across the UK over the past four years has been 72% and the majority of these university towns have performed very well with 12 out of the 15 universities not based in London outperforming the UK over the same period.

Most Popular University Courses

There are now thousands of university undergraduate courses to choose from ranging from Adventure Tourism Management to Zoology with Evolutionary Psychology. However, the top 10 most popular courses remain more traditional.

TABLE A.A

	University/Location	Average £ 1999	Price £ 2003	Increase	(%)
1	University of Cambridge	118,405	220,962	102,557	87
2	University of Oxford	141,495	269,862	128,367	91
3	Imperial College London	177,410	258,865	81,455	46
4	London School of Economics	177,410	258,865	81,455	46
5	University of Warwick	122,428	170,413	47,985	39
6	University of Nottingham	67,765	123,135	55,370	82
7	University College London	177,410	258,865	81,455	46
8	University of York	80,634	157,803	77,169	96
9	Bristol University	90,808	169,847	79,000	87
10	University of Manchester	61,202	1,878	39,676	65
11	School of African Studies	177,410	258,865	81,455	46
12	University of Bath	1,807	227,624	126,817	126
13	University of Birmingham	67,396	117,561	50,165	74
14	Loughborough University	79,479	147,564	68,085	86
15	King's College, London	177,410	258,865	81,455	46
16	University of Durham	72,010	103,7	31,690	44
17	The University of St Andrew's	84,044	160,967	76,923	92
18	University of Southampton	93,669	170,745	77,076	82
19	University of Edinburgh	84,044	160,967	76,923	92
20	University of Sheffield	56,629	109,711	50,082	84

Source: Rankings are combined scores from all university league tables: *The Daily Telegraph, Financial Times, The Guardian, The Sunday Times, Times and Employers,* published in *The Daily Telegraph* 25/6/03.

Top ten most popular university courses in the UK

1	Business studies
2	Computer science
3	Law
4	Art & design
5	English
6	Psychology
7	History
8	Sociology
9	Medicine
10	Electronic engineering

Source: Higher Education Statistics Agency – number of students enrolled on specified named courses, 2001/2002.

In addition to the top 20 most highly rated universities, the following universities are recognised as excellent providers of some of the most popular courses. Many areas around these universities have also seen good increases in price rises over the past four years, compared to the UK increase of 72% over the period.

Universities Outside the Top 20 Rated Highly for Providing Popular Courses

University/Location Subjects	Average Price (£)		Increase	Increase
	1999	2003	(£)	(%)
Sussex University, Brighton, Sociology	87,147	197,783	110,636	127
University of Leicester Medicine	67,599	128,212	60,613	90
Newcastle University Medicine	68,264	127,209	58,345	86
University of Leeds* English	68,27	123,414	55,143	81
University College Northants, Art & Design	86,489	156,362	69,873	81
University of Essex, Colchester, Law	101,666	179,580	77,914	77
Cardiff University Psychology	78,027	136,933	58,906	75
Staffordshire University Psychology	58,229	97,645	39,416	68
Hull University Electronic Engineering	48,186	79,130	30,944	64
University of Lancaster Art & Design	67,1	103,537	36,437	54
Glasgow University* Sociology	69,843	103,436	33,593	48
Surrey University, Guildford* Business Studies	209,344	307,791	98,447	47
University of Dundee Psychology	59,868	83,859	23,991	40
Queens, Belfast Electronic Engineering	72,112	1,233	28,121	39

Source: *The Guardian* University Guide 2003, subject tables.

* University of Leeds is also highly rated for Art & Design and Electronic Engineering; Surrey University is also highly rated for Electronic Engineering; Glasgow University is also highly rated from Computer Science and English.

Buying a Property for University Accommodation

Wherever students are living, accommodation costs will amount to a substantial expense as courses average around four years in duration. Finding suitable safe and secure rental accommodation, at the right price and close to the university, combined with fears over mounting student debt is leading a growing number of parents to consider buying a property for their children to live in whilst at university.

Whether the property is in the parent's name or the child's name a number of financial benefits can be gained:

- Letting the remaining rooms to other students often covers mortgage payments.
- No rental income is paid over the period spent studying.
- The property can be kept as a longer-term investment to rent to other students after they have finished at university.

Jane Pridgeon, Managing Director of Halifax Estate Agencies, said:

"The decision to buy a property for a son or daughter at university ultimately depends on personal circumstances and property prices around the specific university. High property prices in places such as London and Oxford may prove to be prohibitive but there are still plenty of areas, such as Durham and Manchester, which are very affordable and provide good investment opportunities.

"Feedback from our estate agents in university towns and cities shows that potential student properties are in high demand, particularly by parents looking for a good investment."

Students buying a house in their own right.
Students can apply for a mortgage in their own right, usually with their parents acting as guarantors for the loan. This not only enables the student to get on the housing ladder, but it also provides lenders with the safety net of knowing that if payments are not maintained they can turn to the guarantor for payment. Individuals should always take independent legal advice before they consider acting as guarantors because they are legally responsible for payments. A number of lenders, including Halifax, accept guarantors on mortgages.

Tax Implications when letting property
Details of the tax implications for individuals renting their property are provided by the Inland Revenue in Leaflet IR87 (Letting and your home – including the 'Rent a Room' scheme), available from local tax office or from their website, *www.inlandrevenue.gov.uk*.

Sources:
House Prices – Halifax House Price Index, crude average prices Q2 1999 – Q2 2003. Prices shown are the arithmetic average prices of houses on which an offer of mortgage has been granted. These prices are not standardised and therefore can be affected by changes in the sample from quarter to quarter. Figures exclude properties sold for 1 million plus.

Top 20 Universities – combined scores from all university league tables, *The Daily Telegraph*, *Financial Times*, *The Guardian*, *Sunday Times*, *Times* and *Employers*, published in *The Daily Telegraph* 25/6/03.

Top 10 most popular university courses – Higher Education Statistics Agency – number of students enrolled on specified named courses, Subject of Study 2001/2002.

Top universities for the most popular courses – *The Guardian* University Guide 2003, subject tables.

Research by the Halifax, using Land Registry figures, revealed there has been a slight fall in the number of £million properties sold during the first six months of 2003 from 1,212 to 1,181. Overall the figures show that 12,168 properties worth more than £1m have now been sold in England and Wales since 1995.

The research, which looked at house sales across the 377 local authority districts of England and Wales, found that, unsurprisingly, London has dominated the sales of £1m properties with the boroughs of Kensington and Chelsea, City of Westminster and Camden making up 45% of all £1m plus sales since 1995.

To reinforce the fact that 2003 has been dubbed the 'Year of the North', the figures also highlight the very rapid increase in the number of million pound properties sold in the north during the past 18 months, albeit from a very low base.

Key findings:

£1m property sales slow for first time since 1995
Sales of million pound properties in the first half of 2003 were 3% down on the corresponding period in 2002 (1,181 million pound properties were sold in the first six months of 2003 compared to 1,212 properties in the first six months of 2002). Despite this slight slowdown, 11 of the top 20 districts (as measured by £1 million sales) in the first half of 2003 recorded an actual increase in the number of £1m properties compared to a year ago. Camden, Richmond upon Thames and South Bucks all saw more than 20 properties worth more than £1m sold in the first six months of this year.

Since 1995, just over 12,000 properties valued at over £1 million have been sold in England and Wales (12,168). In 1995 there were only 232 properties sold for over £1 million – by 2002 this figure had risen to 3,174. A further 1,181 'million pound' properties were sold in the first six months of 2003.

The £1 Million Ripple Spreads North
The rapid increase in house prices experienced by the North during the last 18 months has impacted the sale of million

pound properties. Although the increase in the number of million pound properties is measured from a low base, regionally, it was Yorkshire and the Humber which saw the largest percentage increase in sales of £1m properties recording a 250% increase (from two property sales to seven). The West Midlands saw a 183% increase in sales on the corresponding period in 2002 – going up from six transactions to 17.

Greater London was the only region to record an actual drop in the number of £1m properties, with sales down 17% on the corresponding period in 2002. There were 703 million pound properties sold in London during the first six months of 2003, compared to 850 in the first half of 2002.

Nine Districts See Their First £1m Property Sales During 2003

During the first half of 2003 nine local authority districts have seen their first million pound property sales. The local authority districts of Castle Morpeth in Northumberland, Dartford, South Kesteven in Lincolnshire, Penrith in Cumbria, Rutland, Chester, North East Derbyshire and Oldham all recorded their first £1m plus sale during the first six months of the year.

The top end of the property market in North Kesteven was particularly active. The area not only recorded its first million pound property sale earlier this year – it actually recorded three £1m plus property sales!

All but 105 local authority districts have now experienced million pound property sales.

Since 1995, £1m plus properties have now been sold in 272 out of the 377 local authority districts. In the first half of 2003 there were sales of at least one £1m property in 145 local authority districts, with sales of more than one £1m homes in 94 of these areas.

Since 1995 the two London districts of 'Kensington & Chelsea' (3,077 sales) and the 'City of Westminster' (1,841 sales) have consistently topped the £1m plus sales table by a wide margin.

Outside London and the South East it is the local authority areas of Poole (89 sales), Epping Forest (58 sales), Three Rivers (57 sales), Hertsmere (55 sales), East Hertfordshire (51 sales),

Trafford (45 sales) and Macclesfield (44 sales) which have recorded the greatest number of £1m plus transactions.

Halifax group economist Martin Ellis said: "Although million pound properties still represent a very small part of the overall housing market the general rise in house prices over the past few years has had a knock on effect on properties at the top end of the scale. The million pound 'ripple effect' is now reaching the north of England highlighting the fact that 2003 is undoubtedly the 'year of the North'."

Figures are compiled from the Land Registry and are based on all residential property sales in England and Wales. The south of England is defined as Greater London, the South East, the South West and East Anglia.

Over 50% Of Towns Are Now Unaffordable For Key Public Sector Workers

New Halifax research published 7th February 2004, showed that buying a home is out of reach for the average key public sector worker – nurses, teachers and police officers – in half of the UK's major postal towns. Housing affordability problems for key public sector workers have largely been confined to London and the South East of England in previous years.

The average house price in 504 (80%) of the 634 UK towns analysed is now in excess of £100,000. This has had a serious impact on key public sector workers. Of the towns analysed, 496 (78%) are unaffordable for nurses. Police officers cannot afford to buy a house in 400 (63%) of the 634 towns, whilst 390 (62%) are now unaffordable for teachers.

Shane O'Riordain, General Manager, Group Economics, commented: "Buying a home is out of reach for an increasing number of key workers across the country. Our research shows the average UK house price is now almost six times the average UK salary for both nurses and fire-fighters.

"In regions where affordability is an issue the recruitment and retention of key public sector workers will become more and more of a problem. The current scheme, whilst available throughout the country, is weighted towards London and the South East. Clearly it is sensible for the government to continue with the London weighting but consideration should be given to extending the scope of the scheme outside the south of England."

Key Findings of Halifax research:

In London, the average price of a property now stands at 8.8 times a nurse's average annual pay compared with 8.21 times in 2002. For fire fighters the ratio has risen from 8.03 to 8.77, whilst the house price to earnings ratio has increased from 6.79 to 7.06 for teachers. Police officers have seen an increase in the ratio of prices to earnings from 6.07 in 2002 to 6.33 in 2003 but, following the trend nationally, are still in a significantly better position than nurses, teachers and fire fighters. However, housing is rapidly becoming less affordable for police officers.

In 2003, the average house price to earnings ratio for key public sector workers was above the average 4.27 for a first time buyer in six regions from the Midlands southwards. The situation replicates the pattern last year when the same six regions were out of reach for key public sector workers. Key public sector workers in East and West Midlands, East Anglia Greater London, South East and the South West are now finding it increasingly difficult to buy their own home. This drive northwards will continues as the old north/south divide narrows.

Four regions – Wales, the North, the North West and Yorkshire & the Humber – have seen the highest increases in house price to earnings ratios, but remain the most affordable for key public sector workers. The North experienced the highest rises and nurses in the region have the highest house price to earnings ratio of 4.41 (in 2002 it was 3.41). Police officers have to find 3.54 times their salary (compared to 2.84 in 2002) and teachers 3.38 (2.65).

Scotland is the most affordable area for all four key public sector occupations. Nurses have the highest house price to earnings ratio amongst key public sector workers in Scotland (3.65), followed by teachers (2.87) and police officers (2.73).

Nationally, the current situation is worst for nurses and fire fighters with the average house price now being almost 6 times the average salary for both occupations. By comparison police officers have an average house price to earnings ratio of 4.44. The average house purchased by teachers costs £139,716, which is 4.61 times the average annual salary (£30,274) for the occupation.

There are already schemes targeted at helping key public sector workers to get onto the property ladder. The Government's £250 million Starter Home Initiative assists health workers, teachers, police officers and fire fighters along with some other key worker occupations to buy a home in areas where high house prices are undermining staff recruitment and retention. The scheme, which will close at the end of March 2004, has so far helped 6,000 key workers buy their own home. A new scheme is expected to be launched in April.

Key public sector workers can also take advantage of one of the shared ownership schemes offered by local housing associations. The schemes enable the homebuyer to purchase a property in stages (usually split blocks equal to 25% of the property value). The outstanding value of the property not purchased by the homebuyer is rented from the housing association.

Half of the towns featured in the 20 'least expensive' list did not feature last year, including Porth in mid Glamorgan which has slipped from 602nd to 619th in the list of 634 towns across the UK.

The 20 Least Expensive Towns In The UK

Rank 2003	Town	Ave. Price 2002	Ave. Price 2003	% change	Rank 2002
615	Carluke, Strathclyde	63,601	70,679	11	588
616	Darwen, Lancashire	71,919	70,512	-2	547
617	Motherwell, Strathclyde	67,348	70,423	5	572
618	Airdrie, Strathclyde	61,660	70,371	14	597
619	Porth, Mid-Glamorgan	61,015	70,293	15	602
620	Accrington, Lancashire	58,783	70,059	19	612
621	Ebbw Vale, Gwent	57,918	69,627	20	618
622	Aberdare, Mid-Glamorgan	54,196	69,205	28	626
623	Arbroath, Tayside	58,391	69,500	18	614
624	Wishaw, Strathclyde	60,336	68,976	14	606
625	Peterhead, Grampian	59,377	68,296	15	610
626	Merthyr-Tydfil, Mid Glam.	48,597	68,057	40	633
627	Barrow-In-Furness, Cumbria	55,073	67,138	22	623
628	Irvine, Strathclyde	51,915	65,305	26	629
629	Port-Talbot, West Glam.	58,018	64,490	11	617
630	Bootle, Merseyside	54,954	63,919	16	624
631	Coatbridge, Strathclyde	58,922	63,754	8	611
632	Peterlee, County Durham	49,149	62,159	27	632
633	Bellshill, Strathclyde	52,474	60,988	16	627
634	Lochgelly, Fife	48,700	54,910	14	634

Jane Pridgeon, Managing Director, Halifax estate agents, said:

"These figures confirm that 2003 has undoubtedly been the 'year of the north' and we expect this trend to continue in the coming 12 months although anticipate that annual house price growth will ease slightly. House price growth in Wales has been one of the most rapid in the UK and it will remain strong over the coming year. We expect house price growth in Wales to be around 14% in 2004 compared to an expected growth in the UK of around 8%.

There has been little change in the most expensive towns across Wales during the past 12 months. The most interesting factor in 2003 was the doubling of the number of towns in Wales that now have an average house price in excess of £100,000. If this trend continues, more and more first time buyers will begin to have difficulty in getting a foothold on the housing ladder."

Post town House Prices shown are the arithmetic average prices of houses on which an offer of mortgage has been granted. These prices are not standardised and therefore can be affected by changes in the sample size. Figures exclude properties sold for £1 million plus.

Regional House Prices are seasonally adjusted, standardised average prices.

Halifax is the UK's largest mortgage lender and produces the longest running monthly housing index in the country. Full historical details of the Halifax house price index can be found at *www.hbosplc.com*

The HBOS group of companies lends approximately one in four of all new mortgages granted in the UK.

PROPERTY PRICES BESIDE THE SEASIDE

The British do love to live beside the seaside whether it's the increasing trend for buying a property abroad or the popularity and convenience of living by the sea a little closer to home.

Halifax estate agents has analysed average property prices for over 100 seaside towns in England and Wales over the past two years. It appears that the desire for a sea view does add a premium to property prices, over 70% of the seaside towns examined have outperformed their region.

TOP 10 SEASIDE TOWNS LARGEST INCREASES 2001-2003

	Post Town	Average Price		Increase	
		Q2 2001	Q2 2003	£	%
1	Padstow, Cornwall	109,833	223,084	113,251	103
2	Pwllheli, Gwynedd	79,424	147,251	67,827	85
3	Penzance, Cornwall	89,650	164,351	74,701	83
4	Porthleven, Cornwall	85,339	154,611	69,272	81
5	Cardigan, Dyfed	67,375	117,799	50,424	75
6	Sandwich, Kent	109,019	190,197	81,178	74
6	Brancaster, Norfolk	1,646	175,253	74,608	74
6	Mevagissey, Cornwall	82,105	142,954	60,849	74
9	Sheringham, Norfolk	1,520	167,374	66,855	67
10	Prestatyn , Clwyd Wales	57,742	95,891	38,149	66

The highest increase over the past 2 years has been in Padstow where average property prices have increased by 103% compared to the regional average for the south west of 42% and the average for England and Wales of 28%. The seaside towns in Cornwall have performed very well with four of the top ten located in the county.

The Welsh coastal towns have also performed well, with average prices in Pwllheli rising by 85% and with three of the top ten seaside towns in Wales.

The most expensive seaside town in England and Wales is Sandbanks in Dorset where the average property costs over £400,000. The seaside towns in the south are the most expensive in the country and eight out of the top ten most expensive towns are in the southwest.

Top 10 most expensive seaside towns, England and Wales

	Post town	Region	Average price Q2 2003 (£)
1	Sandbanks, Dorset	South West	403,594
2	Lymington, Hampshire	South East	273,326
3	St Mawes, Cornwall	South West	245,241
4	Padstow, Cornwall	South West	223,084
5	Budleigh Salterton, Devon	South West	223,066
6	Sidmouth, Devon	South West	209,417
7	Christchurch, Dorset	South West	205,909
8	Swanage, Dorset	South West	204,192
9	Lyme Regis, Dorset	South West	199,228
10	Sandwich, Kent	South East	190,197

These prices may be too high for most of those looking to relocate to the coast or buy a weekend hideaway by the sea. There are, however, many areas around the country where seaside town property prices are more affordable and people may be able to buy a property with their own sea view. The most affordable seaside towns are in the north of England with the north east coastline offering many of the least expensive seaside properties in the country.

TEN MOST AFFORDABLE SEASIDE TOWNS, ENGLAND AND WALES

	Post town	Region	Average price Q2 2003 (£)
1	Withernsea, North Humberside	Yorkshire & Humber	47,678
2	Seaham, County Durham	North	51,615
3	Barrow In Furness, Cumbria	North	57,121
4	Workington, Cumbria	North	58,307
5	Blyth, Northumberland	North	62,901
6	Fleetwood, Lancashire	North West	65,904
7	Hartlepool, Cleveland	North	66,403
8	Maryport, Cumbria	North	66,771
9	South Shields	North	68,998
10	Cleethorpes, South Humberside	Yorkshire & Humber	69,893

It is a mixed picture throughout the country and there are wide variations in average price within the different coastal regions.

Jane Pridgeon, Managing Director of Halifax Estate Agents, said:

"A home by the sea is a dream for many people and it could also prove to be a good financial investment, the majority of seaside towns we have analysed have performed very well against the rest of their region. However, if you're looking for a property with a great sea view you may have to be prepared to pay more than the average price as a good sea view will add a premium to the price of a property."

Source:
Land Registry and Halifax.
Please note all prices quoted are crude averages, and can be affected by changes in the sample from quarter to quarter.

WHICH PARTS OF THE UK ARE EXPERIENCING THE BIGGEST INCREASES IN PROPERTY PRICES?

Source: Halifax reports

UK house prices are continuing to rise, recording a 4.3% increase in September, according to the latest report from the Halifax. The East Midlands has taken over from East Anglia as the UK's property hot spot, with prices rising by 38% over the last year. Here are the latest regional increases over the past 12 months:

- East Midlands +38%
- South West +26%
- North West +21%.
- West Midlands +21%
- East Anglia +21%
- South East +20%
- Yorkshire & Humberside +19%
- Greater London +18%
- North +16%

- Wales +10%
- Scotland +7%
- Northern Ireland +5%

The latest report also shows that the average property price in both the East and West Midlands has now breached the £100,000 mark. In Greater London, the average price is now over £200,000. Prices in London are steadying, though, as shown by the region's eighth place in the table. However, prices in London are still 83% higher than the UK average.

Average house price to reach £1 million?
A recent report by the Halifax states that the number of homes sold for more than £1 million is set to double within the space of just three years. In 1995 just 232 £1 million+ homes were sold. By 1999 the figure had increased to 1,305. But that figure is increasing exponentially and by the end of this year approximately 2,600 £1 million properties will have been sold in England and Wales.

Unsurprisingly the South East accounts for most sales exceeding the £1 million mark with 1,624 in London, and 615 in the rest of the South East. Wales, with just 2 sales in 2001, and Yorkshire and Humberside, with 3, bring up the rear. In London, quite remarkably, 1 out of every 100 homes sold costs more than a million.

It may take only another 50 years before the average house price hits £1 million. If house prices rise at 4.5% over the next 50 years they will cost on average £1 million, but London will break that barrier much earlier – in 2039. So your grandchildren might have a huge mortgage on their hands!

Which region has seen the most growth?
The most expensive counties in which to live are Greater London, Surrey, Berkshire and Hertfordshire. South Yorkshire and South Humberside are the cheapest. These match the statistics on £1 million+ sales, but what is perhaps more interesting is that although London is the most expensive area, its prices have not risen as fast as some other areas since the dark days of 1987.

The average property in County Antrim, Northern Ireland, has increased by a whopping 213% since 1987, whereas London prices have only increased by a comparatively modest 156%. If you had bought a house in County Antrim for £50,000 in 1987 it would now be worth £156,500, whereas your London property would be worth £128,000. County Down, also in Northern Ireland, is in second place, with Shropshire, Cheshire, and North Yorkshire filling the next positions. Oxfordshire, in 6th place, saw the biggest increases in the southeast. The slowest growing areas are Tayside in Scotland and Northumberland where increases have been 73 and 77% respectively.

What does this tell us? The really canny, or lucky investors, have not necessarily been those living in the most expensive areas of the country. For those of you who bought in County Antrim, your house might not be worth a million, but a 213% increase over 14 years is something even an investor like Warren Buffet would be proud of!

HALIFAX HOT SPOTS – FEBRUARY 2004
Isle of Wight (2.5%): Supply continues to outstrip demand and the market has been extremely busy this month.

Cumbria (1.7%): There has been a huge increase in market appraisals from January onwards and at least two people offering on every property.

Northumberland (1.6%): January has seen a very active market with lack of stock keeping sales and prices buoyant, and increasing.

Derbyshire (1.5%): Market activity increased sharply during January, with good instructions and sales following.

Merseyside (1.5%): The market is still very busy and has made a positive start to 2004.

England's Second Home Hot Spots

England has 206,000 second homes worth an estimated £40bn. But where are they located, and where are the current hot spots?

Research from FPD Savills reveals that the second homes market is divided into two distinct sectors; the holiday home in the country, and the pied à terre in central London.

Unsurprisingly the South West accounts for just under a quarter (23%) of all second homes, while London has the second largest proportion with 18% of supply. The South East (17%) and the Eastern region (11%) follow closely behind.

Richard Donnell, Head of FPD Savills Residential Research comments: "The second homes market is made up of two distinct sub-markets. The first is the holiday homes market where the property is used for a weekend or longer break.

"The second is the pied à terre market appealing to commuters and those wanting a second home in the city centre.

"The holiday homes market explains the high proportion of second home ownership around much of the English coast, whilst the pied à terre market accounts for some 38,000 second homes in London."

Pied a Terre
Donnell's figures are based on council tax data and provide a figure for the size of the market in each Local Authority in England. Viewed as a percentage of all housing, the local authority with the most second homes is the City of London (26.6%).

Next comes the Isles of Scilly (23%), South Hams (12%) and North Cornwall (11%). 10% of properties in Westminster are second homes, in Kensington & Chelsea the figure is 9.2%.

But which areas have seen the strongest growth in the last five years? London again tops the table with the City of London seeing a 16.3% increase in second homes between 1998-2002.

Surprisingly, Tower Hamlets comes second (13%), followed by North Kesteven in Lincolnshire (12%) and Richmondshire in North Yorkshire (9.5%).

On the emerging areas, Richard Donnell says: "Interestingly, the demand for pieds à terre in central London has boosted the size of the market by more than 10% in Tower Hamlets and the City of London.

"Tower Hamlets has been the centre of much new development activity in recent years and offers a range of apartments at prices that are more affordable than the traditional second home markets of Westminster and Kensington and Chelsea."

He adds: "Affordability is also driving some of the emerging areas such as North Kesteven in Lincolnshire where it is possible to buy a property within easy access of the coast but for far less money than other more popular and expensive locations.

"It is important to note that the supply of second homes on the Lincolnshire coast is still small but it has expanded off a low base in recent years. Similarly, many of the other areas that have recently experienced rapid growth also offer affordable stock in accessible rural locations.

"There still remain many areas of Leicestershire, Derbyshire and Northamptonshire, within 2 hours drive of London that remain largely undiscovered and which are likely to be attract those who cannot afford the increasingly expensive South West or Suffolk coasts."

Top Ten Areas For Second Homes (as a % of all housing)

City of London (26.6%)
Isles of Scilly (23.3%)
South Hams (12.0%)
North Cornwall (11.3%)
Westminster (10.0%)
Berwick-on-Tweed (10.0%)
North Norfolk (9.5%)
Ken & Chelsea (9.2%)
South Lakeland (7.4%)
Great Yarmouth (7.1%)

Top Ten Movers Since 1998 (Increase in Number of Second Homes)
City of London (+16.3%)
Tower Hamlets (12.9%)
North Kesteven (11.9%)
Richmondshire (9.5%)
East Northamptonshire (9.4%)
Harborough (8.8%)
South Derbyshire (8.7%)
Ashford (8.4%)
Daventry (8.3%)
South Northamptonshire (8.1%)

Bradford & Bingley

Bradford & Bingley have researched the current buoyancy of the market, demonstrating that there is still growth in property value

No Sign of Slowdown

March 2004 figures from Bradford & Bingley Estate Agents revealed what several other reports had already confirmed: that the housing market, which roused itself in the autumn of 2003 after a slow first half, has carried the momentum forward into 2004.

Between September 2003 and February 2004 prices climbed by 6% and the average price of a home, based on the company's completed sales figures, now stands at £185,984.

Every region across the UK, from Cornwall to Lanarkshire, has recorded growth in prices since September, but inflation in the North was twice the rate of the South (10% vs 5%).

Seven Buyers for Every Home

The reason for the revival?
With an average of seven buyers chasing every home on the market, supply is failing to match demand and this is keeping the pressure on prices.

Gary Verity, managing director of Bradford & Bingley Estate Agents comments: "We have witnessed a slowing down of sellers putting their homes on the market.

"Sellers seem to prefer to wait to find a new property to move into before placing their own on the market. This is causing a logjam similar to that experienced in 2002."

Looking forward to the next six months, Verity adds: "The

key to the market growing at a healthy pace is a steady supply of realistically priced properties to satisfy buyer demand, which is growing by the day.

"Despite interest rates rising and a lack of choice in the market, buyers remain incredibly keen. I envisage this enthusiasm growing throughout spring and summer, the traditional home buying season, with the market performing well."

Across The Regions – Buoyant North

The North is again growing at a rate of knots. Price rises in the Midlands, North West and North East have pushed the price of an average home to £153,865.

The North East, in particular experienced phenomenal growth throughout 2003, the cost of home in the region is now £162,402, a rise of 11%.

Gary Verity comments: "The North East is largely being influenced by a hive of activity around Newcastle. Several exciting new developments and the city's continuing regeneration programme are boosting activity and prices across the region as a whole."

South Begins Bounce Back

The South of England is also performing very well with a rise of 5% since September 2003. Increased activity, especially at the top end of the market, has pushed average house prices up to £205,924.

The South East in particular reports renewed interest in the £1m plus market, largely driven by the expectation of improved stock market performance and the return of City bonuses.

To the South West pressure continues to mount on prices, fuelled by an average of five people chasing each home in the region.

Much of the current housing stock, especially in the first-time buyer market, is being snapped up by investors or second homeowners. Although there is demand for all types of homes the level of supply is not matching it, and as such prices will remain strong.

Scotland Upbeat

Scotland remains at the forefront of price inflation, the average home in Scotland now costs £128,147, a substantial rise of 14%. Whilst traditional hot spots, the West End of Glasgow and Bearsden, remain incredibly buoyant with buyer demand showing no signs of subsiding, a new hot spot of Paisley has emerged, particularly popular with first-time buyers finding it difficult to step onto the ladder.

Paisley has grown in popularity with young buyers and represents a good choice of affordable and attractive housing. Coupled with good transport links to Glasgow city centre, the town is now experiencing a boom.

And according to Hometrack's latest price survey – house prices over the month (Feb 2004) rose by 0.9%, the biggest increase since October 2002.

The average price of a house now stands at £148,500, up from £147,200 in the previous month.

Widespread Rises

All 52 county areas in the UK reported price rises, the highest increases being in the Isle of Wight (2.5%), Cumbria (1.7%), Northumberland (1.6%), Derbyshire (1.5%) and Merseyside (1.5%).

Wiltshire and South Lincolnshire were the slowest moving counties with rises of just 0.2%, followed by 0.3% rises in Surrey, North Wales, Leicestershire and Cornwall.

Among the cities, Bath (2.2%), Lancaster (2.2%), Liverpool (2.2%) and Hull (2.1%) all made a strong showing. No city experienced falling values, although Cambridge and Sunderland remained static with no recorded rises.

More Buyers than Sellers

Why this pick up in the market? Hometrack's report reveals that both the number of properties for sale and the number of buyers registered has increased, but the growth in demand has increased at over double the rate of new properties listed.

This imbalance has kept the pressure on prices and, says the report, suggests that further strong house price rises are likely in the coming months.

Given this situation, it's hardly surprising that buyers are finding it more difficult to negotiate a discount: price achieved as a percentage of asking price rose to 95.7% – a level not seen since February 2003.

The average length of time taken to sell a property is 4.6 weeks. There is currently an average of 11 viewings before a sale is achieved.

John Wriglesworth, Hometrack's Housing Economist, comments: "The housing market continues to strengthen. The green shoots that began to appear in January look set to blossom this Spring.

"Despite recent interest rate rises, mortgages are still very cheap by historical standards. With lenders continuing to relax their lending criteria (increasing the multiples of income on which they are willing to lend) house buyers are happy to pay higher prices for their desired homes.

"As the Government was not stupid enough to raise stamp duty in this year's Budget, house prices will continue to rise strongly this year. Speculation that there is going to be an imminent housing market crash has as much foundation as a brick on a pavlova."

Tina's Top Ten Property Hot spots

Having done the research, I have plumped for 10 property Hot spots and given you the reasons I think these areas will do well. Do take into account that once a location is identified as a Spot that is Hot you've probably already missed the boat.

FOCUS ON NOTTINGHAM

LIE OF THE LAND

Nottingham is a vibrant, young and trendy city which is very cosmopolitan. It has earned its reputation as capital of the East Midlands by being home to 50 regional/national head-quarters, including the Inland Revenue, the Government Office for the East Midlands (GOEM) and the East Midlands Development Agency (EMDA).

According to the annual Employment Survey, Nottingham is creating jobs nearly three times faster than the national average. Unemployment has halved in the last four years, and Nottingham is now the UK's third richest city in terms of Gross Domestic Product. Nottingham has over 7,000 businesses and the main employment areas are:

- Education, Health and other Public Sector Services
- Insurance, Banking and other Financial Services
- Retail
- Food, Drink and Tobacco
- Pharmaceuticals
- Clothing and Textiles

Interestingly, office rents rose by 26% between 1994 and 1999.

The City's growth industries include media, telecommunications and financial services.

LEISURE

The leisure market has seen a great expansion, with the number of bars, clubs and pubs increasing from 209 in 1995 to 368 in 2003. The recently opened Cornerhouse is a tangible sign of the confidence in this sector, employing a staggering 700 people. It consists of a multi-screen cinema and top restaurant chains like TGI Fridays and Wagamama. There are plans for the further development of the leisure, retail and hotel sectors elsewhere in the city centre, including Chapel Bar.

Robin Hood Centre in Nottingham together with Sherwood Forest, Chatsworth House in Derbyshire and Alton Towers in Staffordshire are just a few of the local tourist attractions.

SHOPPING

Nottingham is ranked the third best shopping destination in the UK. As well as flagship stores of major chains, such as House of Fraser, Gap and Marks & Spencer, the city has specialist shopping areas, such as Bridlesmith Gate and The Hockley. Nottingham also boasts the Victoria and Broadmash Shopping Centres.

MOST DESIRABLE AREAS

Nottingham is the leading city in the East Midlands and is the most cosmopolitan. It boasts the largest number of women per head of population, out-numbering men 2:1.

West Bridgeford, Wollerton Park and The Park are amongst the most expensive and desirable areas, although the city has had an increase in crime.

The city centre is seeing an increase in the number of loft apartments and trendy wine bars – which could well indicate this 'hot spot' is on its way out. Certainly, there has been a lot of money made.

Development in Nottingham shows no signs of slowing. The major site is Nottingham Waterside, which is a 250 acre development adjoining the world famous Trent Bridge. Other prime sites include the former Royal Ordnance Factory, now renamed Queensgate, and the Nottingham Business Park, now all set to become one of the UK's most prestigious office locations. On the 'Eastside' of the City, too, there will be many changes set in motion by the success of Nottingham's landmark £40 million National Ice Centre all of which will have a noticeable impact on property prices.

UP-AND-COMING

Mapperley Park city centre loft apartments is the up-and-coming area under development now. Outlying areas such as Hucknall and Wilford, Beeston and Toton are areas to watch once the new tram system has been opened.

Line 1 runs from a terminus opposite Nottingham Midland railway station, and then runs via the City Centre and Hyson Green to join the existing heavy rail route linking the city with Hucknall, Mansfield and Worksop, widely known as the 'Robin Hood Line'.

Line 2 is a planned route to the south of the city over the River Trent on the existing Wilford Toll Bridge and along the former Great Central railway line between Wilford and Compton Acres/Ruddington Lane. It then runs south into the Clifton Centre and a new park-and-ride site for the A453 road.

Line 3 will be a route to the western suburbs also linked directly to Line 1 at Nottingham station. The route follows Meadows Way before passing through the Royal Ordnance Factory (ROF) Development site over the Midland Main Line to the Queen's Medical Centre (QMC) site. It then crosses into the University of Nottingham, before running into Beeston town centre. From Beeston, Line 3 will go via Chilwell and Broxtowe College to a park-and-ride site next to the A52(E) road at Toton Lane/Stapleford Lane.

The route links the important transport destinations of

Beeston town centre, University of Nottingham, QMC, Royal Ordnance Factory and city centre.

Focus on Wakefield

Lie of The Land

Wakefield is at the hub of the UK's communications network. Its position at the intersection of the A1, M1 and M62 motorways provides excellent nationwide access.

Leisure

The area has great museums and galleries such as the Yorkshire Sculpture Park, Pontefract and Sandal Castles and the National Coal Mining museum as well as sports facilities, beautiful countryside and a variety of great shops, not forgetting the Wakefield's famous 'Westgate Run' which has over 30 pubs and nightclubs.

Shopping

As well as the usual high street names, there's a lively indoor and outdoor market which boasts 179 stalls and a history that dates back to 1297. Horbury even boasts its own clog shop.

The Ridings is situated in the very heart of Wakefield and offers more than 90 high street stores and specialist shops together with on-site parking and the Garden Food Court.

Most desirable areas

Popular areas include central areas like St John's, handy for both the Wakefield Girls' High School and Queen Elizabeth Grammar school, and southerly areas such as Sandal and Newmillerdam and villages like Wrenthorpe and Horbury.

Combining the best of Yorkshire's old and new, urban and rural, with excellent communication links, Wakefield lies at the heart of the UK motorway network making it an ideal base for business. The city has attracted businesses both large and small in the last few years. It's also just 14 miles from Leeds/Bradford airport and eight miles to the centre of Leeds with its bustling nightlife and great selection of shops both big and small.

The area thrives on service industries, call centres and logistic and tourist industries.

Up-and-coming

The close proximity of Wakefield to Leeds means that it offers all the amenities of major city life close by and any good property in Wakefield will have a good return.

Focus on Birmingham

Lie of The Land

The city of Birmingham is at the centre of the four counties: Warwickshire to the south, Leicestershire to the east, to the west is Shropshire and Staffordshire is to the north.

Leisure

The Five Ways development on Broad Street, City Centre is now complete.

This was a £50million development of a major leisure and entertainment facility that incorporates restaurants, bars and a 12-screen cinema, a family entertainment centre and a casino. The listed public house on the corner of Bishopsgate Street and Tennant Street, currently known as The City Tavern, has now been fully restored.

As part of the Broad Street redevelopment area strategy 1984-87, parcels of land owned by different bodies were brought together by Birmingham City Council to allow the complete development of a major area of under-used land in the city centre.

The 17-acre site is currently the UK's largest mixed use scheme. Work started in 1993 and most of the site has now been developed. Completion of the final phase is expected at the end of 2004 and will be the new Regional Headquarters of the Royal Bank of Scotland, together with a food store on the frontage to Broad Street and other units for retail, restaurant and bar uses.

Brindley Place includes new office accommodation, 143 canalside apartments and town houses, a branch of the National Sea Life Centre, a new theatre, hotel, modern art gallery and a vibrant mix of shops, restaurants and cafes in a canal side setting immediately adjacent to the International Convention Centre. The value of this major development is £250 million.

Office tenants include BT, Lloyds TSB, Regus, GVA Grimley, Royal Mail, Deloitte & Touche, Vodafone, F.W. Pharma Systems and Michael Page International.

Bars and restaurants include Le Petit Blanc, Thai Edge, Bank, Pitcher and Piano, All Bar One, Pizza Express, Baguette du Monde, Costa Coffee, Cafe Rouge.

Shopping

The New Street area and the Mailbox development have plenty of designer shops, and Selfridges is to open a store in the Bullring. Birmingham is also home to 700 market stalls with 20 million visitors a year.

A major retail and leisure development is proposed in the heart of the city centre.

Phase 1 – Martineau Place
Detailed planning permission was granted in March 1999 for the redevelopment of the Martinueau Square shopping precinct, between Union, Corporation and Bull Streets. This first phase was completed in September 2001 and houses new shop units for H&M, Gap, Bennetton, Sainsbury's Central and a variety of other shops and restaurants. A new public square has been created at the centre of the development. The "Bull Street Hump" subway system (at the junction of Bull Street

and Corporation Street) was removed and replaced by a new surface crossing as part of Phase 1, and was completed in July 2000.

Phase 2- Martineau Galleries
The second phase of development is one of the development opportunities opened up by the removal of Masshouse Circus. Land Securities PLC propose redevelopment of the Toys R Us store, and the Priory Square Shopping Centre. The scheme would have 92,985 square meters of retail and leisure floorspace, and a new public square at the junction of High Street, Bull Street and Dale End. There is no detailed planning approval for this development at present.

MOST DESIRABLE AREAS

Edgbaston, south of the city centre, was originally a country estate but is now home to the Birmingham Botanical Gardens, Midlands Arts Centre and Edgbaston Cricket Ground. Other good areas are Moseley, Bournville and Harborne.

There has been significant investment and redevelopment in the city and there are proposals to redevelop the site of the former Central TV studios on Broad Street, owned by Hampton Trust and Central Television. The project would further reinforce the greater Broad Street area as one of the UK's leading leisure and commercial areas. This £4 million development, proposed on a 14-acre site opposite Centenary Square, promises to become one of Britain's most exciting office/ retail/ leisure complexes.

It is also proposed that Arena Central will offer private residential apartments and offices together with leisure entertainment facilities and work began on Phase 1 in 2001 which consists of a 19 storey residential tower with 387 flats, on Holliday Street. This phase will form a new link between Mailbox and Brindley place.

Birmingham is well served for transport. It's the hub of five motorways – the M5, M40, M42, M54 and the M6 (whose new toll road opened recently), runs practically through the centre.

It has a mainline railway station, and Birmingham International airport is only 9 miles away.

Birmingham is third in the league of premium 'Zone A' commercial rental values just behind London and Newcastle-upon-Tyne, and on a par with Manchester.

Major employers include MG Rover, Cadbury and Pilkington. In addition, the National Exhibition Centre attracts hundreds of thousands of visitors to Birmingham from all over Europe.

Up-and-coming

Top of the list is the Mailbox development, which includes the Malmaison hotel, designer shops such as Christian Lacroix, 200 luxury rooftop and canal side apartments, state-of-the-art offices and a 900-space car park. A good location at all the new build apartment sites, especially if you can buy off plan.

Focus on Teignmouth, Devon

Lie of The Land

Located on the south coast and with excellent transport links to the M5 motorway, Teignmouth and nestling below the Haldon hills to the north, Teignmouth lies along a stretch of red sandstone coast at the unspoilt estuary of the river Teign. For over two centuries, the port has handled local ball clay which is distributed in shipments of up to 3,000 tonnes to all parts of Europe.

Lyme Bay's well-spaced arms protect smaller bays peering out over the English Channel between Portland and Start Point.

With it's proximity to booming Exeter buyers of all ages are starting to move in to this tranquil Victorian resort town.

The city of Exeter and Dartmoor National Park can be reached by road in 30 minutes whilst Plymouth is about one hour's drive.

Teignmouth is on the Paddington-Penzance line. The A380

with links to the M5 is at Kingsteignton, five miles from Teignmouth.

LEISURE

Teignmouth has a pier and promenade with a Victorian, seafront which attracts visitors in the summer.

Across the harbour and linked by ferry is Shaldon, which has a zoo, botanical gardens, miniature golf course, inns, shops and cafés.

Annual events include an autumn jazz festival in Teignmouth, and a Water Carnival in Shaldon. Nearby are Shaldon Wildlife Trust Breeding Centre, Exeter racecourse and Ashcombe Adventure Centre; Dartmoor National Park is 12 miles northwest. Canonteign Falls, England's highest waterfall, cascades 220 feet into the Teign.

As a favourite holiday destination for people living in the southwest, there are numerous Bed & Breakfast properties.

UP AND COMING

As older period property comes on to the market there is room for modernisation, as long as it is done sympathetically or look to convert larger family property in to holiday home accommodation.

FOCUS ON TAUNTON

LIE OF THE LAND

Taunton is found nestling in a valley at the foot of the Quantock and Blackdown Hills. The town, which is only half an hour's drive from Exmoor National Park, has been the cen-tre of some of the fastest residential property price increases in the country, over the past year.

Motorway links are good with both the M5 and the A303 being close by. The coast at Minehead is only half an hour away and the south coast resorts of Lyme Regis and Sidmouth are around one and a half hours away.

LEISURE

Boasting a number of leisure facilities, Taunton has a tennis centre, golf course and a number of leisure centres.

With fresh local produce being widely used coupled with creative cooking, the results are a gastronomic delight. An array of pubs, bistros, cafes and restaurants, in both modern and traditional styles can be found and for an alfresco meal you can choose from floral parks and gardens, to the banks of the River Tone.

SHOPPING

Taunton has an intriguing selection of specialist stores together with the best in high street names. A newly enhanced centre, featuring wide pavements with easy car parking and numerous attractive areas, ensures shopping is a pleasure. Explore Bath Place, Riverside, The Old Market Centre and the Courtyard. Browse around Taunton's Antique Market with over 130 dealers.

On the last Thursday of every month you have the delight of sampling and buying locally produced fresh fare directly from the surrounding farms at the Farmers Market held in the centre of Taunton.

UP-AND-COMING

Taunton is becoming one of the UK's top 10 property hot spots.

House price inflation in the town is running at 54 percent, with the cost of the average house rising to £185,995, up from £120,553 only a year ago.

There has been no new industry in the town over that period to create new jobs, so the main drive for change has been the influx of people from outside the area. Some come for the private schools, including Millfield School, Kings School and Queens School, plus some good comprehensives and primary schools. Others buyers are choosing to commute from the town in to London, Bristol, and Exeter.

A major recent trend, is the rush to purchase rental properties. Around 50 percent of people were purchasing properties as buy-to-let investments, because the rental yield that they could get on a property here was far higher than say that of Bristol, for example, where flats and houses were more expensive.

Others are moving into the region because they want a better quality of life for their family. Given the congestion in Bristol's rush hour, it takes almost as long to drive into the centre of the city from the outer suburbs as it does to come in from Taunton. The drive to Bristol takes an average of 60 minutes; to Exeter it is about 45 minutes. There is a fast train service to London Paddington.

FOCUS ON TEESIDE

LIE OF THE LAND

The main road to and through Northumberland is the A1 London to Edinburgh highway. Just to the south of Northumberland, the A1 forms Newcastle's western by-pass; and it provides a direct link from the city to three of Northumberland's main market towns: Morpeth, Alnwick and Berwick-upon-Tweed.

Newcastle's eastern by-pass is formed by the A19, Tyne Tunnel route. The A19 is an alternative route to Northumberland from the south, including from the Port of Tyne International Ferry terminal.

Are you seeking the solitude of a country ramble over a seemingly endless expanse of moorland? Or the thrill of sandy beaches and towering cliffs? Or perhaps the pleasure of a successful day's shopping and fine dining at a chic urban restaurant? Or the excitement of discovering a rich heritage of smugglers haunts and famous explorers? The Tees Valley offers all this.

LEISURE

With its five main centres covering just about every type of activity you could want from aerobics to yoga, football to fitness classes and swimming to climbing.

Cultural needs are catered for with the borough's two main museums, the Preston Hall Museum, set in the rolling acres of Preston Park at Eaglescliffe and the Green Dragon Museum in Stockton town centre. The Billingham Art Gallery, in the town centre of Billingham, provides local artists with a showcase for their art and crafts as well as holding workshops for those wishing to develop their own talents.

Film buffs have a choice of 14 screens at the Showcase Cinema on Teesside Retail Park and Leisure Complex and the area has a varied selection of restaurants, bars and nightclubs catering for all tastes.

SHOPPING

Teesside Retail Park and Leisure Complex also provides supermarkets, home improvement centres, lifestyle stores, fitness and beauty centres, along with a selection of restaurants and ample free parking.

The more traditional shopping experience can be found at Yarm High Street, which is in a traditional village with cobbled streets, with exclusive boutiques and shops with unusual giftware, along with fine dining restaurants and great pubs.

Its traditional pubs and cosmopolitan restaurants are widely recognised by the likes of Egon Ronay. It offers a huge range of educational opportunities. Its housing stock is very varied and realistically priced. It even enjoys its own benign microclimate.

UP-AND-COMING

The major impact on the area is the 'Going for Growth' regeneration project, which is a radical city-wide initiative designed to make Newcastle a better place to live, work and visit, with the project starting in 2000 it aims to redevelop the city over the next 20 years.

It set ambitious targets for creating new jobs and new housing and made the case for a regeneration strategy that would not only be city-wide, but also be long-term.

The first regeneration phase for the Outer East and the West End of Newcastle began in 2001 and plans for the Outer West and North Central areas of the city were produced in 2003.

South Tyneside made it to the top in terms of quarterly growth, with a rise of 5.1 percent. Northumberland saw the highest annual increase at 18.6 percent, enabling the county to move up from fifth to fourth in the region's average house price table.

The Newcastle area is experiencing something of a renaissance as people look for affordable housing and 'buy-to-let' opportunities.

Tyne & Wear is the commercial centre of the North East with over 150 IT and software development companies and 400 new digital media firms have made their base there, including world leading names such as Sage, Orange and games developers such as Reflections, Eutechnyx and Mere Mortals.

Property prices there reflect this. With investment in a network of quality public transport services on the major traffic corridors, including the addition of trams, quality bus routes, trains, guided buses, new rail services and the Metro, this area is set to grow over the next few years, at least until 2020, when the project completes.

Prime sites in the Newcastle area include prestigious developments such as Gateshead's Baltic Quays, 55 Degrees North and new apartments at the Bonded Warehouse.

Focus on Glasgow

Lie of The Land

Glasgow is Scotland's biggest city, with a population of almost 612,000.

Glasgow is the best UK shopping centre outside London and has excellent business, cultural, sport and tourist facilities. That's why the City was 1990 European City of Culture, 1999 UK City of Architecture and Design and is European Capital of Sport 2003.

The city provides over 350,000 jobs in over 12,000 companies.

Today, Glasgow's economy is dominated by the service sector with finance and banking, public administration, education, healthcare, hotels, tourism and other business services being prominent.

The city still retains a strong manufacturing sector with strengths in engineering, food and drink, printing, publishing and clothing as well as new growth sectors such as software and biotechnology.

Leisure

Glasgow has over 20 wonderful museums and galleries, each with its own individual collection and events programme, and all with free admission.

The city that hosted the Great Exhibitions of 1888 and 1901, and was designated European City of Culture 1990 has a full and exciting range of entertainment venues and activities including being home to Scotland's principal performing arts organisations: Scottish Opera, Scottish Ballet, the Royal Scottish National Orchestra, the BBC Scottish Symphony Orchestra, the National Youth Orchestra of Scotland, the Citizen's Theatre.

The name Glasgow means "dear green place", recognising the fact that Glasgow has over 70 parks and open spaces, more than any other city its size. Many of them contain some of the city's main galleries and attractions, facilities for recreational activities, and many fine examples of Victorian sculpture.

SHOPPING

Glasgow is a shopaholic's paradise. The best city in the UK after London provides endless opportunities for retail therapy. Merchant City is the home of the Italian Centre, Glasgow's most upmarket shopping area. This is the home of Armani and Versace, as well as upmarket shops, cafés and restaurants.

In Kings Court, is ESD, which sells funky ladies clothing and retro designs. And of course there's The Barras, Glasgow's famous East End market with over 1000 traders flogging their wares.

The West End is a great place for browsing as it's full of quirky, off beat shops. There are several good jewellery shops.

There are several great delis around here full of treats to help you put together a delicious picnic if the weather's good.

UP AND COMING

Glasgow is witnessing a property boom that shows no sign of slowing down.

Having seen a trend in converting period commercial premises in to residential living over the past few years, the city is now seeing investment in more purpose built office accommodation together with the residential conversion of brown field sites in to trendy city living. For example the former Daly Metals site on Upper Bell Street, Glasgow.

The new hot spots are on the outskirts of the south side, especially Giffnock, Whitecraigs, and Netherlee, and in contrast, the ever-popular areas such as the west end are seeing only marginal rises in property prices.

Bearing in mind that the sale of property in Scotland is different to the way we do things in England, property prices have been reaching offers of 30 percent over the asking price, but in some cases up to 50 percent.

Focus on Wales – Newport

Lie of The Land

Newport, the most easterly of the South Wales ports, is ideally located to serve the UK's main industrial and commercial areas. The port has excellent road communications, being just five minutes from J28 of the M4.

Leisure

Newport is a busy town situated on the south coast of Wales, just to the east of Cardiff. Although fast becoming the Silicon Valley of South Wales, Newport also has a long and visible history.

Newport City Council manages a number of sport and leisure facilities catering for all tastes and abilities, from the Newport Centre to smaller community based leisure centres.

The Millennium Stadium in nearby Cardiff, sees more than its fair share of nail-biting football games: the FA Cup, the Worthington Cup, Nationwide League play-off finals.

And there's golf, with Wales having some of the best golf in Britain and Europe and the Ryder Cup due to be played here in 2010. And rugby is the traditional national game of Wales.

The Newport Waterfront Festivals are a celebration of music, food, family and fun right on Newport's historic waterfront.

With five business and science parks as well as 15 industrial estates and other sites available for development, Newport can provide the environment for emerging technology companies and service industries.

Up-and-coming

Wales has become the latest property hot spot with certain areas enjoying price rises of more than 50%, according to research from the Halifax house prices across Wales are rising at their fastest rate in 10 years, with the average property costing £71,804 in January 2004.

Property prices in Gwynedd have soared by 57 percent during the past year, while in West Glamorgan they have risen by 56 percent.

In January 2004, new property hot spots emerged at Caerleon near Newport, Brynhyfryd in Swansea and the Canton and Grangetown areas of Cardiff proving especially popular.

FOCUS ON NORWICH

LIE OF THE LAND

The Norwich area is easily accessible from all parts of the UK by road and rail. Ferry ports, the Channel Tunnel and two modern international airports provide routes from Europe. Major trunk roads to the Norwich area are the M11, A11, A12, A140 and A14 from London, the South East of England, ferry ports and the Channel Tunnel. The A14, A11, A47, A17 and A1 serve the Midlands and the North.

Anglian Railways operate Intercity hourly services between Norwich and London Liverpool Street and local connecting services within East Anglia. Average journey time from London is 1hr 50 mins. Connecting services from the Midlands, North of England and Scotland via Peterborough. Anglia Railways also operate a direct service between Cambridge and Norwich, which takes approximately 70 mins. Central trains run connecting services from the Midlands, North of England and Scotland via Peterborough.

LEISURE

Norwich has extensive sports facilities. Indoor sports can be pursued at a number of local leisure centres within the city, and outdoor activities have their own centres. Spectator sports are also well supported, with First Division football at Norwich City's Carrow Road ground, and cricket at the Norfolk County Cricket Club ground in Trowse.

SHOPPING

Norwich streets bustle with life on most weekdays and, particularly on Saturdays, a variety of musicians, from string quartets to skiffle bands and South American pan pipe players, entertain the passing shoppers in the city centre. There are still over 200 pubs in the city, many with a unique atmosphere, and the restaurants provide an impressive range of international food. As well as traditional high-street stores and a modern mall, Norwich has many charming specialist shops and a large open-air market.

UP-AND-COMING

Norwich put in a bid to be European Capital of Culture 2008 but despite not being short listed and officially designated as a UK Centre of Culture the city will benefit enormously both from the immediate publicity and tourism, and from the longer term ongoing process, even without government support.

One of the last truly, undeveloped areas of the country, where land is still available at affordable prices. I would expect new build developers to move in to this area in the next 5-10 years.

A House of Commons debate took place in 2000: Mr. David Prior (North Norfolk) stated that the new housing requirement for Norfolk in the period from 1991 to 2016, as assessed by SCEALA – the Standing Conference on East Anglian Local Authorities, which represents the local authorities of Norfolk, Suffolk and Cambridgeshire – is for 86,000 new houses.

The development investment is already starting; a £6m hotel and restaurant is to be built in Norwich. The Travelodge six-storey 104-bed budget hotel will form part of the bus station redevelopment in Queens Road. And the bulldozers are already in the town of Lynn, to redevelop their town centre.

Property prices on the east coast of East Anglia are generally lower than the average property price throughout the UK, and as a result represent an above average return for property investors who want to lead the way.

FOCUS ON MANCHESTER

LIE OF THE LAND

Greater Manchester, located in the North West, is a thriving city comprising of ten districts, each with it's own characteristics. It incorporates the cities of Manchester and Salford, the six towns of Bolton, Bury, Oldham, Rochdale, Stockport and Wigan and the two boroughs of Tameside and Trafford.

Greater Manchester is recognised as the country's single most important financial and business centre outside of London. Renowned for it's vibrant and powerful music scene, Manchester is also the home to the largest student campus in Europe (so buy-to-let will always be a good option here) and it is the city of arts and a Mecca for sports fans.

Manchester city centre is the home of many national and international financial and professional institutions, and has over 60 consulate offices and government bodies in residence.

LEISURE

Manchester has a rich sporting heritage, which was massively enhanced by the City's hosting of the 2002 Commonweath Games and provided Manchester with a legacy of excellent new facilities.

Greater Manchester is already home to eight Premier League or Nationwide League football teams, seven top rugby teams and has over 90 golf courses.

Shopping

Manchester city centre is the main shopping centre for the North West region. Over recent years, Manchester has undergone a huge transformation, turning it into one of the best shopping centres, not only in the UK but also in Europe.

The city also offers a huge range of retail choice, from designer chic to antiques and crafts. There are large chain stores and department stores such as House of Frazer and Debenhams, designer names with Vivienne Westwood, DKNY, Armani and Hugo Boss.

For the out-of-town shopping experience, The Trafford Centre is the UK's third largest indoor shopping centre, four miles west of Manchester and easily accessible from the M60 orbital motorway or by tram and bus links from the city centre.

Bars and restaurants have boomed, doubling in the last five years to 450 licensed premises in the city centre alone. Manchester's Chinatown is unrivalled in Britain and Rusholme's 'curry mile' is famous, and there are a thousand others: restaurants specialising in the best of French, Italian, Thai, Korean, Spanish, Greek, Turkish, Mexican, Japanese or even Mongolian cuisine as well as seafood, sushi, tapas and noodle bars, you name it, there is something for every taste, pallet and wallet. Not forgetting the big name chefs like Gary Rhodes, Paul Heathcote, Raymond Blanc and Nico Ladenis, who have all added Manchester to their list of restaurants.

Up-and-coming

Though Manchester may have blazed a trail in trendy urban living for the past ten years, it still has along way to go to catch up with London.

The virtues of Castlefield, with its canals, open space and Victorian architecture. Even the unlovely Ancoats, as the third designated Millennium Community, will be transformed to provide 1,400 new homes for a broader cross-section of buyers than those able to afford the centre.

The second phase of the Green Quarter involves a huge overhaul of the Redbanks area north of Victoria station and aims to couple quiet, green and watery spaces with the utility of being near the city centre.

The Next Property Hot Spots by Jill Burdett – property journalist Manchester Evening News.

WHAT do Bury, Bacup and Wythenshawe have in common? There may be no obvious connection but according to those who make their living out of buying property these towns will be this year's housing hot spots.

MEN Homes has got some advanced inside info on where and what to buy if you want your bricks and mortar investment to pay dividends.

As a property locator with Old Trafford-based Specialist Property Group, John Russell spends each day looking at houses and it is his job to know which areas are on the up.

He does not hesitate on where's going to take off: "The Rossendale Valley. Drive to the end of the M66, pick any town round there and you will not go wrong. Rawtenstall, Haslingden, Crawshawbooth, all have a lot going for them. I have just bought a house in Stacksteads: a nice three-bed terrace off the main street with fantastic views and a position that cannot be bettered for £85,000. That's the sort of place you want to be.

"A big new Asda is going up in Rawtenstall and although prices there are already pretty expensive, development like that consolidates value. If they get a commuter service into Manchester on the train line it will help things even more.

"But the place that will see the real increase in value is Bacup. It is a bit of a pit at the moment with a lot of tired housing stock and a large council estate. But some of the buildings are very grand and if you buy right, a solid terrace with big rooms, then I think it will see big rises in value.

"There has already been a conversion of a bank into eight apartments so some developers are already spotting the potential.

"It is a case of supply and demand. The big demand is for sub £100k houses and it is in towns like this that you find them."

Bury is the tip of Barbara Goldsmith who runs Stratford Properties.

Sleeping giant

She said: "Bury is a sleeping giant but it is already being shaken awake. Before Christmas I was looking at two-bed terraces near the town centre for £55,000 but they are now more like £65,000 – that's in just two months.

"But even so I think there is a lot more room in the market. I fully anticipate these properties to triple in value in the next five to seven years."

So why Bury? Barbara said: "It already has the basic infrastructure in place: good public transport with the Metrolink, close to the motorway network, good schools and a good town centre and it is close to bigger centres like Bolton and Manchester.

"What I like about these places is that the local people often have a negative social attitude towards them and only an outsider who looks at it quite clinically can see the potential.

"The council is the most improved in the country, they have just won money to improve the parks, they are creating a cultural quarter with a new museum and have spent a lot on improving shabby private housing stock.

"But you have to pick your streets and the individual property very carefully. That is the skill! It is not a random process."

Other areas she sees with a negative image include many to the east of Manchester like Ashton and Denton. She said: "Chorlton was regarded as the pits when I was growing up there but now look at it. You need to get in before perceptions change."

Image makeover

Her other tip for the top could also do with an image makeover. Wythenshawe was the overspill council estate for Manchester, suffered years of neglect and bad press and even now the main shopping centre is bleak.

But, according to Barbara, invest here and you will not lose.

She said: "It is a gold mine, the jewel in the investing crown! It is just off the motorway, is going to get a couple of Metrolink stops and the airport and the hospital provide a huge tenant base.

"The shopping centre is disgusting but that will change and there will come a time when people will not even remember it was a council estate.

"Local authority stock was usually well-built and at the moment you can get a three-bed semi for around £100,000. If you see one on the market, buy it!"

So much for hot spots but where is the market colder?

"I would be wary of places like Gorton, Longsight and Moston which I think have got a bit too far to go yet to be a safe bet," says Barbara.

So now you know where, you simply show up and buy the cheapest thing on the market, right? Wrong.

The professionals follow strict criteria when they are buying and the rules apply just as much if you are looking for a house for yourself as if you are buying for a rental investment. Frank O'Rourke, from Specialist Property Group, said: "Just because it is cheap does not mean it is right and we have stopped looking at stuff much under £40,000.

"And gut feeling should not come into it. There is much more to it that that."

Like what? "We never buy next door to a shop or other commercial property, or overlooking unsightly areas of land. If the second or third bedrooms are below a certain size we walk away and don't buy anything with double yellow lines outside or close to a busy junction."

"We're looking for houses that can be sold on quickly if the investor wants to liquidate their money.

O'Rourke added: "Finding the right property to buy in the first place is the hardest bit." "We invest around £5,000 a year just on people searching and of the thousands we look at we bid on around 30 per cent and perhaps 18 per cent of those bids will be successful. So it's not an easy process!"

FOCUS ON LEEDS

LIE OF THE LAND

London is only two hours away by train and there are direct links to Manchester, Liverpool, Newcastle and Edinburgh.

The M1 north-south and M621 east-west motorways are a stones throw away allowing easy access to towns and cities across the UK.

Leeds/Bradford International Airport is approximately 10 miles from the city and provides daily scheduled flights to many national and international destinations.

LEISURE

There are leisure clubs, health and fitness centres, sports equipment shops, outdoor pursuit centres and sports grounds at your disposal.

Leeds is one of the most vibrant, cosmopolitan cities in Britain, with a great nightlife, fine architecture and excellent shopping. At the centre of the UK, the city enjoys excellent transportation links and it makes an ideal base location to reach the European market place. It is also one of the fastest growing cities in the country, with the financial services sector continuing to drive the economic expansion that began in the 1990s.

SHOPPING

Leeds was once the living embodiment of grim industrial productivity with its bleak wasteland and depressed economy. But now Leeds has emerged as a city with great potential with its booming real estate market, designer boutiques, smart restaurants and a thriving bar culture and has now been awarded the accolade of being named as the best place to live in Britain. Leeds has changed beyond recognition within the past 20 years, much to the city's advantage.

UP-AND-COMING

Around a third of the city's economic contribution is gener-
ated by the financial and business services sectors. Together,
they employ over 100,000 people. On the back of a strong local
market, the financial and legal community is now attracting
business from outside the region and from overseas.

As well as its position as a centre for corporate financial
services, Leeds has become the location of choice for some of
the country's leading household names in banking and insurance services. Major businesses include First Direct, GE
Capital, Alliance & Leicester, Halifax Direct and Direct Line,
have all chosen Leeds as a centre of operations because of the
ability to recruit high calibre staff locally and because they
recognise the importance of Leeds as a major financial centre.

These companies have also been quick to see the benefits of
the city's advanced communications infrastructure. Around a
third of the UK's internet traffic passes through Leeds and one
of the biggest internet server farms in Europe is located in the
city. Cable provision is also widespread and ADSL roll-out is
happening more quickly with the result that Leeds also has
higher take up than elsewhere. It's therefore no accident that
leading international companies such as Freeserve, Firstnet,
Ananova and TEAMtalk have made their home in Leeds,
making for an unrivalled and expanding e-service sector.

Added to the mix, is a fast growing media sector. Recent
figures from the Office for National Statistics show the city's
media, communications and advertising sector has grown by
more than 20 percent in the last two years.

Research carried out by Leeds Initiative found that most of
the people currently living in the city centre of Leeds were
young well-paid professionals and city centre life appealed to
this group because it was close to work and the city's
nightlife.

City Island is one new exclusive waterside development of
404 luxury one-and-two bedroom apartments, duplexes and
penthouses located just a short walk away from Leeds City
station with its national rail network connections.

REFERENCE

Property Portals
An alphabetical listing of useful property-related websites

Reallymoving.com
Property finder reallymoving.com was launched in November 1999, and has become one of the UK's leading providers of online home-moving services. It is an independent and privately financed service that provides everything you need to move home. Instant quotes from solicitors, surveyors, removal companies, and cleaners; UK property database; a movers planning and reminder service; and a wealth of relevant links and information.
www.reallymoving.com
www.reallymoving.co.uk

Rightmove
Rightmove is jointly owned by four of the leading estate agency groups in the UK. Over half of the top 100 estate agencies use rightmove to showcase their properties online, covering 99% of UK postcodes. Rightmove.co.uk is the UK's number one property search website where people view more property pages than on the next three largest property websites put together. You can:
- access details of any property or agent in our database
- keep records of properties you are interested in
- access guides to help you make the right move.
www.rightmove.co.uk

ASSERTAHOME
assertahome features the properties of more than 2,000 estate agent branches across the UK; advertising around 110,000 properties. You can search the property database using a choice of search criteria including price, location and number of bedrooms, and send an email to the agent or developer. Assertahome also has heaps of helpful information. There is advice and guidance on everything from how to spot the hidden fees in mortgages to clever tricks to sell your home, as well as great deals on conveyancing, insurance and mortgages.
www.assertahome.com

THE SCOTTISH BORDERS PROPERTY GUIDE
The Scottish Borders and North Northumberland's largest online property sales database. The BSPC is an amalgamation of lawyers based in the Scottish Borders. Each member firm is dedicated to providing a superb estate agency service for its clients who are selling their homes, as well as offering a complete buying service to the purchaser. When buying or selling, you can find guidance on instructing surveys, arranging a suitable mortgage or submitting offers in correct Scottish legal format. Member firms offer a selling service, which includes pre-sale valuations and advice on marketing. They also cover all aspects of legal work involved in selling your home, providing a one-stop complete selling package.
www.bspcbricks.co.uk

EDINBURGH SOLICITORS PROPERTY CENTRE
East central Scotland's largest online property guide. Whether you're looking to buy or rent, find a solicitor, or arrange a mortgage, Edinburgh Solicitors Property Centre can help.
www.espc.co.uk

ESTATE AGENTS LONDON
A comprehensive listing service of estate agents in the greater London area to make your house buying and selling a more productive time.
www.london-estate-agents.co.uk

FIND A PROPERTY

Find a Property is an independent resource covering the whole of the UK. Properties details are updated daily, making it more accurate than most.
www.findaproperty.co.uk

COUNCIL HOMEBUYERS

Originally set up in 1996 to encourage people to purchase their homes under the Housing Act and related legislation. The company provides a service to help people purchase their home. This is where the person is a tenant and the landlord is within the public sector.
www.councilhomebuyers.co.uk

HOME SALE NETWORK

A network of independent estate agents offering homes for rent and to buy. You can search online for property and get advice on buying and selling.
www.home-sale.co.uk

HOME.CO.UK

A UK Property Search Engine with links to thousands of homes for sale across England, Wales and Scotland.
www.home.co.uk

HOMECLICK

For sale by owner. Advertising portal for those wishing to DIY the sale of their property without an estate agent.
www.homeclick.co.uk

HOMEFILEUK

Combines a database of properties for sale and to let with products, services and information useful for homeowners and tenants.
www.homefile.co.uk

HOMEPAGES
Searchable UK database of residential property, with thousands of homes from hundreds of estate agents.
www.homepages.co.uk

HOMES ON-LINE
Searchable database of properties for sale in the UK.
www.homes-on-line.co.uk

HOUSE MARKET
For Sale by Owner – Private UK property advertising site your property with House Market.
www.housemarket.co.uk

HOUSEMOUSE
Housemouse sell your home and property free in the UK and search for property and keyholder service in East London.
www.HouseMouse.org

HOUSES FOR SALE UK
Houses for sale privately throughout the UK.
www.ukpropertyweb.co.uk

LONDON HOMEFINDER
For sale by owner. Residential property for sale in London.
www.london-homefinder.co.uk

LONDON PROPERTY RENTALS
London property rentals for a selection of London's property ranging from studios to mansions.
www.londonpropertyrentals.com

LONDON TOWN
London apartment rentals – prime London flat and house letting. Features searchable database of property, comprehensive guides for landlords and tenants and online client accounting.
www.l-t.co.uk

NETHOMES.UK

Online property UK search for homes and offices for sale and rent; find residential and commercial property or letting.
www.nethomes.uk.com

NET-LETTINGS

Agents directory with over 50 estate agents. London flats to rent. Holiday flats, studios homes or apartments to rent, real estate to rent or to let.
www.net-lettings.co.uk

PROPERTY INVESTMENT UK

Listings of investment properties, currently has a small number of properties in the North.
www.propertyinvestmentuk.co.uk

ONE SOURCE HOME SEARCH

Provides a complete home-search service for central London.
www.onesourcehomesearch.co.uk

CHAINBUSTERS

Chainbusters specialise in buying residential and commercial property fast, with rapid property purchasers. They arrange exchange of contracts and completion of property transactions to suit your needs.
www.chainbusters.co.uk

PARTAKE

ParTake lists properties for sale, as well as contact details for estate agents nationwide; they offer to help organise your conveyancing, insurance, mortgage.
www.ParTake.co.uk

PLOTFINDER

A land and renovation database. PlotFinder is a service for finding and buying building plots and property for renovation and conversion.
www.plotfinder.net

PROPERTY FOR LONDON

Searchable London property index: including property details and mortgage resources, for residential and vacation homes in London.
www.p4l.co.uk

NUMBER ONE 4 PROPERTY

Property for sale in the UK. Residential, commercial and rural listings plus mortgages, conveyancing and insurance.
www.itlhomesearch.com
www.numberone4property.co.uk

UK PROPERTY SHOP

UK property listings.
www.ukpropertyshop.co.uk

LONDONHOMENET

Private advertising for property sales, lettings and flat shares in London.
www.londonhomenet.com

LINK UP PROPERTIES NATIONWIDE

Link Up Properties established since 1992 and one of the fastest growing estate agencies in the UK, with franchised agents operating in areas across the United Kingdom.
www.linkprop.co.uk

MRA PROPERTY INVESTMENTS

MRA Property Investments Ltd assists individuals and companies based both in the UK and abroad to invest in residential property in the North of England.
www.mrainvestments.co.uk

PROPERTYFINDER

UK property listings.
www.propertyfinder.co.uk

NET LETS

Rent a flat, let a flat, find a flat, find a house or property in London – search and alert service for tenants and landlords.
www.net-lets.com

SOLICITORS PROPERTY SHOP – SPS

A network of solicitor estate agents firms across Yorkshire, Greater Manchester and Lancashire, the Midlands, Wales and Northeast England, SPS offers combined legal and estate agency services to home movers.
www.sps.net

THE AMERICAN AGENCY

UK's only US owned and managed estate agency offering international companies and private individuals a complete expatriate programme for those moving to Britain.
www.american-agency.com

PROPERTY CHAIN

Buy residential property if you are stuck in a chain. Property Chain will normally pay 80-90% of market value.
www.propertychain.com

THE HOME SEARCH BUREAU

Home Search Bureau is a property finder relocation agent for real estate in central London.
www.homesearchbureau.com

THE LETTING INFORMATION CENTRE

Directory of Letting Agents throughout the UK.
www.letlink.co.uk

08004 HOMES

100,000+ Home improvements. Telecoms services. Financial services. Money savers. Conveyancing. Change of address. Building information. Landlord services. Doctors, chemists, Removals Utilities etc.

www.08004homes.com
www.home-to-home.co.uk
www. home2home.co.uk

PROVISER
UK property prices. UK street maps. Detailed, easy to understand analysis of property prices. Easy to use graphs and tables. Easy to use street maps of UK. Easy click navigation.
www.proviser.com

UK PROPERTY SALES
The comprehensive directory of property sales in the UK, classified by area.
www.ukpropertysales.com

UPMYSTREET
The real-life guide to your neighbourhood. All the facts about where you live in England and Wales, including property prices, top GCSE and A Level schools, council tax rates, crime clear-up rates and ambulance response times.
www.upmystreet.com

A to Z of UK Mortgage Lenders

Abbey National
www.abbeynational.co.uk
0800 555100

Alliance And Leicester
www.alliance-leicester.co.uk
0845 303 3000

Allied Irish Bank
www.aibgb.co.uk
01895 272222

Amber Homeloans
www.amberhomeloans.co.uk
0870 601 3233

Bank Of Ireland
www.bank-of-ireland.co.uk
0800 085 0444

Bank Of Scotland
www.bankofScotland.co.uk
0800 810810

Barclays
www.barclays.co.uk
0800 400100

Barnsley
www.barnsley-bs.co.uk
01226 733999

Bath Investment
www.bibs.co.uk
01225 423271
Chelsea

Beverley
www.beverleybs.co.uk
01482 881510

Birmingham Midshires
www.askbm.co.uk
0500 228822

Bradford & Bingley
www.marketplace.co.uk
0800 358 5556

Bristol & West
www.bristol-west.co.uk
0845 3 80 300 800

Britannia
www.britannia.co.uk
0800 013 1140

Britannic Money
www.britannicmoney.com
0800 550551

Buckinghamshire
www.bucksbuildingsociety.com
01753 482100

Cambridge
www.cambridge-building-soci-ety.co.uk
0800 716113

Capital Home Loans
www.chlmortgages.co.uk
01252 365802

The Chelsea
www.thechelsea.co.uk
0800 291291

Cheltenham & Gloucester
www.cheltglos.co.uk
0800 226341

Chesham
www.cheshambsoc.co.uk
0800 966026

Cheshire
www.thecheshire.co.uk
0845 755 0555

Chorley & District
www.chorleybs.co.uk
01257 419110

Cis
www.cis.co.uk
08457 464646

Clay Cross
www.claycrossbs.co.uk
0800 834497

Clydesdale Bank
www.clydesdalebank.co.uk
0800 419 000

Coventry
www.coventrybuildingsociety
.co.uk
0845 766 5522

Cumberland

Darlington
www.darlington.co.uk
01325 366366

Derbyshire
www.thederbyshire.co.uk
0800 085 2020

Direct Line
www.directline.com
0845 246 8165

Dudley
www.dudleybuildingsociety.co.
uk
01384 231414

Dunfermline
www.dunfermline-bs.co.uk
01383 627714

Earl Shilton
www.esbs.co.uk
01455 844422

Ecology
www.ecology.co.uk
0845 674 5566

Egg
www.egg.com
0845 600 0290

First Direct
www.firstdirect.com
0800 242424

First Mortgage
www.1stmortgage.co.uk
0800 080088

www.cumberland.co.uk
01228 541341

First National
www.firstnat.co.uk
020 8909 8000

First Trust Bank
www.firsttrustbank.co.uk
0289 032599

Furness
www.furnessbs.co.uk
0800 834312

Future Mortgages
www.future-mortgages.co.uk
0800 389 1221

Gmac-Rfc
www.gmacrfc.co.uk
01344 478478

Halifax
www.halifax.co.uk
0845 273747

Hanley Economic
www.thehanley.co.uk
0800 542 8790

Harpenden
www.harpendenbs.co.uk
01582 765411

Hinckley & Rugby
www.hrbs.co.uk
0800 774499
0800 072 5726

Holmesdale
www.holmesdale.org.uk
01737 245716

Hsbc
www.banking.hsbc.co.uk
0800 494999

Igroup
www.igrp.co.uk
01923 426426

Intelligent Finance
www.if.com
0845 609 4343

Ipswich
www.ipswich-bs.co.uk
01473 211021

Irish Permanent
www.ipmortgages.co.uk
020 8746 3334

Kensington
www.kmc.co.uk
0808 100 4114

Kent Reliance
www.krbs.co.uk
01634 848944

Lambeth
www.lambeth.co.uk
0800 7928 1331

Leeds & Holbeck
www.leeds-holbeck.co.uk
0800 072 5726

Leek United
www.leekunited.co.uk
0800 093 0004

Legal & General
www.landg.com
0870 010 0338

London Mortgage Company
www.fisa.co.uk
020 7298 8778

Loughborough
www.theloughborough.co.uk
01509 610707

Manchester
www.themanchester.co.uk
08709 900800

Mansfield
www.mansfieldbs.co.uk
01623 6763 00

Market Harborough
www.mhbs.co.uk
01858 463244

Marsden
www.marsdenbs.co.uk
01282 4405 00

Melton Mowbray
www.mmbs.co.uk
01664 563937

Mercantile
www.mercantile-bs.co.uk
0500 295500

Monmouthshire
www.monbsoc.co.uk
01633 844444

Mortgage Express
www.mortgage-express.co.uk
0500 111130

National Counties
www.ncbs.co.uk
01372 744155

Nationwide
www.nationwide.co.uk
0800 302010

Natwest
www.natwest.co.uk
0800 400999

Newbury
www.newbury.co.uk
01635 555700

Newcastle
www.newcastle.co.uk
0845 606 4488

Northern Bank
www.nbonline.co.uk
0800 660033

Northern Rock
www.northernrock.co.uk
0845 601 1581

Norwich & Peterborough
www.npbs.co.uk
0845 300 6727

Royal Bank Of Scotland
www.rbs.co.uk
0800 917 3025

Nottingham
www.thenottingham.com
0115 948 1444

Saffron Walden
www.swhebs.co.uk
01799 522211

One Account
www.oneaccount.com
08456 000001

Sainsbury's Bank
www.sainsburysbank.co.uk
0500 700600

Paragon Mortgages
www.paragon-mortgages.co.uk
0800 375777

Scarborough
www.scarboroughbs.co.uk
0870 513 3149

Penrith
www.penrithbuildingsociety.co.uk
01768 863675

Scottish
www.scottishbldgsoc.co.uk
0131 220 1111

Platform Home Loans
www.platformhomeloans.com
0845 600 7100

Scottish Widows
www.scottishwidows.co.uk
0845 845 0829

Portman
www.portman.co.uk
0800 548548

Shepshed
www.theshepshed.co.uk
01509 822000

Principality
www.principality.co.uk
0800 454478

Skipton
www.skipton.co.uk
01756 705030

Progressive
www.theprogressive.com
028 9024 4926

Southern Pacific
www.spml.co.uk
020 7590 1500

Prudential
www.pru.co.uk
01384 472004

Staffordshire
www.staffsbs.co.uk
0800 216121

Stafford Railway
www.srbs.co.uk
01785 223212

Standard Life Bank
www.standardlifebank.com
0845 845 8450

Stroud & Swindon
www.stroudandswindon.co.uk
0800 618161

Sun Bank
www.sunbank.co.uk
01438 744500

Swansea
www.swansea-bs.co.uk
01792 483701

Teachers
www.teachersbs.co.uk
0800 378669

The Mortgage Business
www.t-m-b.co.uk
0800 203049

The Mortgage Lender
www.themortgagelender.co.uk
0800 197 8951

Tipton & Coseley
www.tipton-coseley.co.uk
0121 557 2551

Ucb Homeloans
www.ucbhomeloans.co.uk
0845 950 1500

Ulster Bank
www.ulsterbank.com
00 353 1702 5128

Universal
www.theuniversal.co.uk
0800 288383

Vernon
www.thevernon.co.uk
0161 429 6262

Verso
www.verso-mortgage.co.uk
0845 840 3020

Wesleyan Homeloans
www.wesleyan.co.uk
0800 092 1990

West Bromwich
www.westbrom.co.uk
0800 298 08

Woolwich
www.woolwich.co.uk
0845 070 5090

Yellow Brick Road
www.yellowbrickroad.co.uk
0800 009977

Yorkshire
www.ybs.co.uk
0845 120 0805

Yorkshire Bank
www.ybonline.co.uk
0800 202122

Zurich&U
www.zurichandu.co.uk
0500 6509

Top UK Estate Agency Chains

League Table of Residential Estate Agency Offices

League Rating	Estate Agency Group	No of Offices
1	Countrywide Assured	865
2	The TEAM Association*	550
3	Connell Estate Agents	487
4	Halifax Estate Agency	341
5	Bradford & Bingley Estate Agents	307
6	Your Move	291
7	Spicerhaart	236
8	Reeds Rains	133
9	Arun Estates	120
10	Kinleigh Folkard & Hayward	66
11	Winkworth	58
12	Hamptons International	55
13	Chancellors Estate Agents	52
14	Andrews Estate Agents	49
15	FPD Savills	46
16=	Bradley's	40
16=	Humberts	40
16=	Townends	40
19	Knight Frank	38
20=	Cluttons	34
20=	Jackson-Stops & Staff	34
22	Keith Pattinson Limited	30
23	Strutt & Parker	26
24	Peter Alan	25
25	The Venmore Partnership	21
26=	Acorn Estate Agents	20
26=	Burchell Edwards	20
26=	Dacre Son & Hartley	20
26=	Lane Fox	20
30	Nottingham Property Services	19

Notes:
League position and branch numbers as at January 2004.

Top 30 estate agents taken from the Top 50 league table of residential estate agency offices produced annually by Estate Agency News (with kind permission from Estate Agency News – *http://www.estateagencynews.co.uk*)

League Table of Affinity Groups and Franchise Operations

League Rating	Affinity/Franchise Group	No. of Offices
1	NAEA HomeLink Network	836
2	Home Sale Network (Cendant)	742
3	The Guild of Professional Estate Agents	714
4	movewithus	673
5	The TEAM Association	550
6	Mayfair Office	342
7	National Homes Network	210
8	The London Office	184
9	Legal & General Franchising	118

Notes:

League position and branch numbers as at January 2004.

Top affinity/franchise groups taken from the League Table of Affinity Groups and Franchise Operations produced annually by Estate Agency News (with kind permission from Estate Agency News – *http://www.estateagencynews.co.uk*).

Useful Contacts

The Royal Institution of
Chartered Surveyors
Parliament Square
12 Great George Street
London SW1P 3AD

The Professional Conduct
Department
The Royal Institute of Chartered
Surveyors
Parliament Square
12 Great George Street
London SW1P 3AD
Tel: 020 7222 7000
www.rics.org

The Law Society
113 Chancery Lane
London WC2A 1PL
Tel: 020 7242 1222
www.lawsociety.org.uk

The Law Society of Scotland
26 Drumsheugh Gardens
Edinburgh EH2 7YR
Tel: 0131 226 7411
Helpline: 0131 476 8137
www.lawscot.org.uk

Office for the Supervision of
Solicitors (OSS)Victoria Court
8 Dormer Court
Leamington Spa
Warwickshire CV32 5AE
Tel: 01926 820082
www.oss.lawsociety.org.uk

Legal Services Ombudsman
22 Oxford Court
Oxford Street
Manchester M2 3WQ
Tel: 0161 236 9532

Council for Licensed
Conveyancers (CLC)
16 Glebe Road
Chelmsford
Essex CM1 1QG
Tel: 01245 349599

Home Buyer Legal Protection
Ltd
8 Broad Street
Wokingham
Berkshire RG40 1AB
Tel: 0118 989 0914

The Chartered Institute of
Arbitrators
24 Angel Gate
City Road
London EC1V 2RS
Tel: 020 7837 4483
www.arbitrators.org

The National Housebuilding
Council (NHBC)
Buildmark House
Chiltern Avenue
Amersham
Buckinghamshire HP6 5AP
Tel: 01494 434477
www.nhbc.co.uk

The Association of British
Insurers (ABI)
51 Gresham Street
London EC2V 7HQ
Tel: 020 7600 3333
www.abi.org.uk

Mortage Code Compliance
Board
University Court
Stafford ST18 0GN
Tel: 01785 218200
www.mortgagecode.org.uk

Council of Mortgage Lenders
3 Savile Row
London W1S 3PB
Tel: 020 7437 0075
www.cml.org.uk

Leasehold Enfranchisement
Advisory Service
8 Maddox Street
London W1R 9PN

Reference Summary

Summary of Useful Tools and Information Sources Referenced throughout this book

www.landlordzone.co.uk
It's an online community, a vertical portal for landlords involved in letting property – novice and experienced alike. It provides free access to information, resources and contacts of value to residential and small commercial landlords, tenants, letting agents and other property professionals.

www.legalhelpers.co.uk
Useful legal documents available online.

www.taxcafe.co.uk
Tax Cafe – A good internet source to get advice on tax.

www.lawpack.co.uk
Lawpack – legal forms, rent book, tenants agreements, and lodgers agreements. Lawpack products are available from most stationers – or buy online.

www.onlineplanningoffices.com
For info on planning permission.

www.hammer-film-locations.co.uk/
www.amazingspace.co.uk
For tips on registering your property as a film location.

www.rhs.org.uk/rhsgardenfinder/gardenfinder.asp
Royal Horticultural Society – Garden Finder. A good source for finding gardens open to the public.

www.sgd.org.uk
The Society of Garden Designers, only professional body in the UK dedicated solely to garden design.

www.gardenvisit.com
The Garden Visit website is a mine of useful information.

www.ngs.org.uk/
The National Gardens Scheme has been opening gardens to the public to raise money for charity since 1927.

www.oft.gov.uk
Office of Fair Trading, free copy of 'Using an Estate Agent to buy or sell your home.' Or call Enquiries on 08457 22 44 99.

www.rightmove.co.uk
The UK's number one property website which contains 35% of all property for sale in the UK.

www.naea.co.uk
National Association of Estate Agents.

www.findaproperty.co.uk
Find a Property is an online property magazine for estate and letting agencies. They publish articles and news about the property industry, as well as directories of properties, with details updated daily.

www.hsh.co.uk
Asset Management.

www.eigroup.co.uk
Auction Watch.

www.propertyauctions.com
For auctions and buying guides.

www.ifap.org.uk
Independent Financial Advice and Planning.

www.mortgagecode.org.uk
Mortgage Code Compliance website.

www.nhbc.co.uk
NHBC. Standards body for the housebuilding industry.

www.thelittlehousecompany.co.uk
The Little House Company – for sale by owner.

www.themovechannel.com
The Move Company. One of the best single location compendiums of internet property services and free information, lists and reviews some 5,000 property related web sites and is a great place to start.

www.hometrack.co.uk
Hometrack provide the most in-depth, up-to-date and independent survey of house prices and market trends in England and Wales. General guides are free, and detailed market reports are available for a fee.

Index

100% Mortgage **106**, 108

Adverse credit mortgage **106**, 108

Assured tenancy **151**

Assured shorthold tenancy **152**

Auctions **84-85**

Base rate tracker mortgage **94**

Bed and breakfast 16, **22**, 25, 30, 33, 264

Birmingham 202, 219, 231, **260-263**

Bradford & Bingley **252**, 298

Building a portfolio**179**

Building survey **113**

Buildings insurance 24, **35**, 78, 79, 85, **111**, 181

Buy-to-let 97, **101**, 108, 120, 180, 182, 192, **193**, **196**

Buy-to-let mortgage 46, 54, 55, 58, 97, **101**, 108, 180, 182, 193, 209, 211, 212

Buy-to-sell 20, 52, 92, **188-190**

Capital gains tax **68-70**

Capital growth 87, 148, 157, **193**

Capped mortgage **95**, 108

Case studies 19, 141, **188-191**

Cash-back mortgage 98, **99**, 108

Completion **79-80**

Contents insurance **111**, 181

Credit rating **18-19**, 107

Current account mortgage 99-100

Demand factors   **58-59**

Devon 195, 244, **263-264**

Discounted mortgage **94-95**, 108

DIY property sale **169-172**, 284

Estate agents 56, 59, 71, 77, 82, **163-169**, 224, 297-298

Estate agents UK league table **297-298**

Exchanging contracts **79**

Exit strategy **186-187**

Expert advice **192-215**

Extensions 72, 114, **136-138**

Film / TV location 16, 22, **36-38**, 303

Fixed mortgage **95**, 108

Flexible mortgage **93**, 108

Game plan **46**

Glasgow 201, 233, 234, 254, **269-270**

Halifax estate agents 104, 169, 171, **224**

Holiday lets **68-70**, 159

Home Buyer's report **113**

Hot spots 68, 104, **199-201, 216-223**

House price changes **230**

House price growth 225, **226-228**, 242,

Housing benefit tenants **158**

Inspections **73**, 75, 83, 113

Insurance 24, **35**, 38, 78, 79, 85, **111, 154**, 181

Interest only mortgage **91-92**, 213

Investment 15, 20 **43-60**, 210

Investor 18, 43, **44-45**, 200, 207, 212, 221, 248

Landlords 28, 149-151, **154-155**, 157, 158, **196**, 207

League tables **231, 297-298**

Lease **149, 150-151**

Leeds 201, 208, 219, 233, 234, 260, **280-281**

Letting agents 28, 56, 61, 62, 63, **161**

Liability 24, 35, **38**, 55, 150

Licence 23, 26, 34, **149**

Life assurance **110**, 111

Location 22, 36, 62, **65-66**, 68

Lodgers 16, **26-31**, 153, 303

Manchester 19, 54, 66, 104, 201, 217, 231, 263, **274-276**

Mark Twain **45**

Midlands 66, 190, 226, 227, 237, 239, 246, 247, 253, **256-258**, 262, 272

Million pound properties **236-238**

Mortgage code **88-89**, 302, 305

Mortgage lenders 88, 110, 156, 193, **290-296**

Mortgage repayment protection **110**

Mortgage types **90-95**

Move channel 172, **216**, 305

Multiple tenancy 46, **149-150**, 156, 212

Net rate of return **186**

Newport **271-272**

North England 195, **225**, 226, 227, 236-237, 239, 246-250, 252, **253**

Norwich **272-274**

Nottingham 141, 201, 204, 205, 217, 219, 220, 231, **256**, 295

Office of Fair Trading **82**, 169

Offset mortgage **99**

Pitfalls **51**

Planning 179, 186

Planning permission 136, 188, 190

Property management 20, 70, 111, **156**, 157, 209

Property promotion **173**

Property selling **163-178**

Property syndicates **55-56**, 211

Property types **64, 219-220**

Reducing the rent **162**

Regional house price growth **227**

Remodelling 20, 61, **144-147**

Renovation **117-147**

    Bathrooms **124-126,** 128

    Ceilings **129-135**

    Floors **129-135**

    Kitchens **121-124**, 126, 128-129

    Lofts 120, 136, **137-139**, **145-146**, 188, 203

Rent Act Tenancy **151**, 154

Rental guarantee insurance **111**

Rental investment **190-191**, 279

Rental property 52, **56**, 155, 162, 196

Rental refresh 54, **161**

Repayment mortgage **91**, 98

Retirement investment 44, 101, **194**

Sale by estate agent **164-169**

Sale by owner **169-172**

Scotland **82**, 225, 227, 240, 247, 248, **254, 269-270**

Seaside towns **242-246**

Second homes **249-251**

Self build **201-204**, 211

Self-certificate mortgage **102-105**, 108

Selling property **162-178**

Shorthold tenancy 151, **152**

Sole agency **169**

Somerset **174**

South England 195, 204, **225**, 226, 227, 237-238, 239, 244, 246-250, 252, **253**

Speculator **44**

Staging 55, **142-143**, **161-162**, 169, **173- 178**, 213

Student lettings 212, **230-235**, 274

Surveys 31, 51, **73-74**, 78, 82, 83, 85, 107, 112, **113-114**

Surveyors 43, 56, 74, 76, 78, **115**

Surveyor, finding a **115**

Surveys online **115**

Taunton 197, **264-266**

Teeside 197, 199, **266-268**

Teignmouth **263-264**

Tenancy 26-31, 46-49, 61-63, **148-162**, 212

Timing 16, 58, **216**

Universities (performance league table) **233**

Valuation 24, 35, 78, 82, 85, 109, **112**, 144, **163**, 165, 169

Variable mortgage (see Flexible mortgage)

Wakefield **259-260**

Wales 40, 43, 195, 225, 236, 238, 239, 242-247, 254, **271-272**

Wealth coach **199-201**

Working from home **31-35**

Yorkshire 167, 177, 189, 197, 199, 237, 239, 245, 246, 247, 248, 250, **259-260**